TEN YEARS' HARD LABOUR
– a personal political odyssey –

TEN YEARS' HARD LABOUR

- a personal political odyssey -

by

Dr Bill Tormey

BLACKWATER PRESS

Design & Layout
Paula Byrne

Broomhill Business Park,
Tallaght,
Dublin 24.

Produced in Ireland by Blackwater Press

ISBN
0 86121 572 9

Contents

Introduction

Politics holds the Irish spellbound, whether here at home, or abroad in Camden Town or Boston. It is the Irish national sport. The PR voting system and the personalised nature of constituency politics encourages a close relationship between the electorate and the elected. Dr Bill Tormey's career as a political hopeful in the Labour Party nationally, and on Dublin's northside, is graphically outlined.

National and local personalities and issues are intertwined in a maelstrom of activity. All human life is there – elections, political struggle, high principle, back-stabbing and farce. Personal friendships, loyalty and group cohesion become very strong and enemies of one become enemies of all. Spring, Desmond, Quinn, Halligan, Finlay, O'Briain, Kavanagh, etc., are all writ large. The building blocks of Labour's successful evolution from the coalition rows of '82, to the local election disaster in '85, the threat of virtual extinction in '87 and onwards to the unimagined heights of '92 are traced through the eyes of a Labour Social Democrat and a supporter of Dick Spring's leadership. Dr Bill learned from experience that politics is like football – "a funny old game".

1
BETRAYAL

General Election 1992

'I will now proceed to eliminate Bill Tormey and distribute his votes,' intoned Dermot Hayes, the Returning Officer from the temporary wooden stage at about 11.15 on a wet and windy Friday morning, two days after polling day as the count for the constituency of Dublin North-West in St Vincent's School Hall on the Finglas Road was drawing to its slow and tortuous completion. Frank Rock, Finian Mitchell, David Core and George Metcalfe were huddled alongside a barrier trying to convince themselves that we did not do so badly after all. We had passed Jim Tunney, the Yellow Rose of Finglas, after the ninth count finishing on 3,842 and that placed us in sixth position, one worse than the '89 election. Beaten again! Was this the ultimate in political futility? Michael Freeman, Noel Cloake and Des St Leger from Fianna Fail offered their sympathy but it sounded more like condolences. The whole ritual left a bizarre feeling. It was like attending your own funeral. Only I was not surprised as I had in truth expected the result for more than a week. The real disappointment was not getting another 500 votes to go over the 3,000 first preference mark. For Fergus Finlay, Dick Spring, Brendan Howlin, Anne Byrne, Ita McAuliffe, Sally Clarke and others who were around when times were tough, I was very pleased. As for the Labour Party in general in its hour of triumph, I felt little empathy, merely betrayal.

After the 54 vote close shave in the 1989 General Election, I had always intended to contest the next outing whenever it would arise because there appeared to be a reasonable chance of success even though the constituency boundaries had to be extended to take in about 11,389 extra people in the Drumcondra area to the south-east and an extra 1,968 in the Magenta/Lorcan area in the north-east going over as far as the new motorway to Dublin Airport.

On Thursday, 8th October 1992, I met Dick Spring in his office in Leinster House to discuss the situation in the constituency. He reminded me that at an earlier meeting in May, he had suggested that I leave the constituency to Shortall and that maybe it would be better if I tried for the Seanad. He told me that he had been assured by Roisin Shortall that she would win a seat and he also suggested without overtly saying so, a nod being as good as a wink, that I would not get elected to the Dail and that I had already peaked electorally and was on the way down. He mentioned the local election defeat as evidence for this and I had to remind him that three of the four Fianna Fail candidates in the Finglas ward had reputedly spent more than £35,000 between them on the election and that Barney Rock, who was reared in Ballygall was sprung by the PD's in a master-stroke considering he was live on television each week-end of the campaign kicking points for Dublin in the marathon Dublin-Meath series of drawn encounters in the Leinster GAA Football Championship. The kids in the streets were shouting, 'Vote, vote, vote for Barney Rock' and Barney's Dublin team mates including Mick Deegan and Charlie Redmond from Erin's Isle in Finglas were canvassing for him door to door. A sizeable number of former Fianna Fail members were also canvassing for him. Barney is a nice personable fellow but in political terms he was and remains an enigma.

Dick knew about the level of support I had in the constituency among his own old core supporters because of the personal letters he had received from them. I told him that he should have replied to or at least acknowledged those letters especially from Paddy Donegan (a man with 50 years continuous Party membership) and from the other disaffected branches in North-West as it was discourteous at best not to have done so even if he was very busy.

I asked him what would he do if he was in my position? But just as he was about to answer, I told him that the question was rhetorical but I presumed that the answer was obvious. He nodded in agreement.

I also told Dick that I was a Social Democrat and would have immediately left the Labour Party had Emmet Stagg and company won in Tralee in '89 and that any honest observer could not claim that much of Labour's official conference economic policy was for real as it failed to take into consideration normal human behaviour in relation to taxation and incentives. There was also no recognition of the effect of an overly bureaucratic approach on the provision of many State services. Complaints from consumers in the Health and Social Welfare Services were well known to everyone. Freezing trains to Sligo, the Dublin Bus timetable, the passport office queues, etc., do not encourage belief in the primacy of the State sector. Just because a service is publicly funded should never be an excuse for the expectation of mediocrity. We have never properly addressed the interrelationships of pay, performance, responsibility and accountability of public sector workers at all levels especially right at the top. More openness everywhere in this area would work wonders. Televised Oireachtas committees on all areas of government expenditure should be routine, not the exception. I also told him it was a pity that there was not a formal German style Social Democratic Party in this country which he should lead and which should include some Labour, Fine Gael, Fianna Fail and Democratic Left people. However, I have never been sure about the reality of de Rossa's commitment to the social democracy speech, which was written for him by Eoin Harris for his address to the Workers Party Ard Fheis in 1989, as he had described himself to me personally as a Marxist in the same year outside a church in Finglas West. Dick reminded me that politics is a hard ruthless business and that he had to fight hard for his position in Cork and Tralee at successive conferences. Sometimes it was better to leave the Marquis of Queensbury's rules to one side, he said. I was left in no doubt that when it came to his own position, Dick would fight rough and tough. I knew well that Stagg and company were well aware of this man's combative abilities. Spring is also brave as a person and when it comes to the crunch, the man has bottle. He did not choke when he played for Munster, Trinity, Lansdowne or Ireland. The comments about the dropped 'garryowen' at Cardiff Arms Park are cheap shots at a good player.

Dick also said that he had seen and did not like the 'Loose Cannon'. This was a double sided A4 hand-out which we delivered to 18,000 homes in the constituency. It was a mixture of satire and local news based loosely on the style of *Scrap Saturday* and *Phoenix* magazine. Dick has a fairly sharp sense of humour himself. But being a politician first, his attitude was entirely predictable because satire and ridicule, even if done badly, are powerful weapons. Most public figures, I would guess, have a fear and loathing of being lampooned. Frank Hall with the Minister for Hardship (guess who?), the Minister for Unemployment and Women (Michael O'Deary), Richie Ruin and the whole Ballymagash scene on 'Hall's Pictorial Weekly' on RTE television during the 1973-77 FG/Lab coalition did a lot to undermine the credibility and certainly the pomposity of those in government.

Dermot Morgan with *Scrap Saturday* on RTE radio in the Autumn of '91 had the country spellbound with 'MAAARA' and the Gerard Collins 'Albert, don't do it, You'll burst the Party, ... political immaturity ', etc. scenario. I cannot look at Gerry Collins or Michael Noonan on TV without Morgan-speak coming into my mind. I can still see Eamonn Morrissey in the collarless shirt as the Minister for Hardship and that was 15 years ago. All politicians realise that their cliches, mannerisms, and foibles can be wickedly exploited to the delight of the punters. Some may like to be featured because it tickles their egos but the cute lads know that satire can explode and you never can tell just where the organic waste might land. *The Phoenix, Private Eye,* etc., are consistently popular with the chattering classes. Ironically when *Scrap Saturda'* was at its height, Charlie was at his most popular. If Morgan returns, will Haughey be far behind?

I told Dick to remember he was now aged 42 and that there comes a time in everyone's life cycle when you must take the main chance. As John Healy had put it in his 'Backbencher' column in the 60's, in politics it can be 'Instant sunshine, instant gloom'. My view, as I told him, was that he should personally go for whatever was on offer because many of those who would get elected would only be in the winners enclosure in his slipstream. I even suggested that he should consider Fianna Fail as a coalition partner particularly if they got rid of Albert. At least it would get rid of the Fine Gael tail tag for good. In Finglas, many of the Fianna Failers that I knew such as Freeman, Cloake, Kenny and company would fit easily into Labour. The other wing of Fianna Fail was ultra conservative. But its conservatism is qualitatively different from that of Fine Gael in that GUBU events never seem to overly bother them. Fianna Fail is in that sense a two-headed animal.

Imagine how perplexed Arts faculty students would be if faced with the following exam question:

Q. Shorn of party labels, is there any substantive difference in the politics of Ruairi Quinn and Bertie Ahern?

Dick then asked me if both he and Fergus Finlay were not in the Labour Party would I have persisted? I replied that I had stayed with Labour largely because I felt in philosophical agreement to a great extent with both himself and Fergus and as long as he was party leader I would remain. There was a definite 'family' social feeling about the whole thing. It may have been naivety but was certainly a big factor for me. What I did not say was that politics becomes a social habit and one's circle of friends and acquaintances becomes intertwined with political meetings and organisation. Loyalty then works both ways or at least it should. He also asked, had we commissioned any local constituency opinion poll, which we had talked about before, to see how the probable candidate list stood at present. We had not. I knew by the end of the discussion that he was not going to scale Everest for me. So we concluded on very good terms and he wished me the best of luck, hoped I would win a seat and asked me had I started preparing yet because he said that the balloon would go up in about four weeks. He reckoned that the Taoiseach's cross examination at the Beef Tribunal would see the PD's pull the plug. He was so right!

I could have added a few more comments but we were having a short meeting and not a didactic tutorial. In the minds of many Labour people, bureaucracy and civil service control of essential services have often been portrayed as an essential of socialism. If it were so then 'Bills of Rights', so-called 'Patients Charters', etc., would not be necessary. Social democracy for me has always been the recognition that man is interdependent and that everyone is entitled to the maximum degree of personal freedom which should not just be confined to a self perpetuating elite. We should recognise that we are all different and thus a grey uniform monotonous government-controlled and regulated equality as in Eastern Europe is a distortion of the fact of human heterogeneity which is both genetic and environmental. We must establish, as best we can how to provide each citizen with the facility to maximise their own talents so that everyone in the country benefits. Essential human services such as medicine should be provided on the basis of the patients' clinical need only. Governments should make sure that their particular health system eliminates possible distorting economic factors on the quality of service provision. Furthermore, all health services are in dynamic change because there is a constant push-pull between the competing demands of practitioners in centres of need and excellence for scarce resources. Real wealth for social distribution is produced in the manufacturing and traded sectors of the economy. Lawyers and doctors consume rather than create primary wealth. The high social status of the professions in Ireland is a contributory factor into our poor economic performance as a nation. The Japanese, the Americans and the Germans have an altogether different view of the value of industrialists. Recent business scandals in 1991-92 have only made the necessary national attitude adjustments more difficult.

Selection problems for me were obvious within a month of the Local Elections in June 1991. Gerry Doyle was talking with Odran Reid outside the King's Inn pub in Bolton Street on the evening of the Count when Ruairi Quinn came along. Quinn was quite happy that Tormey had lost. Ruairi's body language told it all! A month later I phoned Roisin Shortall who had not spoken to me since the local election count. She immediately said that she wanted the sole nomination for the next general election and that she would not run with me. I told her that I obviously totally disagreed and that a two-candidate strategy would be necessary to win a seat considering the constituency geography. She did well in Drumcondra and a combined vote would be very competitive. The question of Des O'Malley's contribution was also brought up by me as I knew he was keen to run. Des was working in the job centre in Ballymun and was very well known in the local community. He had been a candidate for the Labour Party in the 1979 Local Election getting 330 votes but left the Party in 1980. He joined the Workers Party in 1986 and later left them having become disenchanted with de Rossa and their strict party discipline. He rejoined Labour in 1990. Des had run Eamonn O'Brien of the Workers Party close for the last seat in the Drumcondra Ward in the '91 Local Election. Eamonn is a Dublin Bus driver who lives in the Courts in Poppintree, Ballymun and was a sitting councillor since 1985. Des got 942 votes and Eamonn O'Brien got 1,091. Des now felt that he would hold or increase his local election vote in the next general election. He was elected constituency organiser in 1991 but when it came to the crunch to head off a take-over by the Shortall group and to organise and get ratified a new branch in Ballymun and another in East Finglas, Des baulked. As was decided at the meeting in November 1991 in Leinster House with Fergus Finlay and Pat Magner, new people were organised into two branches which had gone into obeyance. Gerry Maher, a former candidate in Finglas agreed to help in one, and Barney Hartnett, another former candidate, agreed to set up the other branch in Poppintree. Barney is the editor of the *Ballymun Echo.* As a political move, it was correct but Des O'Malley saw it as a threat to his nomination and decided firstly to oppose their affiliation at a constituency council meeting in February. Later, he realised the true situation and at the next constituency Meeting, he proposed to review the new branches and organise their affiliation if appropriate. However, within a week, he resigned from the Labour Party without warning citing 'coalition' as his sole reason. After a few months he was replaced as organiser by Paschal O'Reilly from the Militant infiltrated Finglas East Branch and the new branches fell into a political limbo. That was the key incident in our failure to retake control in North-West and it was the final nail in the deselection box.

There was now no possibility of getting new branches ratified because of the attitude of head office and the organisation committee. No one has a proprietorial right to the nomination in any party. But one has a right to expect fundamental eligibility rules to be followed.

When it was obvious that the government would fall, I phoned Dick Spring at home in Tralee on Sunday night 1st November, and he asked me to 'Give me 48 hours' to see whether he could have me added to the ticket. I heard no more. The campaign was very quickly planned at a meeting in the Maples, Iona Road that same night involving Gerry Doyle, Helen and George Metcalfe, and Frank and Phyllis Rock. Everybody was enthusiastic but within a week Gerry had the wobbles and said we could not win. The Metcalfe's and Frank Rock were adamant and Mary Chambers was very definite and determined that we should fight no matter what. Helen Metcalfe said she was busy in the County Council computer room printing the Abortion Referendum polling cards and would be unavailable for canvassing for a week. As luck would have it, Helen could only hobble about having been on crutches for a few weeks due to a foot injury. Gerry Doyle would also be busy in his electrical contract business for the first week and a half but in reality both he and Helen Metcalfe only got out on the campaign about four times each. This was a serious blow for us because of their key influence on other potential campaign workers.

And They're Off!

We contacted the press to publicise the fact that I was going to contest the election. *The Irish Times* reported that Labour's chances of taking a seat in Dublin North-West received a setback when one of its leading constituency activists, Dr Bill Tormey announced that he would contest the election as an independent. He accused the Party's deputy leader Mr Ruairi Quinn, head office and members of the Militant Tendency in his constituency of depriving him of the nomination. 'I have no argument with Dick Spring and I will take the Labour whip if I am elected.'

Dr Tormey added that he was standing in response to demands from his supporters inside and outside the party, in the real expectation of contesting seriously for the last seat. 'My supporters are the true voice of Labour in this constituency and I have a record of 23 years' service in the Labour Party generally,' he said. His election posters would describe him as 'Democratic Labour' but he would be described as an independent on the ballot paper.

Rejecting Dr Tormey's claims, a Labour spokesman said that the selection convention which chose Ms Shortall had been run strictly in accordance with the Party's rules. It was a matter of very considerable regret that Dr Tormey, a long-standing member of the Party, had decided to run against the official candidate, he added.

The Crunch

In the context of my final pre-election letter to the General Secretary dated 22nd October and copied to Dick Spring and to the National Organiser, Pat Magner, the comment from their anonymous spokesman regarding the selection convention in Dublin North-West had the Robert Armstrong look about it, i.e. it was economical with the truth. The letter had been delivered because I had received written acknowledgements within days from Sally Clarke for Dick Spring and from Marion Boushell, the Deputy General Secretary.

The letter questioned the validity of the decision at the selection conference of 6 May held at the Willows Pub on Sycamore Road in Finglas East.

The text read:

> 'At that meeting, there were two decisions taken following a vote. The first was that there would be one candidate to contest the General Election in the constituency for the Labour Party and the second was that Ms Roisin Shortall would be that candidate. I wish to seek a ruling from the Administrative Council that the decisions taken at that meeting be declared null and void because delegates from two branches, i.e. DCU and Finglas East up to possibly six in total were almost certainly members of the proscribed organisation 'Militant'.'

On 11th September 1990, I wrote to Pat Magner, Chairman of the organisation committee with a copy to Ray Kavanagh and reported that specific members of the DCU Branch were members of *Militant.* (copy enclosed).

On 6th May 1992, Gerry Doyle of the Ballygall Branch wrote to the General Secretary reporting the activity of the secretary of the Finglas East branch selling the *Militant* Newspaper in O'Connell Street at a specified time and date (copy enclosed).

On 20th May 1992, Frank Rock, Chairman of the Ballymun branch wrote to the General Secretary with a copy to the Party leader naming members of the DCU Branch who had voted in the recent Dail selection convention and who were selling *Militant* door to door in the Shangan area of Ballymun (copy enclosed). Furthermore, I enclose a copy of a leaflet distributed by *Militant* in the Coultry and Shangan areas of Ballymun which is self-explanatory.

To the best of my knowledge no action has been taken by the Labour Party on the above *Militant* activity.

On Wednesday, 14th October 1992, at the 40A bus stop in Parnell Street at approximately 5 p.m., Ms Helen Metcalfe of the Finglas Branch bought a copy of *Militant* from a Finglas East branch constituency delegate. He had been selling his publication for over an hour at that stage and was somewhat taken aback when he realised that he recognised the buyer.

Clearly there appears to be a serious *prima facie* case of breach of the Party's rules in the eligibility of many members of two branches in Dublin North-West. As both of these branches voted *en bloc* for one candidate at the forthcoming General

Election, it would appear that ineligible people have played a pivotal role in arriving at a decision that frustrated the wishes of the legitimate majority.

For all of the above reasons I wish to have the selection convention declared invalid immediately.

Should the Selection Conference Be Declared 'Null and Void'?

It is unrealistic to expect a political party to cause itself embarrassment going into a general election campaign. I spoke to Ciaran O'Mara, a solicitor who is also a member of the Administrative Council, to ask him should I go to court to seek a review of the Labour Party's procedures in relation to their conduct towards myself. He was familiar with the details and it was his opinion that no judge would interfere in the internal workings of a political party. I asked him about natural justice and he said I should not bother but I should go ahead and run. Anyway he said I was going to run no matter what the outcome. I was not happy with this but I did not want any legal proceedings as I felt the potential embarrassment and public damage to Dick Spring and Fergus Finlay might be too great and loyalty prevented me pursuing the matter further.

The early election in 1992 ensured that this issue could not be brought much further internally at the time but we considered that the weight of Mili evidence was getting too large to be continually ignored and that the Organisation Committee might have been forced to change its view if we had more time. If! If! If! By Sunday 13th December, within weeks of the count, the former constituency youth officer Alan Bermingham, who was a DCU branch delegate to the candidate selection convention in May, publicly confirmed his Militant credentials. I wrote, again without reply to the General Secretary, Kavanagh with a copy to Pat Magner. In it I wrote '...To avoid adverse publicity for the Party during the election campaign, I did not publicise my detailed reasons for disquiet nor did I seek legal redress.

On Sunday, 13th December, 1992, the *Sunday Tribune* published a letter Page A16 concerning Labour in power written by Alan Bermingham as Militant Socialist (Co-ordinator). This surely makes even more solid the evidence of Militant membership of the DCU branch of the Labour Party. Whilst I am sure you are happy to be rid of me and to have had a successful campaign in Dublin North-West, nonetheless, the substance of my complaints has been increasingly validated. Bermingham was, as I had earlier pointed out in my letter to you of 11th September 1990, 'Youth Officer' in this constituency.

I would like to know what action you propose to take to avoid me having to seek outside justice. I have no intention of merely fading away.'

The Campaign Plan

The campaign plan was to get large 4 ft x 2 ft 8 in posters printed and erected. Having heard from Gregory Sparks that 500 was more than enough to effectively cover a local election area for Derek McDowell in Artane in the Summer of '91, we decided to order at least 1,000 and get George Metcalfe to price the hard board backing. Sheets of hardboard 8 ft x 4 ft could be cut to take three posters and we bought bulk tiewraps in an electrical wholesaler in Glasnevin. We had planned to get John McNamara, Chairman of Shamrock Rovers, to direct the campaign but he was tied up by litigation involving his work. John is highly respected as an effective organiser by everyone and has efficiently run Rovers. So we improvised and ran the election by committee. An efficient organiser would have been able to mobilise many more people to come out and canvass but you have to do the best you can with whatever help you have and be grateful for all volunteers. Through the early part of the campaign, we may have been in reality 'independent' but we still considered ourselves the standard bearers for the 'real' Labour Party. We decided on three poster teams, George Metcalfe and his brother Paul for Finglas, Frank Rock in Ballymun and Denis Carr for the South East. They were to operate independently. This turned out to be totally impractical because Frank Rock was let down in Ballymun by non-performers and George Metcalfe clearly operated better in a team. So we decided to all work together. Eithne Costello found Paul Mulholland from Barry Avenue in Finglas to help with postering which was quite a hard physical task. Unfortunately, both he and George Metcalfe fell off ladders and injured themselves after a few days. I took an each-way bet ordering the posters. Having gone to the printer, George Goodson, to find out who printed the large portraits, George played it close to his chest and would not say but took an order for 500. I gave him a recent photograph and a drawing of the poster design. I based it on our local election '91 poster as I presumed that the Labour Party's generic design would be similar. This turned out to be spot on! Rather than call ourselves Name X only on posters, I decided on the title 'Democratic Labour' which was at least amusing. The red rose is a European social democratic symbol and so cannot be exclusively used here as a trade mark by the Labour Party. I phoned Michael Freeman, a personal friend of mine in Fianna Fail to find out who printed the Brian Lenihan posters in the Presidential Election in 1990 and we got Pat Synnott of Lithospeed on St Margaret's Road in Finglas. That was a stroke of good fortune because he was able to immediately print posters. When I called to see him, the first thing he made clear was that he worked for Fianna Fail! I told him I was fully aware of that fact but all that was required was the work. There was no messing about from him. The posters hit the lamp-posts on Friday night. We were first up and had the anticipated impact locally. This was the first election in which I did not have to do a major part of the postering myself. Meanwhile, the Labour Party's poster campaign had hit a major hitch. The work had been contracted out to Wexford where the printing machine broke down. I heard about this and phoned Fergus Finlay to tell him I could arrange an alternative and passed on the information to Pat Synnott. By Sunday morning, I saw Shortall posters rolling off the machine first – 600 rather than the 500 for other constituencies. Do them a favour and get a kick in the teeth – we all live and learn. We postered as quickly as we could but after about three days when more than 300 posters should have been in place, it was obvious that there was more than mere gravity at work taking down and removing our offending objects. We then got reports via a Fianna Fail candidate and from Mary's patients that people were seen pulling down our posters. While out postering, Frank Rock was told by a resident from his front garden on Home Farm Road that a rival candidate's people would have our posters down as soon as he had left. That was the third poster on that particular pole and it was replaced by another large facial apparition when we passed by the following day. Talk about being obvious and unsubtle! Over the course of the election, we reckon that about 1000 posters were downed. I protested to my contacts in the city centre Labour Party but these protests were ignored. This created great difficulty in controlling some of my supporters who demanded immediate retaliation. They held off for a week and then acted once only. Our message was ignored. I should have gone to the police immediately but we did not ourselves catch them red-handed. I also did not know what was the exact legal position.

Grundy and Spence

I went to see John Grundy, a well-known Finglas poet and writer and Jimmy Spence, another well known Finglas character to get them to agree to help us dropping literature. John Grundy, author of a published historical verse history of the state called 'A Grocer's Republic', has always come to our rescue in elections and has a number of local youths to help him distribute leaflets, an activity run as a part of a community service. John is active in the Finglas writers group. He is also a pacificist and is quite opinionated on local issues often writing to the *Sunday Tribune* which he reads with great interest.

Jimmy Spence on the other hand is a born and reared Finglas man who is a real character and likable in the old Dublin sense – a former Rank's Flour Mills worker, loud and gregarious. His 'office' is the Drake Inn on Main Street, Finglas. Jimmy's late father Jack Spence lived in Ballygall Crescent for nearly 50 years and was a solid Labour supporter having being a shop steward in Alec Thoms Printers in St Mobhi Road which is now Smurfit's. Jimmy did not get it off the trees. His wife Molly is a diehard Fianna Failer and is a fanatical supporter of Alderman Pat Carey from the time she was involved with Summer projects for kids in Finglas South in the early 80's. Pat has for years used her house in Fairlawn Road, Finglas South for 'clinics'.

The canvass started on Monday, 9th November. I made arrangements in Beaumont for consultant cover from Rory O' Donnell, Shane O' Neill and Derval Royston and I was first on the list at the Sheriff's office in Fownes Street with the formal nomination and the £300 deposit. I opted for a blank space after my name on the ballot paper rather than non-party or independent because I was still not used to the idea of not being Labour. Being placed alphabetically immediately under Shortall on the ballot paper should at least facilitate transfers, or at least that was the theory.

We planned to maximise literature drops with four into each of the approximately 27,000 housing units in the area during the three week campaign. The idea was to reinforce the candidate's name and image tying the poster picture to the literature drop. We again used two printers to maximise our efforts. The first drop was a double sided A5 with a picture on one side to identify with the poster. As a result of a warning from a local former Fine Gael activist Jim O'Higgins, the second drop was to feature a family picture of myself, Mary, Tommy and Aoibhinn to head-off a personal whispering campaign which had been done during the Local Elections. The third drop was to be a straight-forward political issues affair with the rose symbol, etc. We then wanted to finish with a montage of newspaper cuttings set out on a double sided A3. The main problems we faced were that some of the drops did not in fact go where they were supposed to, particularly in Ballymun and in the east end of the constituency but we could not afford to complain too much for fear of alienating our droppers. The other problem was the slow and often late delivery of literature by printers. Every candidate probably makes similar complaints and the printers on the other hand are often left with unpaid bills for their pains. Because of the relatively dry weather, we were able to deliver most of what we planned except that we only printed 15,000 of the last A3 leaflet. All of these were written by myself before we started canvassing because the campaign was going to be so short and we were without a propagandist. Declan Cassidy, Finglas publicist was now running another local paper called the *Finglas Forum* and was unavailable.

At a 'Race night' fundraiser for the Finglas Old Folks in Martin's Pub on Ballygall Road West, on the night after the dissolution of the Dail organised by Molly Spence, Cyril Chaney, Sylvia Byrne and their committee, there was a noticeable move towards Labour among people who voted Fianna Fail or the Workers Party previously. From the first doorstep canvass, one thing was clear – Labour was a certainty to win. I had never seen anything like it before. Everywhere you went, it was the same story. Labour's opinion poll ratings jumped from 14% in Dublin when the election was called to 19% after a week and then into orbit at 32% just before polling day. Nationally, Labour's MRBI opinion poll ratings were 10% in June, 14% in September and 19% in November. I phoned Barry Desmond at home on the first weekend in his capacity as Director of Elections and told him that I would not release potentially damaging information and that our campaign would be honourable. I hoped the official effort would follow suit. He was slightly taken aback by the call but friendly nonetheless. I sent a message to Fergus Finlay that I was still willing to run as a second candidate and that second runners should be added at least around Dublin before the close of nominations on Monday 16th. No new action was taken. That no second candidates were added anywhere when there was still time to react to the rising poll surge for Labour was a huge managerial error and is a clear demonstration of the incompetence of the Head Office decision- making apparatus. There was an obvious case for an additional candidate in Dublin North, North-West, South, South-Central, South-East, West, Wicklow, Waterford, Cork North-Central, and maybe Carlow-Kilkenny. I suppose a few more TD's might not have meant a lot but it might have resulted in John Bruton and Dick Spring rotating in the Taoiseach's chair.

What we had to do was to stay associated with the Party. This was to prove impossible due to a very thorough uncoupling job by the Shortall camp. At the end of the first week of the campaign, RTE phoned the practice to arrange to film a short piece focusing on the challenge to Mary Flaherty of Fine Gael. Their intention was to film Roisin Shortall in Omni Park, Mary Flaherty in Ballymun flats and myself at the local 'Our Lady of Victories' church. The filming went ahead on a bright crisp Monday morning and went very well indeed for me with no one giving any verbal abuse. It was quite funny when familiar locals such as Kay Bermingham, a long time friend of my late mother and Kitty O'Malley came over to talk. The RTE producer wanted a bit more bite so he took us up to Ballymun Shopping Centre, which is in a disgraceful state of disrepair to see if there would be any fireworks. We walked into Maggie Murray's son-in-law just released from prison after serving a few years sentence. I remembered him from our Poppintree clinics in the early 80's. The RTE lads did not want his contribution and it was funny watching them trying to escape from the friendly verbal pasting. The piece was shown on the Six-One news and I was described as the 'disgruntled former Labour candidate'. That TV appearance was one I could have done without. The following morning Dick Spring was on the Pat Kenny Radio Show phone-in and was asked why I was not a Labour Party Candidate. He tried to duck the question but he did state that he had confidence in Roisin Shortall as the properly selected official Labour candidate. It might have been interesting to have heard his reply to a 'what about' question. What about the Militant votes at the selection convention? I heard of the broadcast secondhand on the doorsteps that afternoon. Roisin Shortall was to feature on film with Dick Spring outside Superquinn in Finglas the next evening again on the main RTE news bulletins and again the following night when she was seated in the background at a press conference involving the Party leader. The Shortall Campaign then ran a drop which featured a letter from Dick Spring endorsing her as the Labour Party candidate selected alone in order to insure a seat. All of her literature including the election address featured on this one message. Shortall also distributed a two colour double sided A5 with 9 photographs and a brief comment on the main issues such as housing, unemployment, law and order, health, high finance, honesty, Aer Lingus, and social welfare. One section was more banal than the next. According to Roisin Shortall, Labour was committed to giving interest relief to £5,000. I presume this referred to mortgages, whether per person or per household was not clear. Redundancies in Aer Lingus were out. There was also an announcement that jobs are the only way to get the country working! Wow! There was no detail on any of the issues. Given the result, there is obviously a lot to be said for the 'Gotcha!' Sun newspaper approach to the electorate. The contrast with the similar sized 'Election News' from Proinsias De Rossa of Democratic Left was total. De Rossa's headline was '301,000 reasons to vote for Proinsias de Rossa' and the text was reasoned and well written with a broadsheet rather than a tabloid flavour. There was also more targeting on strictly local constituency problems. Frankly, it was good literature.

About 90% of the early queries to me at doorsteps had been simply why was I not running for Labour officially. The impression received by many voters at doorsteps around Finglas East was that I was purely a spoiling candidate out to mess up Labour and that I couldn't take my beating. Other comments like 'crap doctor' 'millionaire', etc., were being put about. I did not mind the 'crap doctor' bit too much but the £1 million lottery prize had escaped my clutches. On the other hand, I had been holding a winning Labour ticket since the 1989 near miss only to find it reefed from my hand as I attempted to collect the winnings in 1992. Strange that most of the old Labour members in the constituency were still actively supporting me.

After the RTE exposure, I knew that I was beaten but it was important to keep up appearances for the sake of the canvassers. Betrayal was the only apt description for how I personally felt and I told Fergus Finlay and Dave Grafton this precisely in those terms. It was ironic to have been the only Labour candidate on the Northside of Dublin to have overtly and publicly supported the Party leader, Dick Spring, when his name was quite a definite 'no-no' and then to be simply rolled over by an overwhelming Spring tidal wave when it was going to someone else. The official Labour campaign also used Oireachtas free post envelopes to mail shot voters with a personalised letter from Roisin Shortall using a 'mail merge' on a word processor. How many individuals were targeted, I do not know, but it showed me that Shortall had good quality backing with a very formidable organising capability and access to appropriate technology for sophisticated voter targeting by experienced personnel.

Because of the shortness of the campaign, we did not organise a Tormey election address because I would have had to write it myself and then organise the printing. I didn't have the mental energy for either at the time. That was where I badly needed Dave Grafton, Ita McAuliffe and Fergus Finlay. Fianna Fail did not use an election address either but Fine Gael, Labour, Democratic Left, the Greens, the Christian Centrist Party, Sinn Fein and the Worker's Party all used the free post. I also felt that we had sufficient drops and that the election address was in reality just only another drop except it was delivered by the postman. Paddy Dunne was the one person who gave me a lot of verbal stick on this subject constantly pushing us to do an address. Sinn Fein dropped literature some of which detailed a candidate picture and policy information yet never mentioned Sinn Fein or Northern Ireland. They also postered early. John Murphy of the Greens went on the hustings around the streets with Aidan Meagher and a solid group of workers. The Greens have a steady vote in the constituency and have been consistently active for years churning out policies on Dunsink dump, transport, air pollution, recycling, and small scale industry. John's mother in Casement had voted for us for years and promised a No 2 this time. Done, says I at her hall door.

On another showery Wednesday afternoon we were accompanied by Noreen Hegarty and Kevin Clancy from the *Evening Herald* when we went door to door down along Johnstown Gardens and Griffith Road. The reception was very pleasant and we had a good laugh. Mary Chambers, Andy Earley and Gerry Maher all insisted on coming along despite the weather. It is amazing the effect that a reporter and a professional photographer can have on the morale of the troops. The *Evening Herald* had it two days later including a photograph with Patsy Lindsay and Breda Higgins. We were all pleased that night.

The Fairbrother Case – Damages Agreed

Derek Fairbrother's case for damages was settled out-of-court on Friday 20 November and I was interviewed by Des Nix of the *Sunday Press* about the affair. Shortly before this, I was asked by one of the Fairbrothers if I was aware of any other potential assault incident involving the Gardai in the area and I told them that I could not go to court unless asked by a patient and that I would not breach patient confidentiality. They appeared quite happy to accept this. It was only later that I remembered an incident from late 1986 that they could possibly have heard about but which as far as I am aware, was not pursued. Under a heading 'I was right to blow whistle on beating, says doctor' the *Sunday Press* carried the following:

> Dr Bill Tormey, the medical man who brought the Fairbrother case to the attention of Labour Party leader Dick Spring, who then raised the matter in the Dail, says Friday's settlement of the case vindicates him and justifies his action.
>
> Dr Tormey, a friend of Mr Spring and a candidate for Democratic Labour in the Dublin North-West constituency in the general election next Wednesday, says he took 'a lot of hassle' over his initiative in bringing the case to public attention.
>
> He raised the matter after examining Derek Fairbrother the day after the incident. 'I was shocked at his clinical state,' he said. Dr Tormey reckons that Friday's resolution of the case is a watershed for the state. 'I think the outcome is a tremendous example of the success of the open courts system in shining light,

which underlines why all inquiries should be open to the public. I trust and believe that the garda authorities will take every step now to restore the traditional goodwill which had existed up to this in Finglas between the gardai and the general public. Just because some gardai misbehave should not reflect badly in any way on the other gardai who do a tremendous job in this area, although under-manned, under-paid and under tremendous pressure.'

He suggests that the evidence given at the trial should be closely looked at by the authorities. The Fairbrother case will now be investigated fully by the Garda Complaints Board, who decided in December 1988 to defer a decision until the civil action had been dealt with by the courts.

I believed that the £375,000 compensation and the ward of court aspects spoke for themselves.

The *Irish Press* also noted that a preliminary report by Superintendent Pat Jordan then of Store Street, for the members of the Complaints Board members was the basis for the DPP's decision not to prosecute the five Gardai. I did not raise any further public questions in this regard during the course of the general election.

Ballymun was targeted with an extra 5,000 leaflet drop aimed solely at the estates problems during the final week at the insistence of both Eithne Costello and Frank Rock. But Pat Grant of Fianna Fail told me outside St Canice's Church on the last Sunday morning of the campaign that he had found a big swing to Shortall in the Shangan houses and flats in east Ballymun on Friday. Eithne Costello who lives in Shangan and was organising our effort there, did not think that this was true and on a Sunday afternoon canvass of the area, we got a good friendly reception which was misleading because the tally at the count told a different tale.

That Sunday night, Gerry Doyle and I called to the Greenfield Park Social Club on Shanliss Avenue where there was the usual Sunday night session with Eddie Ormond, Barney Hempton and Hugh Conkey on stage. There was no shortage of volunteer singers and the atmosphere was very congenial. That club is an example of great neighbourliness and togetherness in a community. Tony Quinn and John Mason were behind the bar. Pints of Guinness were the order of the night. Emma Marie Regan, a well-known person in Shanard in Santry and Paddy Caulfield from the Smithfield Fruit Market had been actively canvassing for me. Charlie Haughey's absence from the scene was just too much for Paddy. Paddy Caulfield, like many others on the Northside, was 'Charlie' first and the rest last. 'Bertie' would have a long way to go with these people before he would rank in the same class as Charlie. As far as they were concerned Charlie is a likeable rogue and they loved him. He could do no wrong or if he did, then he must have been slipping because he shouldn't have got caught. It must have been age catching up on him. The way the word 'Charlie' was spoken was special. You were left in no doubt which Charlie was in question. The surname was unnecessary. Chaarlie was elongated and caressed in the throat and then followed by a short eh! such was their affection for him. A lot of old age pensioners believed that it was Charlie who had personally given them the free electricity and the bus pass and the Succession Act. I would have personally preferred if the same Mr Haughey had been obliged to declare his interests and the sources of his wealth. It would have ended so much speculation idle or otherwise. The British had the House of Windsor, northsiders had 'Charlie!' I was made feel very welcome and it was clear that I was going to receive quite a few first preferences from the people I knew there.

Overall, Santry was very well disposed to us on the canvass as Barry Desmond discovered when he got it in the ear about my deselection from Mrs Dixon in Omni Park Shopping centre.

It was also obvious from our canvass that Jim Tunney was in trouble unless he was taking Ahern's Fianna Fail votes from the area that we had not canvassed but from talking to him, it was clear that he really did not believe it. Jim was behaving in his usual expansive all embracing fashion. In an interview with Mark Hennessy in the *Cork Examiner* on December 30, 1992, Jim confirmed that his first preference total of 3,054 came 'as an awful shock at the start'. It was strange to see letters from a Leas Ceann Comhairle to individual voters asking for No 1's mainly on the basis that he was your 'local man'. The flavour of Jim comes out clearly in another letter which he circulated from his Dail office. The letter never mentioned Fianna Fail and was headed – Jim Tunney Local TD No1. The text read: 'Dear Friend, You and yours are well, I trust. When you asked me to assist by making representations and enquiries for you, I was happy to do so. You know that I did my best. Now I am asking you to do your BEST for ME by giving me your No. 1 VOTE on ELECTION DAY. Yes — —

1 Tunney Jim PLEASE.
I will be very grateful.
Best Wishes.
Jim

The Yellow Rose was true to the end. It was very interesting watching him operate. He was a Victorian gentleman with decent instincts. He never bad mouthed his opponents and he himself had to suffer a whispering campaign from his own side. His reputed age was increased by the week and he was said to be somewhat reticent about speaking out on abortion. Jim himself told me after the late Tim Killeen's funeral that a large volume mail shot had been sent out by Bertie Ahern, Minister for Finance, in support of his brother Noel. Jim's problem was possibly that too many of his voters were interred in Glasnevin. Tempus fugit.

Interestingly the three Fianna Fail candidates aided their own destinies by each having separate election headquarters: Pat Carey with the Medjugorje prayer group near the Slipper pub on Ballymun Road, Noel Ahern in St Luke's on Drumcondra

Road and Jim Tunney used Taaffe's Law office in Finglas village despite the Fianna Fail Election HQ being directly across the street. Mary Flaherty, Proinsias de Rossa and the Workers Party all had election offices on Finglas Main St. This was clear evidence of just how bad business really was for traders in Finglas.

Following a canvass session in the Walsh Road/Ferguson Road area, which was Bertie Ahern heartland in Dublin Central before the constituency revision but remained strongly tied to his brother Noel, we headed for the Comet Pub on the Swords Road, Whitehall where we met Noel Ahern and his Fianna Fail team who included Mary Foley, the local election candidate from Walnut in Courtlands Estate on Griffith Avenue. Noel Ahern was very tense and clearly worried despite the obvious fact that as the top named Fianna Failer on the ballot paper with the same surname as his famous brother, he would have no problem finishing up on top or nearly on top of the poll. Fianna Fail knew by this time that Roisin Shortall would romp home if she held the Labour vote and Mary Foley warned us about how formidable Shortall's tactics had been in the local election as far as she was concerned. Comments door to door can be very effective. I told her that we were only too well aware of the possibilities. As well as a separate canvass card, the Noel Ahern campaign also used an expensive large A5 message sheet on good quality Art paper. Noel's forte was obviously the attention to local detail such as playgrounds, public lighting, grass cutting, landscaping, speeding traffic, street names etc. The general election issues were clearly for another occasion!

Finian Mitchell, Gerry and Betty Maher and Andy Earley were enthusiastic canvassers during the daytime from the beginning, while Anya Pierce came out on her days off following overnight 'on-call' sessions in Toxicology at Beaumont Hospital. We got on with the door knocking while Frank Rock and George Metcalfe kept the postering going ably assisted by Denis Carr and Paul Mulholland. A good crowd came out from Beaumont hospital after work in the evenings organised by Pat O'Brien and Maria Ennis and they included Luke O'Sullivan, Mick Carney, Derval Royston, Reighnall Glasgow, Roly FitzGerald. I kept out of any arrangements in the hospital because I feel that political involvement must remain totally free from consultant pressure but I was very grateful for the help given with such good spirit.

The Whitehall/Santry Branch held a meeting during the first week of the campaign and agreed to adjourn until after the election having decided that their members could support either candidate as their consciences dictated. They had serious reservations concerning the validity of the selection process and had written to Dick Spring on the subject but never received the courtesy of a reply. This irritated and disappointed their members greatly, especially the Donegan family, Tom Dunne and the former chairperson of the Constituency Council, Maura Doolan. Tommy Dunne who works in SIPTU with the Joint General President Billy Attlee came out to support our campaign. Tommy is a talkative, jolly, and entertaining man, relatively short in stature and often a few pounds over the odds. He knows the local scene very well having been elected to officerships in the Glasnevin North Community Council. Despite his chat and easy manner, Tom is principled and determined, probably still influenced by caring characteristics from his early training as a clerical student with the St John of God Order. He also recognises the pretence in many a public statements made in the political arena. Tom was a very busy man on the hustings as he also gave time, as usual, to support his good friend and union colleague, Brian FitzGerald, on his way to a great victory in Meath. Senator Jack Harte made futile phone calls to both Tom Dunne and Gerry Maher to urge them from supporting me. The lads were anything but impressed. Jack Harte's brother Richie continued to help Gerry in our campaign. We all wondered just who was leaning on the bold Jack Harte? The whys and wherefores of the Labour Party's local tactics were vigorously debated over pints in the Jolly Toper by Gerry Maher, Richie Harte, Jack FitzWilliam and other pint commandoes. The nomination question was the central issue.

The former Labour Lord Mayor of Dublin in 1975-76, Paddy Dunne, and his son Pat also helped us out. It was great fun canvassing in Larkhill with Paddy who was born in Leland Place in the North Wall area and reared in Thatch Road, Whitehall from the age of nine. Paddy personally knew most of the residents. The banter and general slagging of all and sundry was hilarious. Old friends were remembered, past incidents recalled, condolences offered to Paddy on the death of his wife Marie, since the last election, the whereabouts of emigrant children regretfully described, Luke Kelly remembered, and then a few shots fired across the bows of Fianna Fail. We might have lost the election but we did have some great crack. Evelyn Higgins, a bubbly character who knew John McNamara from her time with ICC in York Road, Ringsend, and her husband Bill and son David who is the manager of Crestfield United U14 team, canvassed in Crestfield and in Larkhill. They certainly were well received but did tell me that they found a good few people going to vote for Roisin Shortall because she was remembered for running a playschool at her house in Gaeltacht Park. Joey Malone, who played football for St Patrick's Athletic, Dundalk and was the manager of Galway United when the FAI Cup went west to the City of the Tribes in 1991, also agreed to help us out. He is also heavily involved in local schoolboy football. Another night canvassing on Clancy Avenue, Paddy and I effectively invaded an executive committee meeting of the East Finglas Residents Association where Paddy's sister-in-law, Carmel Quinn, Miriam Connolly and about fifteen neighbours were gathered. They were all very friendly in an area that is traditionally a very conservative Tunney/Flaherty stronghold.

Mary Flaherty's mother was still quite influential locally in Finglas because she had been a nurse/midwife on the district when home births were commonplace. The personal touch still counts for a lot. Mary still advertises on election literature her mother's nursing contribution and her father's St Vincent de Paul work in Finglas South and their commitment to meals on wheels in Glasanaon. The Fine Gael campaign did not appear as well funded as previously . But Mary Flaherty is a wily old campaigner who gets out the Fine Gael conservative vote very effectively. Rumours of her political demise have proven premature to say the least. Mary Flaherty is not a populist and she has been consistent in her political outlook over the years. She is essentially a true blue Tory which fits well with her party's Christian Democrat partners in Europe. Having a colour piece, which included a photograph, in the *Irish Independent* at the end of the campaign can have done her chances no harm at all. It must be great to have well positioned friends –I'm only jealous.

Gerry Doyle and I called to Paul Brien in Kippure Park to seek his support because of his valuable work in election '89 and after taking a few days to consider he agreed to help out which he did at the churches on Sundays. Unfortunately for us, Paul was working long hours at insulation in the new Irish Life development on Georges Quay and did not arrive back in Finglas until the canvass was well on. This was a reconciliation because of the arguments before the previous local election. The early finish in the winter gloom was one hell of a nuisance. Paul's brother Liam, former manager of Drogheda Utd and assistant manager at Shamrock Rovers and Dundalk, contacted some of the local footballers for us as did Noel King, then manager of Limerick FC whom I had got to know and respect when he was both player and manager for Shamrock Rovers. He was a key figure in rescuing Rovers from the death rattle at Tolka Park following the disastrous sale of Glenmalure Park, Milltown for property development. During and after the election some local fans of Bohemians in Phibsboro gave me some 'stick' for being a Rovers man both verbally and by a detailed anonymous letter from someone familiar with the internal politics at Dalymount Park. Michael Kelly, a longtime Labour stalward and an active St Vincent de Paul Society man went door to door across Finglas South accompanied by his family and friends and he was very disappointed because he anticipated a better result. Again the confounding issue towards the end of the election was simply –why was Bill Tormey not the official Labour candidate?

Illness affected many of our usual team in the Santry area. Within a month of the election, both Maura Doolan and Jack McCarthy had died and Paddy Donegan and Mick Purdue from Glentow Road were both at Beaumont Hospital during the campaign. Michael Tierney, John McNamara, my cousin William Tormey, Charles Glass, Karl Vogelsang, Reginald Moore, Breda Higgins, Nora Carroll and others all canvassed hard despite the weather. The Costellos organised a separate group in Ballymun and they canvassed through the Shangan and Coultry area. David Core came out every night and had an interesting social arrangement with his wife Bernie who spent every afternoon canvassing for the Workers Party. They minded their kids for alternate sessions! Very egalitarian! David brooks no messing and is very well organised. He looks a little fierce at times because he has some residual redness in his eye following a successful corneal transplant by Michael O'Keeffe in the Mater after an industrial accident. We knew that the W.P. morale was very seriously punctured by de Rossa's defection and the setting up of Democratic Left. His former supporters were very bitter at what they saw as his betrayal. The Workers Party posters were put up for the last week and they concentrated on canvassing their core vote in Finglas and Ballymun. Despite press comments, our relations with WP supporters in those areas had been quite cordial, particularly since the election campaign for Mary Robinson where John Dunne of the WP had conducted the postering. He couldn't resist sticking some WP labels on the bottom of the Robinson posters which I had delivered but which the WP people had stapled to lamp posts. Such trivia are quickly noticed by each party's troops on the ground but I'm sure are of no consequence to the great majority of the electorate. John Dunne is himself the son of the late Tony Dunne who died shortly after being elected city councillor for Labour in Finglas in the 1979 Local Government Elections.

At a post canvass meeting, attended by more than 10 people including Tom and Paddy Dunne, Helen and George Metcalfe, Andy Earley and Frank Rock, they unanimously insisted that the offending word 'democratic' be removed from the second drop. Continuous questions about this word 'democratic' were driving the team crazy, so like any tumour it must simply be cut out. However, this caused predictable consternation within the Labour Party HQ where they considered serving me with a court injunction. Having printed and given the droppers 25,000 leaflets for distribution, there was no way these could be withdrawn but it was agreed to overprint the word 'democratic' on a third leaflet which was printed and ready for distribution. Our 'lads' were really angry, however I was not surprised as I had told them that I would have done exactly the same thing myself had I been the sole Labour candidate. The RTE television news coverage of North-West made the whole episode irrelevant within days.

Holding an Abortion and Travel and Information Referendums with the General Election was strange as many of these issues became buried under the general election avalanche. I would not personally vote for abortion and made that perfectly clear. Restricting the right to travel and information is absurd. After the X case, the sort of bizarre scenarios which could possibly happen just did not bear thinking about. The abortion row can be boiled down to two main foundations. Firstly, in its essence human life begins at fertilisation and continues until death occurs following a miscarriage or by planned biological obsolescence at an average of 70 to 80 years. Some of my colleagues in the hospital consider that human life begins at implantation but from a genetic point of view I disagree. Deliberate interference with this process is a social decision. If the definition of the potential for human existence requires the presence of an anatomical cerebral neocortex and I think it does, then there is a philosophical biological question regarding the appropriateness of the abortion of anencephalic foetuses. The issue of rape, incest and unwanted pregnancy is psychosocial and is answered by society's mores. I am against killing including the judicial death penalty and I'm also opposed to killing in wars. You have to be able to live with yourself and I am against abortion. There were many people who would disagree with me and I respect their viewpoint.

Thankfully, we did not have to pester people at polling booths this time as the law had changed which made polling day a new experience. The obvious activity was to ensure that the appropriate voters on a marked register actually made it to the polling station and that voters who needed transport were collected and returned home. This needs a fair degree of organisation and transport which we simply did not have. Some people were collected as arranged and we offered lifts to others in houses using a good mobile public address system which we had borrowed from Ken O'Duill. The speakers had seen service in Dr Noel Browne's successful campaigns in Dublin North-Central.

Shortall's campaign had a number of vans for transporting people to the polling stations and they made a great effort in Ballymun and Finglas to make sure any Labour voters did not 'deviate' to Tormey by accident or design. We were taken aback by this degree of organisation which certainly outgunned anything Fianna Fail had done at previous elections and they were the masters. Eamonn O'Brien, a local city councillor who lives in Ballymun was one of the Workers Party candidates. He had hired two buses which were decked out with streamers and a public address system so there was plenty of razzamatazz to attract the attention of any floating voter. I have been on good terms with Eamonn for years. Eamonn was driving a CIE nipper and did not have a rosette when I met him on Silloge Road. I gave him one of mine and stuck an O'Brien label over the centre. We gave his supporters a big hello, hope we beat you, etc! I asked him to suggest a transfer to Tormey and he readily agreed. There was a considerable degree of good humour on nearly all sides during the election. The strangest contrast was seeing Proinsias de Rossa apparently canvassing alone on a Sunday afternoon in Albert College Estate where heretofore he was always surrounded by a considerable number of party workers. His campaign was very low key in comparison to the showpiece effort of the Workers Party during the '89 Dail/European election. The speed of change in politics even locally is truly astonishing.

Pat Carey was very worried about the anti-FF swing in the polls and distributed a written undertaking to address crime with a police crackdown as a main priority if elected. John Grundy attacked me verbally about Carey's law and order attitude which he thought ignored the widespread sense of alienation and disaffection of the youth population in Finglas South and Ballygall in particular. It is amazing in elections how you can be made a sounding board for anger directed at other politicians simply because you are prepared to listen. The crime and vandalism problem has been a serious local nuisance for a long time but the street killings in

Finglas in the recent past have greatly disturbed and frightened the public. Outside the Masses on the last weekend, he and his personal troops were handing out Carey only hand bills without a Fianna Fail logo. This was a classic example of candidate panic. He finished up acting as a virtual Finglas independent much to the great annoyance of some of the Fianna Fail faithful. Pat had intended to do a revamp of the 'PAT CAREY – councillor' local newspaper similar to his local election blast for distribution at the final effort but he was prevented from going ahead by the Fianna Fail organisation. I did not know this until much later and I'm glad they stopped him. Twice on the receiving end of that effort was more than enough, thank you Pat ! On polling day Fianna Fail mainly manned the voting registration tables in the Polling booths. They were not particularly noticeable on the ground in the free transport business. Fianna Fail's morale was in rag order compared to the local elections and previous generals.

When reviewing constituencies, the press seem to look at what happened at the last election, often years earlier as a strong indicator of current likely outcomes when opinion polls are clearly much more reliable. Who would have thought that Labour would go from a 5% opinion poll rating in 1987 to more than 30% by 1993?

I fortunately received a large black and white picture of Dick Spring in a brown envelope through the post. Having realised that the chance of winning was probably gone, a last drop consisting of a picture of Spring and Tormey on one side backed on the flipside by a copy of the '89 count from Nealon's Guide with the exhortation to 'Join the Dick Spring Supporters Club by voting No1 Dr Bill Tormey' was a nice one but it didn't work. We rushed out about 16,000 on the last two days and continued to drop right up to mid-morning on election day. John Grundy and Jimmy Spence were physically wrecked from the effort and were counting the hours until close of play just in case we got any more wild ideas for a new leaflet. How good our distribution was in the rush was hard to know. It certainly lifted our morale and I found the whole idea very amusing. We could just imagine Shortall, Kavanagh and company going bananas and that thought alone gave us all a real buzz. The message itself was essentially true – we were all Spring supporters.

Bingo and Churches

Finian Mitchell reminded us that the most efficient way to meet voters on a Sunday evening was to meet the crowd of people, largely women, attending bingo sessions. Despite the cold and wind, on the final Sunday night before polling, waves of women rushed determinedly into the bingo sessions in St Canice's school in Finglas village at 7.30p.m. and at the WFTA Hall in Finglas West at 8.00p.m. We had our team with Tommy Tormey, Finian Mitchell and Frank Rock covering all entrances. The village session was organised by Pat Grant and Terence Christie of the Barn

Church Restoration Committee and Una Polion, Angela McGrath and Paddy Cromwell were selling the various books. They kindly allowed me to meet the people there. The locals were very friendly and there was a good buzz in the hall because virtually every seat was taken. The persisting high popularity of bingo is a real social phenomenon. About 90% of the players are female. It is a relatively cheap way to meet and mingle with your friends and neighbours. The gambling aspect is very much a minor part of the scene.

Hard Labour

The 'Hard Labour' leaflet distributed by Fianna Fail after advise from Saachi and Saachi attacked the Labour Party on its taxation record in the 1983-86 coalition period. The rushed out reply by Labour to reassure voters about property tax, VHI insurance reliefs etc was an ironic episode considering the self-styled coalition for change that emerged in January. Change is a very elastic word. The Fianna Fail desperation tactic reminded me forcefully of the newspaper advertisement 'Is the Left Right for the Park' which they placed in the national press at the end of the Presidential campaign. The tactic failed then and it failed again. The voters are turned off by that stuff.

The Count

When the scale of the Roisin Shortall-Labour Party victory became evident early in the count, the unbridled hostility towards us from her largely anonymous-to-us schoolteacher camp and from Odran Reid, Peter Daly and company remained. There was no magnanimity in their victory. At least they were consistent. I personally congratulated Roisin Shortall and went upstairs to the tea room to cheer up my despondent son, Tommy, and the rest of the lads.

At the count, long-time Labour activist Finian Mitchell was surprised at the number of official Labour Party supporters who expressed worry at the prospect of Mary Flaherty losing her seat. A number of them claimed to Finian that they had looked for transfers for Mary. John Horgan and Geraldine Cunniffe, both Shortall supporters were clearly worried for Proinsias de Rossa's electoral health. The Shortall-Labour Party were definitely not interested in transfers to Tormey. With David Core, George Metcalfe, Finian Mitchell and the rest of the lads, we headed over to Kavanagh's Gravediggers Pub in de Courcy Square where we met an even more dispirited Workers Party group including Bernadette Hughes and Brian Whelan. Where do we all go from here? There appeared to be no immediate answer but we will fight on.

Politics moves on and the young voter is now very volatile. There is no longer the tight family commitment to Fianna Fail or Fine Gael. This vote has been building since Jack Lynch in 1977 and has been netted at different times by Garret

FitzGerald, Des O'Malley, Mary Robinson and now Dick Spring. Door to door canvassing, political clinics and clientelism, local branches, etc., may still have a role but it is fast diminishing. Media profile and political fashion is everything. This time any Labour candidate was really Dick Spring incarnate in any constituency and this vote will ebb just as it flows. Who then will be the next Irish political Messiah?

Coalition With Fianna Fail

When the numbers for a coalition of the Democratic Left – Labour and Fine Gael became untenable with the defeat of Democratic Left's Eric Byrne by Ben Briscoe of Fianna Fail following the marathon recounts in Dublin South Central, and with Fine Gael being strident in their fear of Democratic Left, as shown by their overblown antipathy to de Rossa's group, the clear next move was for Dick Spring to present his options to Fianna Fail. Reynolds' quick response and very adroit manoeuvres left Fine Gael out in the cold. Other than Austin Currie's post election comments about Spring for Taoiseach, neither John Bruton nor the rest of the Fine Gael Front Bench seemed to realise that they were the biggest election losers.

The Political Plague

The Labour Party headquarters moved against some of my supporters before the Special Delegate Conference on January 10th at the National Concert Hall. Tom Dunne was told by Ciaran Bookey, who was organising the SIPTU delegation that the Labour Head Office had refused to accept him as a delegate as he was no longer a party member. Apparently, the General Secretary had removed him from membership simply by deleting his name from the automatic renewal list for 1993. Mr Kavanagh had no right to act unilaterally in this manner as any such move is a matter for the Administrative Council. Stalin was still stalking the Gardiner Place area in 1993. That's a good laugh when you remember what used to be freely said about our socialist brethern in the Workers Party across that same Dublin street. Tom was irate at an effective expulsion without the right to defend himself or to reply. It is apparently much better to be a Militant than an ordinary Labour member. Paddy Donegan, as secretary of the Whitehall Santry branch had received no communication about the position of any member or about the Special Conference. Tom Dunne phoned Ray Kavanagh who told him that he knew he supported and worked on the Tormey campaign but that there should be no problem if he wished to re-apply as a Head Office member in a number of months. This is, of course a form of political ostracism. Kavanagh said, 'If you went to that conference you would infuriate the Shortall crowd'. Tom told Kavanagh he would think about it. His main concern was the proxy insult to his own union SIPTU.

There is no provision in Labour's constitution for such actions by the General Secretary and I confirmed with Ciaran O'Mara, an Administrative Council member that the issue had not been on, either raised or discussed.

This was a stupid move by Kavanagh and company and only firmed up my support in the constituency. The clever alternative would have been to isolate me and to ignore all those who supported me. The ironic aspect of this new partnership government is its commitment to 'an Ethics in Government Bill' when a report on ethics in the party would make quite interesting reading.

By December '92, I appeared to have acquired a previously undescribed infectious disease – a form of political plague – when I met many Labour Party people. Honourable exceptions were Fergus Finlay, Dave Grafton, Pat Upton, Pat Magner, Ita McAuliffe and Anne Byrne.

It was funny to receive commiserations on my political plight in the 'Hoops Upside Your Head', a Shamrock Rovers fanzine at the RDS at the Rovers v Limerick game in December. It read ...... 'Bill's failure to get a Labour nomination this time out must have been an extremely bitter pill for him to swallow. If you think you've had a rough year, think of the poor doctor. He's been shafted left, right and centre.' It is a pity that more Rovers fans are not on the electoral register in North-West.

In *The Forum* local newspaper at the end of January 1993, there was a profile interview with Roisin Shortall. It read: 'Running as the Labour Party's only candidate in the area, the recent election's historic trend of support for the party was reflected somewhat but not entirely in her vote, she says. Whether the Labour Party could have brought home two seats is something she doesn't linger on but: 'I suppose in theory you could say, there could have been alright' admits the former school teacher.' Tormey had already been before the electorate four times and and in many ways this election took place last year at the local election.' '.... It was agreed locally in the Party and also from Head Office that the right strategy was to run one candidate. We were looking for one seat and that was the recommendation from Head Office and was endorsed locally by the Party here. I won the selection convention then on the basis that people thought I had the best chance of taking the seat'.

From the satirical verse of the great Dean of St Patrick's, Jonathan Swift comes a strangely prophetic description of the unchanging nature of man's behaviour. On this evidence, Irish politics hasn't changed much. On the Irish House of Lords which he called the Irish Club he wrote:

Ye paultry underlings of state,
Ye senators, who love to prate;
Ye rascals of inferior note,
Who, for a dinner, sell a vote;

Ye pack of pensionary peers,
Whose fingers itch for poets' ears;
Ye bishops far removed from saints,
Why all this rage? Why these complaints?
Why against printers all this noise?
This summoning of blackguard boys?
Why so sagacious in your guesses?
Your effs and tees, and aars, and esses?
Take my advice; to make you safe,
I know a shorter way by half.
The point is plain: Remove the cause;
defend your liberties and laws.
be sometimes to your country true,
Have once the public good in view:
Bravely despise champagne at Court,
And choose to dine at home with port;
Let prelates by their good behaviour,
Convince us they believe a Saviour;
Nor sell what they so dearly bought,
This country, now their own, for nought.

2
TEN YEARS' HARD LABOUR

The 1956 Hungarian uprising is my earliest political memory. This was most likely because of the role played by Cardinal Mindszenty and the response of the Soviet Union in rolling the tanks into Budapest. My mother was an ardent Catholic and was very concerned about these events to the extent that there was much talk at home of helping Hungarian refugees. Both my parents were civil servants and strangely, to this day, I do not know how my father voted though my mother was a solid Fianna Fail supporter reared in West Clare who, under pressure from my brother and myself, voted No1 for Barry Desmond until he opted for Europe. She salved her conscience on the basis that Barry just might lose his seat and she wouldn't want that.

I was sent to Marian College in Lansdowne Road when I was 7 years old. At the time this was a fee paying school run by the Marist Brothers who also ran the school in Athlone which my father attended. The entrance interview was held personally by the Principle Brother Declan Duffy and I was asked to read a little book with the word 'potato' in the sentence. The impression from the shining marian blue floor tiles, lighter blue walls and the echo around the entrance vestibule was memorably intimidating to a nervous lad. Quite a contrast to the convent school in Booterstown where Sr Malachi had welcomed nearly every kid in the neighbourhood as virtual babies. The odd man out in baby school was Eamonn de Valera – future *Irish Press* boss – who was driven to school in a large black car and was allowed slide around the classroom to his hearts content. Maybe the nun was FF!

Domestic help ladies were retained from the same street in Booterstown for six or seven years. The Dunnes and Murphys became extended parts of the family. We took care of an old, partly invalided spinster for years, both in her own home in Sandymount Green and in Trimleston, until she died. In retrospect, she had an undiagnosed neurofibromatosis.

It is surprising how little things make a disproportionate impact on children. In my fourth year at Marian, a religious brother made a very nasty remark to a classmate about his father's occupation. The man was an official in the Amalgamated Society of Woodworkers (now UCATT) union. I have no idea what might have provoked this but I have never forgotten the incident. The irony was that the lad in question was the best and brightest in the class. I remember protesting at the time and getting two cane belts across the hands for my trouble.

When I was 12 years old, the class was divided into two. The top five in the private junior school were placed into the 'A' class with the winners of the Dublin Corporation and County Council scholarships for secondary schools. I dropped 14 places in the class according to the Christmas report and was nearly eaten alive at home so I quickly did something about that by the summer. Experience had taught me that national schools were more on the ball than fee paying private junior schools because the neighbourhood kids at home that I palled around with, most of whom attended Blackrock College or Oatlands in Stillorgan did not appear to be much better than me. The other remarkable thing at the time was the speech and accents of many of the scholarship lads. I had not come into regular contact with anyone who spoke with a 'Dublin" accent until then. The nearest meeting would have been at Shamrock Rovers matches away in Tolka Park or Dalymount because I nearly always went to Milltown with a local group of parents and children. There were many fights in the side lanes along the Dodder river, some with the new lads and some with fellows who were now in the 'B' class about little or nothing and the trick was not to beat your opponent but never to be beaten yourself. That stopped after a few bouts and the class settled down. The kids from Ringsend were completely different from those who were there before in the junior school. Some were very good soccer players and we became very friendly. There was a high degree of social apartheid existing in Dublin then and it probably still remains in certain places. Charlie Gannon's father played football for Sheffield Wednesday, Shelbourne and Ireland and Tommy Brennan's brother Fran played for Drumcondra and Dundalk. We formed a team and played many matches in Herbert Park alongside the Dodder. Tommy Brennan was on the UCD athletics team with me years later and tragically died in his early thirties from a malignant melanoma having won the Irish National Cross Country Championships and competed internationally. The school discouraged soccer and we played with a tennis ball or a stone on concrete during breaks. I only remember playing soccer against another school on two occasions at Easter. Gaelic Football was played by one fellow in the class. He played at Kilmacud Crokes and it could have been a foreign game as far as the rest of his classmates were concerned. The GAA ban on foreign games had clearly erected a perverse kind of cultural barrier. Rugby, basketball and athletics were the main school sports. Barry Carty and Alo Munnelly who played for Monkstown and Louis Magee who later captained Bective Rangers and played for Leinster were the best rugby players in my year. The swimming pool was built later in the mid sixties. I ran in many races in Santry and elsewhere during the cross country season and I wasn't really fit enough to say I enjoyed them. Disorganised street soccer and schools rugby were very big at home and the Rock boys were the kings. Many of them played on the winning side on St Patrick's Day at Lansdowne in the Leinster Schools Cup. Years later I was on a winning Lansdowne 3rd team when we beat a Rock outfit 10 - 8 at Stradbrook – one of life's pleasures.

The election of John F. Kennedy as US President was a major influence in this country. I was in Eyre Square, Galway when he was on his triumphal tour around the country in June 1963 and the excitement was enormous. JFK became a family icon after his murder and joined the Sacred Heart and the Pope over the hearths of Irish living rooms. The Berlin Wall in 1960, the Cuban missile crisis in 1961, the space race, Harold Wilson's government in 1964, the Arab-Israeli war in 1967, Alexander Dubcek and the Prague Spring in 1968 were very real in our house. These events helped shape my attitudes. The *Irish Independent* daily, *The Irish Times* on a Saturday, the *Sunday Times*, the *Observer* and the *Sunday Independent* were bought regularly except when the family had no money. Their 'Opinion writers' did influence me. I liked the bias that I was reading. Douglas Gageby and Harold Evans were my idea of VIPs.

School was demonstrably religious and the Second Vatican Council was heavily influential. Ethical, moral, religious and political issues were debated in the classroom with teachers, both lay and religious. These debates were very stimulating. There was a lot of genuine questioning of the ways of the world and even in retrospect there was little bigotry and no racism.

There was much discussion at the school about what choice should be made when 'free secondary education' was introduced by the Minister for Education Donagh O'Malley, and finally the school made the correct decision to opt in. I was very pleased with this development and had reason to be so in later years.

On holidays in Clare in the '50s, paraffin lamps were a common mode of lighting in farm houses before rural electrification. In Galway, many children walked barefooted to school. Dun Laoghaire Borough where we lived occupied another world. In the early '60s, houses in Fenian Street collapsed into the street and I became aware of the terrible housing conditions in which many people lived. I realised that where you lived was important and that we were a very closed exquisitely stratified society. Every Protestant in the whole area was known as that and was somehow 'different'. My mother did not see such people as different however, and she had a wicked sense of pious hypocrisy about her. The late Sam Bateman, a retired civil servant who was Church of Ireland, visited our house on Sunday nights a few times a month and spoke animatedly at length on different subjects including some hilarious anecdotes about Brian O'Nolan 'Myles na gCopaleen' who had worked in the same office as both himself and my mother. Apparently, when Myles was out of the office he would leave a hat on the stand and any higher officer looking for him was told that he was only out of his room but was certainly in the Customs House because his hat was still on the rack. My father's sister had married Victor Swanton, a Quaker from Nenagh who was a thorough gentleman. All their children went to Terenure College and were Catholic. The real cultural imperialism of the 'ne temere' decree was quite clear to me from an early age. John Charles McQuaid had become an overwhelming influence on Irish thinking. He appeared a bit of an ogre in kids social circles, even at Confirmation in Sandymount. The old claim that you had to be a Catholic to go to heaven was also clearly absurd even to a fourteen year old. My father had no time for the Knights of St Columbanus or the Free Masons for that matter. His passions were golf, racing and to a lesser extent football where he was a Rovers hater. His father had been an Athlone Town director when they won the FAI cup in 1924.

Imperceptibly, I realised that the world was unfair and that many of the deficiencies were man-made. The psychology of emigration was widespread. I had many first cousins living in England, Australia, Canada and the United States whose names I did not even know. A few infrequent visits from aunts and uncles were the only real contacts other than Christmas cards.

Sean Lemass was obviously, a dynamic taoiseach. Hope was really alive and palpable in this country in the 60s. RTE television started from Marian College studio before Montrose was fully operational. I could not easily forget the opening night because I had been picked to stand in the school group that was being shown on that historic occasion and we went to a neighbour's house to watch the event on their television. I earned some money after school delivering coal and briquettes around the district from a fuel supplier and also delivering papers in the morning and evenings. Johnson Mooney and O'Brien in Ballsbridge gave me a job one summer as a helper on a bread delivery electric truck where I was assistant to the late Denis O'Brien who shared a passion for greyhounds with our neighbour George Williams. They once took me to a coursing meeting as a kid and I'm glad that I really did not see nor did I realise the barbarity of what was going on.

My parents separated in a bitter squabble and we were hard up for money for many years. I was glad of the 'free education' system and we survived largely because of the help from neighbours and friends quietly given to my mother. My uncle Tommy bought us books and gave me a credit card for Hanna's and later for Hodges Figgis to encourage us to read. Fortunately three of my four brothers received school scholarships given to those at the top of the class and we survived. My brothers often had to walk the three miles into school in Ballsbridge. One incident in particular sticks in my memory. The sheriff's man called to the front door due to some problem with the nonpayment of rates. He could see three youths behind the glass panelled door and he asked politely to be allowed into the house to see the furniture. He was told very bluntly that he would not be admitted. My brother Peter, who is now an army officer, was a straight talker and did not mess about with the caller, insisting on impolitely advising him to leave immediately. Tempers were high because we knew why they had called. The sensible man turned to his helper, passed an inaudible remark and then left. We went back into the kitchen to tell the Ma and we were in a state of high excitement. Life was not dull. Around that time the lights were cut due to the ESB taking a poor view of the nonpayment of bills. Out came the candlesticks, but we survived, and those are the kind of events that are best left in the deepest recesses of the memory. Time heals an awful lot. Some deal must have been done between my parents because these incidents did not recur. Dunne's Stores in Cornelscourt was a weekly destination with Millie Cole delivering the groceries and my mother to the front door. To our good neighbours in Booterstown, I am forever grateful for all the things done quietly for us. To Millie, Mary Walsh, Ma Scally and co, I copped on but never said anything to preserve mother's dignity.

The sixties boom was a good time to be a student. When I left school, my father arrived to get me to sign forms for the civil service. I refused, telling him that I wanted to study medicine and would not budge from that. Then I went to work as a ward orderly in a hospital in London where I was kindly put up by my aunt Jo Higgins. Her in-laws included Albert Duffy who was Labour MP for Sheffield Attercliffe and a junior minister in Harold Wilson's government. The money saved paid the £100 fee for pre-med in UCD and Belfield was ten minutes walk from the house. No busfares, I was in business. UCD was hard and competitive. It was a survival course. I joined the Labour Party in my first year in college in 1968 and joined many demos against the Fianna Fail government. Justin Keating made a lasting impression when I heard him speak at a Saturday morning first years debate in the Science Block. I have had a great regard for the man ever since. Fianna Fail had become tired and their ministers seemed arrogant and aloof. Money and men in mohair suits had taken over or so it seemed. There was a whiff of corruption in the air with a lot of comment about land deals and strokes allegedly involving well known FF politicians. Fianna Fail had become a 'no-no'. TACA turned me off. Fine Gael had a taint of fascism from the '30s so their 'Just Society' left me unconvinced. The British Labour Party and the welfare state attracted me and I was very taken by Tony Benn's technological revolution stuff. I was a still an innocent kid. (Cynicism came much later). I can still vividly remember the 'We want Fianna Fail out' slogan re-echoing down Grafton Street as hundreds of young students chanted in unison. I got a sharp toe in the behind from a law enforcer when we sat down on O'Connell Bridge on a housing action march. I was at some of the mass meetings in the Great Hall at Earlsfort Terrace in UCD during the so-called 'gentle revolution'. Garret FitzGerald came to support the students and speaking for what seemed like an eternity, he succeeded in defusing a charged atmosphere through a very effective filibuster. Many of the audience left to head home or to the pubs. Ad hoc meetings took place with the staff and I was a class representative at some of these. A chaplain warned me to be careful lest I become a marked man and be failed in the Summer Exams. In the event I suffered no mishaps. It was a very interesting time to have been at UCD. The Labour Party membership cost five shillings and my brothers took great delight for years in referring to Labour as the five bob party.

Labour, Fianna Fail and Fine Gael held their final rallies of the 1969 General Election on successive nights from a raised platform erected in Lower O'Connell

Street. These were great street theatre. Fine Gael had the diminutive figure of Richie Ryan bobbing up and down before the microphone while working up a head of indignant steam deriding Fianna Fail on one evening. On another night Kevin Boland had just bragged that he had fired the Lord Mayor when someone cast an aspersion on him that he did not like and he swung a fist in their general direction. It was priceless stuff never to be seen again. Labour had no such dramatics but there was plenty of 'the seventies will be socialist' and other slogans.

For three summers I earned the money in New York or Toronto for the next year's fees in UCD and then my father stepped in. The people I met in North America were the most welcoming, generous, open and friendly that one could wish for. John Campbell from Cookstown and his wife Bernie from Irvingstown, Co Tyrone looked after me like an adopted son. He had served in the US Army in Germany and was an American citizen. I spent many weekends in Hackensack, New Jersey with his family and he got me a better paid job in Manhattan. Pat O' Neill who was in my class in UCD and who played for Dublin was the best paid of any of our lads in New York because of his GAA connections. We were delighted for him because he is such a decent guy. We gave him a right slagging one evening in Gaelic Park in the bar when he had been sent off for laying out a player who had kicked him. Pat simply blushed. I ran out of cash at Easter in 1971 and luckily after a quick dash around the building sites, I got a job in Stephen's Court on St Stephen's Green for three weeks working for Sisks, the builders. That dug me out of that particular financial hole.

During the summer, I met a US army nurse who invited me to visit the Walter Reid Army Medical centre in Washington. The sight of soldiers with half their faces burnt away and others with amputations and multiple wounds from the Vietnam War was shocking. Their aggressive attitude to the 'gooks' as they called the Viet Cong was in contrast to my own opposite sentiments which I kept very much to myself. There was a feeling of controlled violence about many of the injured officers and they were also very racist, being grossly abusive to the black gate sentry on the way into the camp. He had merely reasonably asked who was I, when a torrent of abuse greeted him with the final comment that I was OK, I was an Irish kid. I was fed and kept there on the house. I'm sure the military authorities did not know of my presence.

These experiences, taken together, politicised me and I can never forget that I was lucky, very lucky. The previous summer in Toronto, many of the residents in the University fraternity house, where I rented a room, were American draft dodgers avoiding the Vietnam War. One of these, John Tormoen was the son of a high ranking US Airforce Officer from Georgia. His father arrived in August in a Lincoln Continental limousine to visit his fugitive son. The whole experience was chock-a-block with contradictions. The bombs in Dublin in 1974 which killed many people in South Frederick Street and in Talbot Street were instantly recognisable in

Earlsfort Terrace Library where I was reading at the time. Some of the injuries seen in the city hospitals were awful. Jaw Jaw is better than War War at any time. It is worth remembering that it is the poor who suffer most in wars and who are most vulnerable to the attractions of militant nationalism. Violence is a human plague.

My youngest brother was born with Fallot's tetralogy, a congenital disease of the heart and spent many months over many years in the Mater Hospital where he ultimately died on the operating table undergoing repeat cardiac surgery at the age of 18 years in 1976. While in hospital he was visited at least once every day by my mother – a huge commitment. He was quite a character, bright, talkative and not at all self-pitying or neurotic. He was in the pre-med year in UCD when he died and I encouraged him when he had asked me whether he should go ahead and have more surgery. He was greatly missed by both my mother and myself. The 1973-77 coalition promised much and the cabinet was very talented individually. The heavy gang allegations about police brutality forced me to stop paying my membership for a few years until I moved to the Merrion branch in Dublin South-East in the late '70s when Labour was again in opposition.

My mother spent more than ten years in receipt of social welfare payments, either deserted wives or pension. She jokingly called them her 'Barry Desmonds'. Despite her income she had certain itinerant families as callers and she also gave clothes and food to a tramp called 'Jonjo'. She was very upset when she heard that he had been burnt to death in a caravan fire out past Rochestown Avenue in Dun Laoghaire. I am very aware of the effects of low income and what the whole system entails.

I qualified in medicine in UCD in 1974 from St Vincent's Hospital and after a year as Clinical Lecturer in medicine at TCD Medical School at St James Hospital, I got a job as a Lecturer at Leeds University. The Department of Chemical Pathology at Leeds General Infirmary had a definite left wing bias among the staff and I worked there from 1978 until 1982. Tory supporters were in about a 30% minority and the unions ruled OK. There were a few Ecology fans but Labour was the overwhelming popular choice. The Professor's father had been an official in the National Union of Mineworkers in Wales but Brian Morgan himself was a tough operator against shoddy work attitudes, being a complete workaholic. In experiencing the 'Winter of discontent' which wrecked the James Callaghan Labour government and lead to uninterrupted Tory rule ever since, I quickly came to the realisation that the British Labour Party was quite a broad church coalition internally. The more extreme elements can quickly make the whole body virtually unelectable. The winter of 1979 in Britain saw bodies unburied, graves undug, garbage uncollected, hospitals on emergencies only, etc., etc. It was chaotic and all for what?

The Irish Labour Party is also a coalition of political views and Dick Spring's campaign to rid the Irish Labour Party of the Trotskiist Militant Tendency was in my view a necessity although it spoiled the fun for 'the nationalisers of the commanding heights of the capitalist economy'!

For election '81 in June, I took holidays from Leeds and came home to help the campaign in Dublin South-East. I was kept informed by the very efficient branch secretary Kathleen Gill a nurse in St Vincents Hospital. Mary Freehill and Ruairi Quinn were the two candidates and Caroline Hussey was a tough organised no-nonsense campaign director. She addressed the troops from a raised platform every night before the action. The whole operation was run with great efficiency from a rented building in Charlemont Street and morale in the campaign was terrific. Postering, canvassing and marking a register, literature drops and answers to voters enquiries were handled with almost military precision. The 'Mighty Quinn' as he was styled in his car p.a. signature tune was surprisingly beaten having had a high profile for the previous four years in the Dail. Mary Freehill was a very good second candidate and the campaign was completely unified. I learned a lot from watching what was happening. There is no doubt that the team of Caroline Hussey, Denise Rogers, John Long, Natasha Browne and a host of others was crucial to any chance of victory.

Fortunately for Ruairi Quinn, the government fell on the budget and there was another election in February 1982 when Fianna Fail scraped back into government with the help of the Gregory deal. I had returned from England and helped again in the General Election. The election machine sprang into action to try to regain the seat for Quinn and Labour. Dave Grafton, acting on behalf of the Tanaiste Michael O'Leary went to the Taoiseach Dr Garret FitzGerald to negotiate a deal for Dublin South-East in which all the Fine Gael election literature would include the name of Ruairi Quinn as a fourth preference. This strategy, combined with the selection of only one Labour candidate, was the best way to ensure success even if Quinn was in effect tied into any possible Labour/Fine Gael coalition. A special effort was made on polling day to reduce the possibility of wholesale voter impersonation in the flatlands of Rathmines and Rathgar because it could have a crucial effect on the ultimate result and was reckoned to have been a factor in the recent defeat. I spent the day with Vikki Somers at a polling station on Rathgar Road where we did discourage quite a number of mid-twenty males trying to return to the station for a second helping. Labour in South-East was sufficiently organised to man the tables inside the polling stations. Some contrast with North-West where we often struggled to cover the entrances to all of the polling stations for the whole day. Caroline Hussey ran in the Senate election for NUI without success and we gave her some help with envelopes etc. The unbounded joy in Bolton Street when we won was fantastic. Many of the gang were unashamedly and openly weeping with joy. It was undeniable that Garret FitzGerald was brave and peerless at vote management in his own bailiwick.

Shortly after the election, I discussed seeking a nomination to run for election for Labour somewhere in Dublin with Ruairi Quinn and Mary Freehill and because the Richmond and Jervis Street hospitals were being transferred to Beaumont in the near future, a northside constituency was suggested.

Flor O'Mahony was a Senator from Dalkey who had been a candidate with Barry Desmond in the Dun Laoghaire Rathdown constituency 1969. He moved into the Dublin North-Central constituency which included Beaumont Hospital about June 1982 at the time when I had decided to do the same. So, at the instigation of Ruairi Quinn, who had suggested that Brendan Halligan could do with a bit of competition in Northwest, as he had lost the seat to de Rossa of Sinn Fein The Workers Party after a huge row with local Labour councillor, Paddy Dunne, I decided to enquire further about moving there. Ruairi said that the area had a history of great acrimony within the Labour Party which needed to be sorted out and healed. He had introduced me to Gregory Sparks in late February who had been Director of Elections in North-Central and who knew the Finglas area. Sparks met me on a few times in June to discuss North-Central and later North-West. Gregory was a competent organiser and he produced a plan of action for North-West which included which branch to join, where to organise a medical practice and how to contact northside local newspapers. His advice, of course, was not necessarily followed. There were meetings over lunch with Sparks and Ruairi Quinn in Leinster House and Mary Freehill was advising me independently. Greg also organised a meeting in the Burlington Hotel to discuss North-East with Tony Browne who was the Party's International Secretary. Tony's wife Mary O'Hanlon was a close supporter of Brendan Halligan in Dublin North-West. She died very suddenly after a short illness a number of years later. When the decision was made, Gregory drove me around the constituency on a Sunday lunchtime pointing out the high level of obvious vandalism and deprivation. Some areas looked straight out of the set of an 'Urban Jungle" movie. I was very idealistically driven and I thought that perhaps I could contribute to the resolution of some of these problems. Experience has taught me circumspection and humility in relation to my expectations of what I could achieve in the political and social spheres.

The Dublin West By-election following Richard Burke's surprising elevation to EC Commissioner by the Fianna Fail Taoiseach Charles Haughey was held in May. Liam Skelly of Fine Gael pulled off a tremendous win over Eileen Lemass of Fianna Fail and the Workers Party benefited from the backlash to the PRSI increases in the earlier harsh budget. The election was being run from Ballyfermot Road and the whole organisation was crawling with Militants. What a turn off! I felt sorry for our candidate Brendan O'Sullivan who polled 703 first preferences compared to 16,777 for Skelly and 6,357 for Tomas Mac Giolla. Michael Conaghan of the DSP, later elected for Labour in the 1991 Local Election, got 667. I showed up dutifully three times and that was that. Liverpool wasn't the only place where Labour appeared synonymous with Militant Trotskiism.

The Galway East By-election followed quickly afterwards in June. A big effort was made to boost the Labour vote there even though we knew that winning was a non-starter. Morale needed a lift and it was a question of all hands on deck. The Labour candidate was Kevin Dwyer from Tuam. I travelled to Ballinasloe three times for the campaign. We canvassed housing estates, streets in the towns particularly in Ballinasloe and also some country areas. It was a completely new experience for me and I do not know how much benefit obvious Dubs would be on the Galway doorsteps. Gerry and Margaret Mansfield put us up in their house and treated us with great hospitality. John Kelliher and I canvassed the large St Brigids Hospital in Ballinasloe and I also took the opportunity to see Portiuncula Hospital which had better laboratory equipment than the Richmond at the time. Dick Spring, Billy Coady, Niall Connolly, Seamus Patterson, Mary Freehill and a number of others were in Haydens Hotel helping in the war effort. On the following weekend the local Party organised a social in the Imperial Hotel in Tuam on a Friday night which was attended by Michael D Higgins, Toddy O'Sullivan, Ruairi Quinn and local man Pat Joe Gavin. Michael O'Leary was apparently well liked when we went around on the Saturday morning and by Sunday Sally Clarke, Michael Moynihan, Joe Bermingham, Tim Conway, Alan Finnegan, Ray Kavanagh and Ciaran O'Mara had all appeared. It was like a meeting of the clan. Palermo next stop!

The scene outside the polling station in Ballinasloe on a sunny and warm summer's day was amazing. Perched across the door was Padraig Flynn the Mayoman, like a King Kong dwarfing everyone and dropping 'Noel Treacy' chants in the voters ears. All the candidates had many supporters covering the entrance and the general heaving was incredible. The local Gardai had to referee the scrum regularly to insure that foul play was kept to a minimum. The Taoiseach Charles Haughey and Garret FitzGerald and their entourages were all in the Ballinasloe area and the atmosphere was terrific. Noel Treacy won the seat for Fianna Fail with 16,337, Ulick Burke FG got 13,610 and our man Kevin got 1,741 a respectable total.

Nurse Bridie Gargan was attacked and murdered in the Phoenix Park while lying in the summer sunshine. When the suspect Malcolm McArthur was arrested in a flat at Pilot View near Dalkey, which was owned by the Attorney General Patrick Connolly, Mr Connolly offered his resignation in mid-August even though there had been no wrongdoing on his part. The Haughey administration seemed dogged with bizarre events and an election was on the cards. Later that week, Michael Mullen met me in his office in Liberty Hall and gave me copies of the biographies of the great union leaders of the past. He also presented me with a personally signed copy of the history of the ITGWU by Desmond Graves. He wanted to discuss a possible role for me as consultant on health policy to the ITGWU and also wanted to help me win back his old seat in Finglas for Labour. He said he would do anything he could in that regard. Mickey was a scheming bright man and sometimes phoned me at work to meet him for lunch particularly in Nico's restaurant in Dame Street. On one occasion, I was unaware that he had invited along Dolores Price who had been convicted of terrorist bombings in England but had later been released on humanitarian grounds by the Home Office. She was interesting to meet.

On 24th September, I collected Barney Hartnett in Balbutcher Lane. An unmistakable figure in Ballymun, big black haired with a round kindly face, Barney dominated meetings and measured political decisions in Leinster House and in City Hall by a simple yard stick; what were their effects on Ballymun? He was politically anarchic and hated coalition with a blathering passion. Leon was the name he insisted on calling his son and that was no accident. Barney was the chairman and guru of the Ballymun branch and I took him down to the Lincoln Inn to discuss local politics. Sally Clarke got me the names of the members of Finglas East branch and arranged a contact with Stephen Dowds whom I met for a drink in Kavanagh's pub in Glasnevin on Saturday, 25th September to discuss the constituency. He was a member of Finglas East. So I transferred into that branch on 29th September, 1982. The Finglas East membership was active and met monthly in a room in the Tolka House opposite the Bons Secours Hospital. Niamh O'Doherty a social worker friend of mine from UCD days, joined the branch with me. Senator Jack Harte was national organiser and with the help of Finian Mitchell, they got me as much information on North-West as I required. Ten years later after much water under the bridge, I was to run in the same area as an Independent.

3

ARRIVING IN NORTH-WEST FOR THE 1982 GENERAL ELECTION

With a GUBU government in power, coalition was in the air. Brendan Halligan wrote in *The Irish Times* that another coalition with Fine Gael might prove disastrous for the Labour Party. He was correct. I wrote in reply that, 'Coalition with either of the major conservative parties should be removed from Labour's agenda until the Party has at least 30 Dail seats and can be seen to deliver on its own policies without 'contamination' by reactionary budgetary mistakes of the 'VAT on food and children's clothes' variety. Otherwise Labour becomes a self deluding irrelevance destined to disappear into the mists of history'. Labour can inspire our rapidly growing young population away from the cynical 'me feinery' of the *laissez-faire* capitalism of the conservative parties towards an all-embracing concern for social justice and advancement for all of our population both urban and rural. While on this road, the party's democratic traditions must be jealously guarded to insure against Stalinist centralism. New members from all walks of life must be actively sought to develop policy options to face the reality of an increasingly complex specialised industrial world.

The extra Dail seats can be won by implanting our policy options in the public mind with professional marketing expertise and dynamic leadership; thus identifying Labour as the party for young people to support. The trade unions have a pivotal role to play in oiling the machinery and in trying to politicise their membership to widen their vision and recognise the broader implications of their previous voting patterns. Labour has the will to do it and can go forward 'Mitterand-like' to a great and exciting renewal and leave the conservative parties with no option except to bury their Civil War past and amalgamate.

Michael Mullen

Michael Mullen was due to fly to Frankfurt on the 15th October and I had lunch with him on the previous Wednesday in Nico's of Dame Street. Terri McDermott joined us and there was much light banter and general slagging about what the bold Mickey might or might not do in Germany. Terri was well able to verbally joust with the General Secretary and he really enjoyed the contest, some of which consisted of in-house jokes above my head. Maybe she should go to Germany to keep an eye on him herself. I slagged him about his vulgar language to our great Taoiseach, his friend Mr Haughey, in my presence. Did Charlie know or was he ever aware that a Labour Party man could not avoid overhearing one end of their telephone conversation on August 20th? In fairness it should be said that the call had been incoming.

The following Monday, 18th October, I had a phone call from Liberty Hall and I was stunned to hear that Mickey had suffered a stroke in Frankfurt. He had earlier commented about his blood pressure and said that he disliked taking tablets. I had told him to do what his doctor, Jim Finucane, an eminent consultant had advised. On the weekend before he died, I was phoned at home from Germany by Susan Bowler-Geraghty and by Michael's family and they got me to phone the doctor in the Intensive Care Unit where he was being treated. I advised the family that Jack Phillips the neurosurgeon should be asked to see Michael and they wanted me to supervise the chemistry. Mr Phillips was willing to help and arrangements were made to fly to Germany. John Carroll had heard that there was a rumour that the government jet was to be used and he phoned me highly annoyed and said that the Union would pay for us to go across to London and on to Frankfurt. Early in the morning of Monday 1st November before anyone had gone anywhere, Michael Mullen died and a great union man was lost.

Michael had told me that he wished to engineer the amalgamation of the Transport Union with the Workers Union of Ireland and he would have been very jealous of John Carroll's success in that regard some years later. Some people slagged John behind his back but I found him to have a sharp incisive mind and I personally like both himself and his opposite number Billy Attlee.

The Galway Conference

The Labour Party conference started on Friday 22nd October with Michael D. Higgins delivering a brilliant speech full of inspiration, fire, passion and theatricality. Anguish then amusement, fierce anger and blazing commitment shone from his face. He held his audience spellbound. He would pause, wipe his brow and fix his gaze at the audience. I often thought he would have made a frighteningly effective fundamentalist preacher in another context. I loved it and those about me loved it. Conservatism was excoriated and the mood of the conference set.

Michael D. said, 'The Labour Party in its 1980 programme, declared itself to be a party of change, the party of equality, the party of planning for justice and for full employment. It is not the party which is on everybody's side. It is the party of the worker, of the ordinary men and women of the country, yet in particular the party of the poor and underprivileged and of those who are the victims of an unjust and often oppressive economic and social system.'

I was a member of the ITGWU delegation. This was a useful experience because one gets some insight into the way the General Officers think. Individual decisions are out and the vote is organised collectively. What the Union pays for in votes, it ensures delivery without slippage by having one coordinator in each group overseeing all ballot papers. John F. Carroll and Christy Kirwan were the main dealers and they made many decisions on the day, following a huddle with advisers on the delegation. The Frank Cluskey compromise on coalition was supported and many went home disgruntled. The vote, 671 to 493, was against involvement in a further coalition without prior approval by a special party conference. Most of the Dublin North-West branches voted against coalition or support for any minority government in line with the views of Brendan Halligan at that particular time. This was Michael O'Leary's last stand as Party leader but none of us had any inkling of what his intentions were. The Labour Women's National Council held a lunchtime anti-amendment meeting on the abortion issue and this was very well supported. The dissenters on this subject did not put their case.

Some of the conference motions were pretty wild. Resolutions included opposition to all public spending cuts; nationalisation of banks, financial institutions and major industries and all mineral, oil resources etc with compensation only on the basis of proven need; workers democratic control and management of all sections of the economy; a guaranteed job for all school leavers; nationalisation under workers control of all industries threatening redundancies. Unemployment was 15% or 160,000 and the national debt was £11 billion. There were also many constructive proposals including investment in the railways, opposition to nuclear waste dumping off-shore, the abolition of the status of illegitimacy; a National Development Corporation for joint ventures with the private sector targeted at import substitution and at some high risk projects and a stop to land rezoning scandals.

The Administrative Council's 'Towards Economic and Social Recovery' was constructive suggesting a National Planning Board with a Department of Economic and Social Planning to cover incomes, prices, employment, taxation, social expenditure, budgetry policy, investment and economic growth. A new Oireachtas Committee on Public Finance and a National Understanding with the social partners were also proposed. It is interesting how Labour policies turn up years later dressed in new clothes. Michael O'Leary's conference speech on the detailed proposals for the National Development Corporation has relevance for the 90's. There was also a partnership emphasis involving the Universities and the Third Level Institutions in the initiation of new projects. That whole message was damaged by the subsequent actions of the messenger.

The following Monday I went into the College of Surgeons to help Dr Magnus Oman carry out a study on some people running in the Dublin City Marathon. When I heard how long we were going to have to wait for their return, I decided to run myself. My rugby gear and running shoes were in the car so off I went. It was a crazy thing to do but I finished a long time later. I slowly jogged the first 10 miles with a few guys from Lansdowne rugby club until I got fed up and then I finished the rest with an unknown female at a better pace. By the end of the week, Michael O'Leary had resigned as Party Leader and from the party. That was a huge shock. However when you consider the level of personal vilification suffered by him, resignation might have been understandable. On 5th October, the headlines in the *Evening Herald* read 'O'Leary slams 'false' claims'. He denied all allegations made about him in a memorandum to the AC. The accusations had been made by Dan Browne, the Lord Mayor of Dublin at the time, and by Brendan Halligan and referred to the disposal of payments by the state to the Party Leader. These were his party leaders allowance and a personal transport allowance and O'Leary refuted the allegations in detail. Within days Dick Spring was elected Leader, Michael O'Leary joined Fine Gael and Fianna Fail were defeated in the Dail.

Paddy Dunne phoned me to meet him urgently. On Saturday afternoon, 6th November, the Finglas East Branch met at the Tolka House under the baton of Noel Wheatley. Niamh O'Doherty proposed my nomination as a Dail candidate and was seconded by Stephen Dowds. This was passed unanimously. That night I met Gerry Maher and Jack FitzWilliam at the Village Inn in Finglas and they said that their branch in Finglas Northwest was considering supporting me. We discussed the nomination interminably and moved back to Jack's house at closing time. The issue was not resolved until the following morning just before the Selection Convention which was held at Beneavin College. I was supported by four of the nine branches in the constituency. But before the vote Brendan Halligan asked for a short adjournment in which he considered withdrawing from the contest. When the meeting reassembled, I told them that I would not stand as a single candidate as that would seriously damage our chances and I told Brendan Halligan that two candidates was the best option. This suggestion was turned down and Halligan was then nominated as the sole candidate. Liam Pike was the constituency chairman then and again ten years later at the 1992 election. Finglas East, Finglas North-West, Ballymun and Santry Whitehall supported me and Wadelai, Deanstown/ Kilshane, Ballygall, Beneavin and Finglas 'Billy Rigney' branches were for Brendan Halligan. There were comments about paper branches etc but a newcomer ought not to be able to beat a former TD and Party General Secretary. Rooms were rented above a garage on Ballygall Road West and the campaign started.

I canvassed for Brendan Halligan virtually every night and at week-ends as did nearly everyone who had supported me at the selection conference. Peter Daly, Dan Proctor, Ben Kearney, Kevin Halligan, and Noel Wheatley were regulars and manpower was not short. At that point Seoirse Dearle, Liam Pike and Mollie Bracken were solid Halligan people. Ben Kearney and myself frequently teamed up to canvass Finglas West. The campaign was organised by Katie McKenzie and Mary O'Hanlon and we believed that Halligan had a fair chance. Dermot Timmins, Odran Reid and Stephen Dowds were active dropping and organising posters with a youth group. Marked registers were kept and queries followed up but there were too many people hanging about at the HQ in the evenings when they should have been canvassing. Many of the election helpers came from outside the area and kept themselves aloof. The branches who had supported me were excluded from any planning or organising of the campaign. Vandalism was a problem and the arrival of a brick through a plate glass window at about 7.15 one evening was a practical demonstration. A four page tabloid newspaper on art paper was produced supposedly by the Youth Section but it strangely reported that 'the Youth Section in Dublin NW is still getting established'! The weather was often cold and damp and winter campaigns are unpleasant. This one was no exception.

There was a series of political debates in the student societies in UCD Belfield. The panel at the Commerce and Economics society in October before the fall of the Government was Niall Andrews for Fianna Fail, Rhona FitzGerald for Fine Gael, Eamonn Smullen for SFWP and myself for Labour. Niall Andrews and Eamonn Smullen were quite a contrast. Smullen was serious, analytical, intense and didactic whereas Andrews gave it a lash straight off the shoulder, without a hint of embarrassment over the GUBUs of Fianna Fail. I summed up in the debate by saying, 'Reality respects ideals when we are in power, says Fianna Fail; ideals reflect reality when we are in power, says Fine Gael; Labour compromises its principles when it wants power; and Tony Gregory could be described as an expensive voice for the poor in society.' I also pointed out the low paid workers subsidise the rich and that many religious orders educate the children of the elite to ignore the poor. Debating societies in College had much difficulty getting competing candidates to talk during election campaigns. I again found myself asked to speak at the same society during the campaign. Ruairi Brugha, standing for Fianna Fail in Dublin South claimed that nothing would change under a new government and that this had created an anti-democratic situation where a handful of deputies had an undue influence in policy. Without stable government, there would be a marked deterioration in economic and social conditions. Roger Garland for the Ecology Party (later the Greens) said he had no quick answers to 15 years of bad government. He believed in National Government because it was more democratic. In the last Dail, Tony Gregory and the Workers Party had more authority than the whole of Fine Gael. I said, that reducing the budget deficit to zero in four years as intended by the conservative parties would have a devastating effect on the life of the country. Two days later, I addressed the L&H in Belfield. Maurice O'Connell spoke very well for Fine Gael and Peter Gibson a candidate in Dublin Southeast batted for Fianna Fail. Following the election, the UCD Commerce and Economics Society had Professor John Kelly, Fine Gael TD for Dublin South, Michael Conaghan of the Democratic Socialist Party, Liam Lawlor TD of Fianna Fail and myself to debate 'That Ireland unfree shall never be at peace'. John Kelly and

Michael Conaghan had definite anti-republican rhetoric views and there was a fair amount of good humoured banter with the few hundred students in the audience. Hecklers always liven up the proceedings.

Nationally Labour were at about 10% in the opinion polls after a boost from the new leadership of the youthful Dick Spring. The strength of Fianna Fail in West Finglas and around Tolka Estate was very obvious on the doorsteps. There was no difficulty covering the gates of the polling stations in North-West and I was allocated to Ballygall Road and Ballymun for a number of hours. Mary Freehill had asked me to go to Cumberland Street in South-East that evening and I arrived as promised.

North-West Results

In this second election of 1982, Brendan Halligan, running alone, polled 2,053 whereas Proinsias de Rossa had progressed to 6,291. Halligan was seventh on the list of first preferences at 6.4%. Halligan had been ninth on the list in 1981 when Paddy Dunne beat him by 564 votes. Having walked out of the previous campaign earlier in the year, Brendan Halligan left Paddy Dunne holding the torch and Dunne polled 2,412 but de Rossa took the seat, having increased his vote by almost two thirds from 1981 to 3,906. The electoral situation for Labour in North-West was going from bad to worse.

The state of the parties at the second election of 1982 was Fianna Fail 40.17%, Fine Gael 30.33%, Labour 6.45%, Workers Party 19.78%.

Countrywide

The election resulted in FF 75, FG 70, Lab 16, WP 2 plus Blaney, Gregory and O'Connell. The numbers were right for a coalition with Garret FitzGerald.

Tony Kinsella invited me to write a report for the Party on the cutbacks in the health services and suggested that I call to see Dermot McCarthy, an official in the Department of Health, in Hawkins House on Friday 3rd December. McCarthy was sceptical of many of the things I thought should be done but he had an excellent command of the subject and provided me with helpful documentation. I wanted an Irish National Health Service based on the then British NHS model with merit awards for excellence, a review of the GMS drug list cut by Fianna Fail in their July minibudget and more control of drug prices taking into account the findings of the Telesis Report. Psychiatry, mental and physical handicap, and general practice were to receive special attention. Over the next three days I summarised what I thought would be appropriate as an opening negotiating position and delivered it to Head Office where it was to be typed late on Sunday. On Saturday night there was a meeting in an office in Hatch Street followed by steaks cooked, as far as I can remember, by Tony Kinsella. Dick Spring, Joe Revington, Ruairi Quinn, John Long and Ciaran Murphy were also there. Because of the GUBU government which had just lost the election, I thought that Labour would have to enter coalition but the economic position was such that we were really in a 'no win' situation. On Saturday afternoon I bumped into Dick Spring and Joe Revington watching Lansdowne and Wanderers. Nothing unidimensional about those boys, I thought. Dick met with Charles Haughey and Tomas Mac Giolla but, for FF, coalition was out and he found no basis for co-operation with the Workers Party in the Dail. The meetings with Garret produced a detailed plan presented to the Special Conference.

Michael D. Higgins had been defeated in Galway West and phoned me. He was understandably very upset and I met him in Powers Hotel with Niall Andrews later. The Senate election on the NUI panel was his next target and with the help of his many friends, including media people, he made it safely. A review of his Galway conference speech was featured in *The Irish Times* around the time that the ballot papers were being posted and that certainly helped.

Special Conference, Limerick

The Special Conference was held in the Savoy Theatre in Limerick on 12th December. Most of the branches friendly to me travelled by train to vote 'yes'. Liam Kavanagh was in the street surrounded by the Wicklow organisation. He was looking for 'vote yes' people and entrance to the conference to do so could be arranged. There was much coming and going and meetings in pubs. The tension was real with a lot of doubt about how the vote would go. I was still an ITGWU delegate and was mandated to vote No! The coalition question caused enormous tension and antipathy and some members and groups felt almost blind hatred such was their hostility towards those on the opposite side. An arrangement with Fianna Fail would not have been even remotely conceivable.

Dick Spring produced a policy document which proposed the setting up of the National Development Corporation, the elimination of the current budget deficit within five years, an incomes policy, an employment task force, tax credits instead of allowances, income related residential property tax, derelict site tax, a Commission on Social Welfare, one of the objectives of which was to ensure that cash income from work was kept ahead of the level received while out of work, private patients were to pay more for the use of public hospital facilities, and a national drugs company to manufacture some drugs and supply the GMS was to be set up. Capitation fees in the General Medical Services were to replace the fee-per-item system and 35,000 houses per year were to be built.

Coalition was passed by a margin of 324 with 846 votes for the policy package and 522 against and the new government was in place by the following Tuesday. The Labour Ministers were: Tanaiste and Environment Dick Spring, Labour – Liam Kavanagh; Trade, Commerce and Tourism – Frank Cluskey, Health and Social Welfare – Barry Desmond.

4

1983 COALITION – WAS IT JUST BACK TO THE FUTURE?

The formation of new branches in Poppintree and in Glenhill, Finglas was the priority in order to get to grips with the constituency and I set about recruiting and organising people in the Belclare and the Courts areas of Ballymun. Brendan Core and Alan Boyle were to be the key people if I could keep them interested when the inevitable objections from opposing branches were raised. Party development often comes a long way behind covering a local political powerbase even where votes on the ground are very thin. Billy Keegan, a former city councillor and candidate for Labour and for the breakaway Socialist Labour Party, started to reappear at branch meetings in Finglas East. He interjected and rambled on interminably on every possible issue and was forever attacking Labour at Labour Party meetings – a strange state of affairs. He was sincere but very strident, long winded and dogmatic.

In association with the local branch, we decided to set up a Poppintree advice clinic in the local community complex. At the constituency council of 20th January, Mary O'Hanlon, a close supporter of Brendan Halligan, objected and led an opposition filibuster. This continued at the next meeting on February 3rd, when Liam Pike and Sam Nolan led the charge against any new branch in Glenhill. There was also a lot of debate about the question of the degree of responsibility which the candidate bore for the constituency election debt which was several thousand pounds. In the interim Greg Sparks and I met to discuss tactics and it was simply decided to keep up the pressure.

I tried to get support for a senate nomination by contacting Michael D. Higgins, Pat Magner, Ruairi Quinn and Liam Kavanagh but the exercise was both naive and futile. In the background, the Fianna Fail phone tapping scandal was breaking. Michael Noonan was making an immediate impression as Minister for Justice. Mr Haughey survived a third vote of confidence in his leadership of Fianna Fail and Garret at this point was still 'good'.

The Finglas East branch met regularly with about six to eight members present and the constituency AGM on 17th February in Beneavin College had about forty in attendance. One older branch member, Sean Mulready, died suddenly. The education cuts and school transport charges inflamed these meetings as did the suggestion from Transport Minister, Jim Mitchell, that CIE workers might have to take a pay cut.

Brendan Halligan and Flor O'Mahony were nominated as the substitute Euro MPs at the Mansion House in the following week after Halligan had campaigned vigorously to win his place. They beat Mick Brennan from Dublin West and Jane Dillon-Byrne from Dun Laoghaire.

In reviewing Garret's first hundred days in office, Olivia O'Leary in *The Irish Times* on 23rd March asked what have the Labour Party contributed to Dr FitzGerald's first 100 days? She wrote, 'They've kept him there, every day, through thick and thin, like an undersized Atlas holding up the world. They have supported a budget which has done nothing to create jobs, but plenty to tax workers, a budget with laughable capital taxation measures. They have supported a Government which charges the unemployed for the privilege of applying for public service jobs. While adopting a free vote on the anti-abortion amendment, they rowed in easily on the Forum for a New Ireland. Did they even dare to think about it?

'They have been the most amenable of colleagues. Dr FitzGerald must be very grateful to them .... whenever he remembers they're there.'

Advice Centres

Clientelism has always been a feature of Irish politics and it was considered absolutely necessary to organise such a service for the public if you wanted to be elected. I believe that their impact is diminishing due to the improvements in the public's access to information from radio, TV and the newspapers. Community information services in local libraries and in social welfare offices were also improving. The Poppintree branch advice centre started on 15th February and was held every Tuesday night. Ina Gould and Noel Wheatley helped out regularly. A leaflet was printed and distributed around Poppintree outlining our aims and stating that I would be personally present. By the second month, we had between three to six people per week attending. The main problems were the desire to leave Ballymun and transfer, often anywhere, but usually Tallaght. This sentiment lasted for about seven years until that particular wheel turned full circle and there was a queue to get a flat in Ballymun. Poverty and problems which were easily resolved by the community welfare officer were also common. Having written to the Corporation in relation to housing matters, the constituent was usually then contacted in writing. I began to notice that frequently the person involved did not seem to appreciate that what they had requested had already been done. Finally the penny dropped, illiteracy was a widespread problem. I changed my tack and brought everyone back for the answer to their queries and I read out any council correspondence. A few people then admitted that they found reading difficult and that they had left school very early. Trying to head off evictions for nonpayment of rent required a personal visit to the corporation and I visited Mr Bodley to sort out an arrangement for a family. I mostly found the officials very reasonable regarding people's problems and they were willing to come to any halfway agreement. Money lenders were in operation in the area but the subject was very difficult to get people to talk about. I never knew whether this was due to fear or embarrassment.

By the middle of March, I approached Shay Carbin to see whether the Finglas South branch would be interested in running an advice clinic perhaps in the social services centre on Welmount Road where Jim Tunney operated. Finglas South were keen to discuss a clinic but they would not allow themselves to be tied to a timescale. Branch meetings and constituency councils were held at least monthly and together with a busy job in the Richmond Hospital, the time flew by. However, I did lobby Barry Desmond on behalf of the geriatricians to get an improvement in the psychiatric services for the aged and I also lobbied the Department of Education in support of Alexander Silke of Scoil Ide on Cardiffsbridge Road who had started his ultimately successful campaign to get the building improvements that were agreed in 1977.

In April, I called Gerry Maher to arrange with his wife Betty to visit the Mellowes Court old folks community on alternate Tuesdays at lunchtime to offer them any assistance that I could. Brendan Core, Tommy Gallagher, Eddie Uzell, Denis Molloy, Tony Greene, Philip Clarke and Ina Gould had begun to argue about officerships and local issues as the Poppintree Branch got going and within one month Brendan Core had been voted out of the chair to be replaced by Tony Greene. Government rows about social welfare cuts and about the wording of the anti-abortion constitutional amendment gave the appearance that Labour was in chaos at parliamentary level. The government wording on abortion was defeated 87 votes to 65, and the Fianna Fail wording was subsequently carried by 87 votes to 13. This impression of chaos was seeping deeply into the public's consciousness and the party was heading for deep trouble.

Party Developments

In May, Dermot Timmons, on behalf of the constituency, invited Senator Jack Harte to an organisation meeting in North-West about new branches. New MEP Brendan Halligan made an effort to resuscitate the constituency through the appointment of Odran Reid as organiser but the deal fell through. However, the Poppintree Branch was ratified but Barney Hartnett and the Ballymun Estate branch left the party over the participation in coalition. Halligan was facilitating the establishment of Labour Left with a view to withdrawal from government and presumably to remove Spring as leader. Emmet Stagg, Frank Buckley, Brian Kavanagh, Frank Butler, Sam Nolan, Joe O'Callaghan and many others were active supporters. They ran their own panel for AC elections. But they never made much progress outside of Dublin and Kildare. I strongly opposed them.

Barney Hartnett, Ina Gould and myself joined the local councillors walkabout in Ballymun just before lunch on May 18th to get to grips with the local physical conditions. Barney had managed to cajole them into this through writing, telephoning and ridiculing them in his paper the *Ballymun Echo*. Tony Gregory, Diana Robertson, Paddy Dunne, Luke Belton, Ned Brennan and Hannah Barlow turned up with the council officials. Ina was representing the tenants in Poppintree who were complaining about the blocked sewage pipes and the inadequacy of the general drains where pools of stagnant and often stinking water were left lying in alleyways and outside some hall doors. Action was promised but it was a long time coming.

Greed Wins

The Tories won the British General Election on the 9th June. Michael Foot was a disaster as Labour leader despite the fact that he is a decent and honourable man. The glorification of greed was to be the worthy characteristic of the decade. Rolling back the state became a religion and the loss of the sense of community led to alienation of the unemployed underclass on a huge scale. Riots, unemployment, vandalism, drug addiction, crime and despair resulted from policies where the poor got poorer and transferred their taxes so that the rich got richer. Financial dealing became economically more important than primary industrial production. What happens in Britain impacts forceably on the other offshore island and the British emigration escape valve became a much less attractive option for Irish people.

Parallel Drugs Importation

In June, I went to Harrogate in North Yorkshire to meet Malcolm Town a pharmacist who was interested in parallel importing of proprietary drugs from low cost European Community countries. He had been blocked by the Department of Health from importing drugs into Ireland from Belgium. I had tumbled on a means of greatly reducing the cost of drugs in Ireland if the state was willing to break the price fixing cartel between their own Department of Health and the Federation of the Irish Chemical Industries, which was probably in breach of Community competition policy. Even if done commercially, there was more than £10 million available in profit with the minimum of effort. Maybe I should have gone ahead and done the job myself for personal profit and put it up to the Department of Health to block me, but instead I started campaigning on behalf of the whole community to have the rules changed which would have dramatically reduced the costs to patients and to the Irish taxpayer. This had nothing to do with generic drug substitution, an issue often used by vested interests to confuse the issue and block change. The best part of that trip was the Saturday spent at Lords at the West Indies versus Australia in the cricket World Cup – Viv Richards, Malcolm Marshall, Clive Lloyd, Alan Border, Denis Lillie, Geoff Thompson *et al* on a beautiful day in the Mound Stand with champagne on ice. All in all, the sort of thing for which you could develop a taste!

In the following week, I gave a talk on a comparison of the Irish Health Service with the British National Health Service at the Palmerston Branch in Dublin South-East and afterwards they bought me a few pints in the Barge Pub in Charlemont Street. Whenever I was in Leinster House, I listened to Brendan Howlin, Eileen Desmond and Toddy O'Sullivan anytime I could because their backgrounds and experiences were quite different to mine and their ways of approaching issues were more oblique. Justin Keating still remained high on my list of impressive thinkers on the Left. Consideration of other viewpoints before arriving at a conclusion is important to minimise wilful mistakes. Blind prejudice and arrogance can often be a substitute for well thought out policy. With Labour in coalition, I was simply embarrassed when Dr Andrew Rynne was fined £500 at the Naas District Court for selling condoms without prescription. What an immature country!

Sunshine or Gloom?

Many summer evenings were spent meeting people in the different branch areas. I met the security men in the Rivermount Pub in Finglas South where keeping order was a first priority. First hand experience of conditions in all areas of the constituency is necessary because the diversity is enormous. The middle class affluence and conservatism of Glasnevin and Griffith Avenue contrasted sharply with the disaffection and lawlessness of parts of Finglas where many residents live in fear of their neighbours. Santry, on the other hand, had a great community spirit and there was a thriving social life centred on the Greenfield Park Social Club and also on the club attached to Sanbra Fyffe on Santry Avenue. Ballymun continued as a satellite town with its own unique well publicised characteristics.

Colm O'Briain was appointed General Secretary of the Labour Party and he visited the constituency council in July. His introductory meeting was a particularly rowdy affair and Liam Pike and Brendan Halligan were in belligerent form. Halligan was trying to shore up his position in North-West yet he never competed on the ground with Proinsias de Rossa, the recently elected Workers Party TD. I was not sure what O'Briain would make of it all but I continued trying to lobby the branches for support and to try to get them involved in some local political activity. Inevitably there was a backlash. It was alright to talk of doing things but actually carrying out what you said clearly upset some of the local activists. Shay Carbin and Stephen Dowds decided to oppose me in the Finglas East and South branches on the same night but fortunately for me, there were sufficient of my supporters present to head off real problems. Shay Carbin had ambitions to stand in the local election due in 1984. Another frustration was that some of the local members wanted meetings about meetings to dissect and discuss any movement on policy or on local issues. Statements had to be dressed up in socialist cliche otherwise you were a suspect rightwinger. There was also a definite ingrained prejudice against doctors and especially against consultants. Dublin's games against Meath and Offaly in Croke Park were the best parts of July and Eamonn Coghlan's 5,000 metres victory at the Helsinki World Championships in August lifted the political gloom for a while. Greg Sparks, Finian Mitchell and Peter Daly who was with Finglas West branch, were actively helping me and Finian arranged for information leaflets to be printed in Leinster House where the Party had a small printing machine. Seorse Dearle met me in the Tolka House in September to try to arrange an outbreak of peace in the Constituency Labour Party which had been riven by faction fights for so long. David Thornley, Brendan Halligan, Matt Merrigan, Billy Keegan, Paddy Dunne, Robert Dowds, Sam Nolan, Gerry Maher, Mick McEvoy, Tony Dunne, and Diana Robertson had all stood for election during the previous decade. Factionalism was the norm in North-West. I agreed with Seorse to try for peace but I pointed out that some people seemed to thrive on internecine political warfare and seemed to regard the whole charade as an elaborate and inexpensive game.

The £50 water rate charges, which the government introduced were the political equivalent of shouting fire in a theatre and it allowed the anti-coalition members of Labour to have a field day. I supported the Party in government even if I disagreed with many of their moves because to do otherwise would have been essentially undemocratic. I was, after all, present in the Savoy in Limerick when the package was agreed. If I had felt otherwise I would have resigned. By October, I had called to see Diana Robertson, Larry Quigley and Shay Hackett of the Deanstown Kilshane branch at home to try to reduce the political temperature because they had refused to admit a local recruited by me into branch membership. Things did settle down later. Dick Spring visited the constituency on 20th October and he must have felt some of the barely suppressed hostility from the anti-coalitionists – at that time mainly Halligan supporters. I also spent a considerable amount of time talking to people in the popular pubs around Finglas such as the Drake Inn and the Shamrock Lodge to try to recruit people for our branches. Drink was a lot more popular than politics and it was to be a long hard road forward. Having bought a house on Glasnevin Avenue in October, there was no chance of me fading away from frustration, futility or disinterest.

Pro-Life Constitutional Amendment

On 7th September, the Pro-Life Amendment was voted into the constitution by 841,233 to 416,136 on a 53.67% turnout despite the flaws in its wording which would later become apparent with the 'X' case in 1992. There was much passion and inaccuracy vented during the debate and I felt that the whole subject should be part of legislation and not form an article in the constitution because it underlined the confessional nature of the State and would have no effect on the 'de facto' abortion rate in Ireland. The danger of censorship of front line medical journals and other publications existed and the 'X' case and the banning of the *Guardian* newspaper in 1992 merely proved that we were right to oppose that amendment. I put up the Vote No! posters across the constituency. Labour and the Workers Party officially called for a No vote. Fianna Fail stayed ostensibly neutral but in fact Mr Haughey in his final broadcast called for a Yes vote and Dr Fitzgerald said he would vote No. It was irritating to be called a killer and subjected to other verbal abuse when in fact I have always been personally opposed to abortion. The local Labour Party split on the issue and those for the referendum simply stayed away from the campaign.

Dublin Central By-Election

The unfortunate death of George Colley while in London for treatment for a heart condition precipitated the Dublin Central by-election. The selection convention in the FWUI Hall in Parnell Square nominated Jimmy Somers to fight the election. The meeting was addressed by Barry Desmond, the Minister for Health and Social Welfare. We attended as observers and afterwards Gerry Doyle and I joined John Horgan and Senator Jack Harte to go for a drink in the Belvedere Hotel. Labour was clearly in trouble and we all knew it. The cut-backs were making political campaigns very difficult. The following week, I took a crew from North-West to a fund raising effort for Jimmy Somers in the ITGWU club on Clogher Road in Crumlin. I decided to take half days' annual leave to canvass with Jimmy when he was particularly short in the afternoons. Jimmy, Junior Rice who was one of Mickey Mullen's men, and myself, sometimes with Shay Carbin hit the road. Smithfield, O'Devenney Gardens, Arbour Hill and around the NCR were covered during the day. The Labour Party was very unpopular and the hostility was palpable, not to Jimmy Somers personally but to the Party. The issue of the big 19% increase in TDs incomes was used as a stick to beat the government. The Taoiseach had suggested £500 million cutbacks in publlc expenditure in October. The Criminal Justice Bill had been published and it restricted the right to silence and gave the Gardai power to detain people for twelve hours for questioning. These issues were very controversial within the Party. The Irish Council for Civil Liberties had condemned the Bill and I agreed with them. It must have been very demoralising for the candidate. Labour and not Fine Gael was getting most of the blame because it was the Labour voter who was hurting most.

Local solicitor, Michael White, had a much easier time as the Workers Party candidate, as had Mary Banotti for Fine Gael. Labour was getting it in the neck. Greg Sparks was Director of Elections and made as much of the campaign as he could. He divided the constituency into six areas and allocated one each to other Dublin constituency organisations to help out on the canvass. On Sundays, we covered the churches in Halston St, Arran Quay, Church Street and on up to Aughrim Street with the Dun Laoghaire helpers and even Barry Desmond was not as chipper as usual. I still remember being directed around Glasnevin by Eithne FitzGerald who is a native of the place. The area was not exactly fertile Labour soil! Down Clonliffe Road was a different matter, but many people were still very angry at the defection of Michael O'Leary to Fine Gael and were giving Labour a miss on this occasion. There were more than 100 people out canvassing on some nights. We all knew Jimmy was in for a hiding, but the extent was still shocking. Fine Gael Minister for Defence, Paddy Cooney, and myself stood together in the gloomy dampness outside Halston Street polling station for the last hours of the campaign on 23rd November and voter interest was very disappointing. The result was disastrous and an upset Ita McAuliffe, her sister Helena, Greg Sparks, Junior Rice, George Murphy and myself held our wake in the 'Four Seasons' in Bolton Street. To what extent the Pat Carroll factor in Cabra had worked against us was unknown. Pat had resigned his City Council seat in October to go on overseas service in Tanzania. The co-option for his replacement had been a draw between Jimmy Somers and Barry Fottrell, but Jimmy was appointed by the Administrative Council.

Barry Desmond went on TV to explain away the obvious. Jimmy Somers was in no way to blame because it is impossible to swim against a torrent. Sometimes the role-playing in politics can be overdone. That day Barry was at the crease and he was finding it hard to put his political bat on the ball. Later that night, I was roundly slagged at a debate in the UCD Law Society where I was representing Labour; Michael Woods, Fianna Fail; George Bermingham, Fine Gael; Chris O'Malley, Young Fine Gael and Eamonn Gilmore, the Workers Party. Those were tough times for the party and they were to worsen a few weeks later when, on 8th December, Frank Cluskey resigned as Minister for Trade, Commerce and Tourism over the retention of the Dublin Gas Company in the private sector. Ruairi Quinn was promoted to the Cabinet as Minister for Labour.

The Result

Labour slumped into sixth place with Somers at 1,966 (6%), Tom Leonard of Fianna Fail got 15,236 (46.6%), Mary Banotti Fine Gael 7,362 (22.5%), Michael White WP 4,342 (13.3%), Christy Burke Sinn Fein 2,304 (7%). Jimmy Somers had polled 3,337 (7.5%) at the previous general election.

5

1984 - HALLIGAN GOES, CLUSKEY LOSES IN DUBLIN, NORTH-WEST DISINTEGRATES

The first constructive item of the new year was the continuation of the grant of £30,000 per year for the Coolock Law Centre. That was public money very well spent. The demand for its services was huge. The solicitors were processing up to thirty cases per day. I felt that such a service would be very welcome in Ballymun and that we should look for it.

Alan Dukes' Budget in January was roundly condemned by the ICTU who stated that it would do nothing to stimulate employment and that the Government lacked the will to effectively tax property and wealth. The 7% increase in social welfare was considered too little despite an expected inflation rate of 8%. The PAYE sector were hit again and their purchasing power would fall during the year because take home pay was expected to rise by only 1.5%. Ironically as it turned out, Mervyn Taylor was reported in the *Irish Times* to have expressed relief that food subsidies were untouched because such a measure would cause hardship.

The issue of appointments to Beaumont Hospital Board arose and Dick Spring wrote to Barry Desmond on my behalf. Barry Desmond made it clear that my services were not needed. At least there was no obfuscation with Barry. The Richmond Hospital board was in need of reform and I have long been an advocate of industrial democracy for such boards to prevent abuses and bullying. I had to guard my own right to see patients in the Richmond Outpatients against interference.

Gregory Sparks' wife, Catherine, expressed an interest in working in general practice. She was recently qualified and was not working regularly at the time. I asked her to fill in the forms for the CIE list for Dublin 11 area that had recently been advertised and she was appointed, following an interview. The practice opened on Glasnevin Avenue in April and she continued there for three and a half years.

Ticket to Rio

In the public sector, it is important to guard against being effectively bought by supply companies. The most obvious example that I encountered was an invitation to attend a Clinical Chemistry meeting in Rio de Janeiro in Brazil, around the time of the Mardi Gras. The invitation was accompanied by the air tickets and hotel booking. The company that sent these was a leader in the manufacture of major laboratory autoanalyser equipment. Much, I'm sure, to their surprise, I returned the tickets with a 'Thank You' but really 'No Thank You', note. The sale of equipment to the new laboratory at Beaumont Hospital was their interest. I had previously been to a meeting at their expense in Monte Carlo, which turned out to be a thinly disguised advertising production well attended by people who were in the front line for equipment purchase in Chemical Pathology and Haematology. Such meetings do influence decisions and it would be very naïve to think otherwise. The main benefit of these is the opportunity to meet your peers and swap ideas and information at first hand.

In May, Technicon donated a new RA 1000 autoanalyser machine to the laboratory at James Connolly Memorial Hospital in Blanchardstown. The Minister for Health, Barry Desmond, attended to accept this gift with Liam Flanagan from the Department of Health and the Minister gave a brief address. Barry was not overly friendly for whatever reason. As Minister, Barry gave me the impression that he enjoyed seeking out argument and confrontation on health issues rather than reasoned agreement. The removal of medical cards from students and the treatment of the student protesters left a bad taste. Noise generation was maximised but forging constructive change – forget it.

I spoke to Greg Sparks about setting up a drugs' importation company to force the pace on drug prices in the State because of his professional interest in business organisation and I did a short interview on *Today Tonight* on RTE about the Clinical Pharmacology unit run by Dr Austin Darragh at St James Hospital. The death of Niall Rush, a young drug testing volunteer there, was a dreadful tragedy for all concerned and underlined the importance of very tight controls on the testing of new drugs in normal subjects. He had been given proxindine, an experimental drug for the treatment of irregular heart beats. It was suspected that the new drug's toxic effect was exaggerated by a severe interaction with a second drug which the volunteer was taking without the doctors' knowledge. The incident hastened the Bill regulating the whole drug testing industry in Ireland. Dr Darragh did not skimp on standards in his unit when I had personal experience there during the '70s. The man is a very complex and controversial character and many people are in truth jealous of his abilities.

Poppintree

On a bitterly cold bright day at the end of January, the Corporation arranged another walkabout for councillors and officials in response to local pressure because the Authority did not seem to want to know. Ina Gould and I went along to find out what was happening. Housing maintenance, cracks in the main structure, local flooding, vandalism, broken lifts, rubbish disposal, rats and vermin and derelict flats were the main issues. Local man Tommy Morrissey was holding a watching brief for sports clubs and he was also involved in the community centre in the Sports Hall in Poppintree. The late Ned Brennan, a councillor for a different area in Dublin North-East, was most helpful and came to aid people in Ballymun when he was asked. Ned Brennan had a good reputation for delivery in contrast to the usual politician's promises followed by nothing. The fact that he was a Fianna Failer was neither here nor there.

Labour Politics

At the AGM of the Finglas East Branch, the secretary Stephen Dowds produced his brother and three new members out of a total attendance of eleven to vote me off the constituency delegation. A coup! Jim Harvey was elected chairman, Mary Boothman vice chairman, Stephen Dowds secretary and a young militant Eamonn McNally was the fourth constituency council delegate. Dowds was a town planner by profession and a boy scout leader. He apparently had political ambitions, a rigid attitude and a proprietorial approach to the branch where he and his two brothers had been members. His brother Robert, a gentleman to the core, had run in the '79 local election but had moved to Clondalkin. Gerry Doyle and Noel Wheatley were not impressed and had the decision reversed within a short period. This was easily accomplished because the newly elected officers stopped attending shortly after the novelty wore off. We wondered from where and why these people arrived in the first instance. I was unavoidably held up in the hospital and was late for the meeting much to the annoyance of Gerry Doyle. After the meeting, Gerry and I were asked by two of the Milis to buy a copy of the Militant newspaper. You needed a sense of humour to survive.

In Ballymun, I met with John Byrne, Con Rainey, Willie Cooper, Joan Byrne, Bernard O'Connor and Paul Johnston to try to coordinate their efforts in the community regarding facilities and support for sports clubs including boxing and pigeons. The Poppintree clinic continued weekly. Paddy Dunne and I regularly visited the Greenfield Park, community club in Santry. It was very lively and had regular sing-a-longs, pool competitions, variety shows and talent contests. I also kept in close contact with many of the local branches which were in varying states of disarray.

At the AGM of the constituency in February, the officers elected were chairman – Liam Pyke, vice chairman – Peter Bermingham, secretary – Shay Carbin, treasurer – Dermot Timmins, organiser – Stephen Dowds, minute secretary – Katie McKenzie. Within two years all but one of these had left the constituency.

Euroselection – The RDS Conference – Reagan

The Euroselection conference for Dublin was held on 4th March and Brendan Halligan and Frank Cluskey were selected to contest the June election. The Labour Party conference was held in mid April at the RDS in Ballsbridge. It was a fairly low key event. There was an air of political lassitude about and there was a clear indication that the Party hard core were becoming disillusioned with the Government. Two local members Sam Nolan and Maeve (Ann) Carbin were defeated in the election to the Administrative Council. Between them, they got by no means all of the votes of the branches in their home constituency. The conference passed a resolution against the visit to Ireland of US President Ronald Reagan because of the American support for the right wing dictatorships in Chile, El Salvador, Guatamala and in the Phillipines. The record of human rights violations by these regimes was despicable. Labour would support the 'Campaign against Reagan's Foreign Policy' by joining peaceful demonstrations when the visit was due in June. Many Labour TDs, Senators and Councillors boycotted the official functions. The behaviour of the police at the time of President Reagan's visit – detaining 34 women for 30 hours for the offence of protesting in the Phoenix Park where the maximum fine was £5 – was outrageous. No bail opportunity was provided and the object appeared to be the mass arrest and detention of people who were simply a nuisance. Even Michael Noonan as Minister for Justice offered a very weak defence when subsequently questioned by John Kelly and Monica Barnes in the Dail. The special temporary licences given to the US secret service to carry arms, when they were mingling with citizens peacefully, protesting caused great offence. It was not this State's finest hour.

In his leader's address at the RDS, Dick Spring spoke positively of Brendan Halligan whose 'long years of service to the Party, whether in office or not, and whose deep commitment to socialist principles make him uniquely qualified to serve the people of Dublin'. At the constituency council meeting on the following Thursday night, in Beneavin College, where a report on local traveller camps was to be discussed, Brendan Halligan announced his decision to opt out as a candidate for both European and Dail elections. At the meeting, he did not say that he had quit the ticket because an opinion poll showed him at less than 2% in Dublin. This minor consideration was published in a *Sunday Tribune* editorial on the following weekend. Dick Spring famously replied to a journalist's question on this issue, 'Brendan is a bollocks and you can quote me on that'. Who was I to disagree with the leader's assessment? Halligan's actions created consternation among his followers in North-West but I was not surprised at his lack of 'bottle' because he had nearly withdrawn at the selection conference for the previous general election, even though he had a certain one branch majority.

However, as an MEP, Halligan showed real talent and ability. For example, his analysis of the implications for Ireland of the proposed new Common Agricultural Policy reforms presented to the Irish Co-operative Organisation Society Conference in November '83 was quite astute. The likely effects of the proposed super levy on the Irish economy would be to freeze dairy prices and reduce agricultural incomes; to disemploy up to 30,000 dairy farmers and cause massive job losses in the dairying and meat industries with consequential job losses elsewhere in service industries through the multiplier effect; to reduce our export earning potential; to restrict our potential for developing a grassland-related food industry; to reduce the Exchequer tax take and increase expenditure covering the under-employed and the unemployed. His conclusion was that the super levy was a national agricultural quota system and nothing else.

The European Election Campaign in Dublin North-West

With polling day set for the 14th June, the campaign was launched with a cheese and wine party in my house on the 14th May organised by Brendan Halligan. About 25 people attended the function but only about four turned up for the first two weeks of the campaign outside of Ballymun. Liam Pyke was appointed Director of Elections and he managed to get about seven or eight people canvassing for the final fortnight of the campaign. Stephen Dowds and Dermot Timmins put up most of the 3,000 posters that we received while I put them up repeatedly in Ballymun. The posters seemed to have a downing tendency in some areas. In all, we managed to put up a total of 2,200 which was not a bad effort. With posters, canvass cards, election addresses and polling cards being supplied from head office, constituencies were expected to use their own funds to mount their local campaigns. Believe it or not, North-West demanded money for stationary, hoardings, a headquarters, phones, transport of canvassers and meals on polling day. Funny that, when there were usually fewer than ten people involved in the main campaign.

Liam Pyke asked me to run the campaign in Ballymun. Ina Gould and I kicked off the campaign in Poppintree on Wednesday 30th May. Together with Noel Wheatley, I rounded up the Poppintree branch by calling at their doors at meal times – a very good way of meeting avoiders. 'Good to see you Bill. Sorry you caught me at home!' We had Ina Gould, Tony Greene, Brendan Core, Ed Uzell, Paul Maguire, Josephine Gorman, and Mary Elliott. Fair dues to Greg Sparks and my brother Philip, they came out a few times to help out. At least they provided a different brand of bull in the pub afterwards. Barney Hartnett and his other Ballymun supporters had withdrawn from the Party because of their opposition to the Coalition Government, but they were still politically active on the ground. Barney was venomous against coalition. Such was his distaste for the word itself that on having to utter the dreaded noun, he dropped a syllable shortening the agony to 'co-lishon'. In the Labour Party, some things never change. All the flats and houses including the seven tower blocks were canvassed. We have never done that before or since and it was a terrific physical effort. We used canvass cards and copies of *Labour News*. Reliable and working lifts in Ballymun, you must be joking! Git, Snodzer, Dutzer, Whacker and many other heads were highly visible graffiti stars on the walls, in stairwells and on basement steel doors. Even on Sunday mornings, it was early to rise to cover the Masses at St Joseph's in Poppintree, the Holy Spirit in Silloge and the Virgin Mary in Shangan. So Dick Spring could not say that his supporters did not give it a lash for Frank.

I well remember Des O'Malley giving us some verbal abuse when we casually met him in Silloge Gardens. He was supporting the Workers Party at the time and had been a Labour candidate in the '79 local election. I would avoid further contact with this political gadfly after his brief flirtation with Labour again in time for the '91 local election and subsequent withdrawal when things got tough.

Frank Cluskey visited the constituency three times officially, although he lived in Glasnevin (formerly Ballymun) Park just behind the Autobahn pub. I do not think that he had a very high regard for the local Labour Party and he kept a distinct distance. On polling day, all the Ballymun area was covered and we had no problems other than a shortage of votes.

The tally showed that Frank Cluskey polled from a low of 5.8% to a high of 16.8% in Ballymun, with an average of 11.46% up from 8.78 % and 7.02% that Labour got in the two 1982 general elections. This improvement was achieved against a local background of a very unpopular Government, and it showed that the campaign in Ballymun had some effect on the ground.

The election address was looked after by Katie McKenzie, Joe Coleman and Colm Hanlon and was completed by June 2nd. The 'main campaign' canvassed Wadelai estate and Albert College and some parts of Finglas East, West and South and some other areas were 'dropped'. Participation by members varied from a high of 60% in one branch to a single person in another. Considering Halligan's status as a former General Secretary, TD and Senator and that Paddy Dunne was a former Lord Mayor and Senator and that both he and Diana Robertson were current sitting City Councillors, Dublin North-West was a political shell with the receivers – in the form of the electorate, waiting outside the door. The constituency Labour Party was fast becoming a political Disneyland.

The Result

Fianna Fail won two seats with Niall Andrews and Eileen Lemass and local North-West TD Jim Tunney lost. Richie Ryan and Mary Banotti won for Fine Gael. Labour was left sucking a dry lemon. The single candidate strategy was blamed by the *Irish*

Times editorial of June 20th entitled 'Labour's Inquest' for the loss of the seat and the poor transfer from Des Geraghty of the Workers Party did not help.

Why Labour Gets The Blame

I met Stephen O'Byrnes who worked on the features' page in the *Irish Independent* and we argued the toss on the fate and plight of Labour over a few pints. He invited me to write a piece on the subject and this was published on Friday June 22nd under an article by Dick Spring which was entitled 'Labour Organisation, Marketing Failed'. I wrote:

'Labour is a democratic socialist party which has partly sacrificed itself on the altar of political expediency by avoiding an ideological answer to the crux question in Irish politics of whether there is a real difference between Fianna Fail and Fine Gael, when the ad-man's gloss has been stripped away from them.

The avoidance of a hung Dail is often cited by leaders as the reason why Labour should, or must, enter a Coalition arrangement with a Party that we are philosophically and politically opposed to: namely Fine Gael.

Why the media do not strenuously press the two conservative forces to 'coalesce' has always seemed mysterious to me, as approximately 80% of the country votes for their conservative economic policies, only to receive at present a hybrid of two distinct groupings.

The result is that Labour gets most of the blame and very little of the kudos, ensuring continuous conservative or largely conservative governments. The evidence for this is the almost constant size of the left vote in Ireland of 20%, despite rising unemployment and falling living standards. What should Labour do?

In an objective analysis of the Euro-election results, the most glaring figure is the decline in the Labour vote in Munster from 11.2% in November 1982 to 7.6% in the Euro election, despite having 7 TDs and 2 Senators in that constituency. This immediately suggests organisational sloppiness and lack of commitment.

Whether these are 'Labour' seats or personal fiefdoms, which disappear on the retirement of the principal, is crucial. The experience in Cork South-West with Michael Pat Murphy; in Waterford with Tom Kyne; in Wexford with Brendan Corish, and in Meath with Jimmy Tully, suggests the latter and if this is so, demands immediate depersonalisation of the organisation.

The danger of repeated single-candidate campaigns in a constituency leading to no 'heir apparent', and subsequent disappearance of the seat, is glaringly obvious in many areas and should be rectified in the Party's long term interest.

In Connaught, the party chairman and everyone's favourite son, Michael D Higgins, should be heartened by the tally in Galway city which indicates his good prospect of a quick return to Dail Eireann.

In Leinster, the vote in 1979 was 13.1%, falling to a low of 10% in June 1982 and rising to 11.9% now. This shows a consistent pattern below a Euro quota this time.

The small rise in the votes recently being probably related to the hard graft constituency work of Frank McLoughlin in Meath and Brendan Howlin in Wexford and Justin Keating's personality factor.

Frank Cluskey's outcome in Dublin is the real disappointment, reflecting the Party's long, slow decline in the capital, but amplified by convenient 'leaks' from Fine Gael that Cluskey would head the poll, which affected voter behaviour.

What has happened recently in Dublin, and why? Wherever there is a good candidate, backed by a professional constituency organisation, electoral gain and ultimate success has been the pattern. A primary prerequisite for success by any of our candidates is a good contact with the mass of constituency problems. Any disinterest in this area is immediately reflected in a loss of votes at a subsequent election. The 'late' Michael O'Leary's declining fortunes in Dublin Central were a direct reflection of this phenomenon. Internal party wrangling, complacency and disillusion with the party's general direction in many Dublin constituencies had led to the party's parliamentary obliteration in the North City.

Because of the basic peripheral democratic nature of the Party, Head Office has been ineffective in remedying the obvious ills. The whole repeated debate on Coalition has often overridden consideration of policy, and led to bitter clashes within constituencies. Selection of candidates by branch delegate votes has ensured the setting-up and continuance of paper branches by prospective candidates, giving a false sense of activity and security.

The strident slogans of Militant Tendency supporters has made some branches very difficult for non-Trotskiists. Often more members attend constituency council meetings with a controversial agenda than will campaign during an election.'

Paddy Dunne's main concern at this time was not the Euro election, but in lobbying for his own election as Lord Mayor of Dublin for another term. He asked me to accompany him to visit Councillor Diana Robertson to try to persuade her and she gently told him that she was otherwise committed. Michael O'Halloran was ultimately successful and impressed me by his stewardship of the office for the year. It is only fair that the honour should go around.

Colm Toibin, writing in *Magill* in July, pointed out that many Labour members still suffered from the feeling that it was the people's fault that the Labour vote was declining rather than Labour's. This view permeated the Party from Cabinet Ministers to Brendan Halligan to the grassroots. He detailed thirty-one major commitments from the '82 Labour election manifesto and showed that progress had only been made on six. On the basis of the Euro election results, Gerald Barry in the same publication, predicted that Labour would return to the next Dail with five seats. He also wrote that the Workers Party could gain three in Dublin.

National Drug Company

I spent a lot of time and effort in July getting the precise details together for a 'Today Tonight' TV programme on the pricing policies of pharmaceutical companies in Ireland. Barry O'Halloran interviewed Barry Desmond and myself live on the July 26th programme. The simple case for a major price reduction was outlined. From the Trident report onwards, the high price of proprietary drugs in Ireland was widely known particularly within the Department of Health. The case for benefiting from lower prices in other European countries was also obvious and the great variation in prices of common individual drugs was graphically displayed. A lot of research went into the programme and many of the local generic drug manufacturers were also visited. As I have outlined elsewhere Ireland was the big loser. Yet, the Irish patient was stuck with an agreement between the Department and the Federation of the Irish Chemical Industries (FICI) which kept prices high and also tagged to Britain. My point was that import restrictions from other European Community countries should be lifted and that the State could save approximately £20 million. Barry Desmond debated this with me across the studio floor live on air. He defended the civil service position and never addressed the issue in real terms either that night or subsequently before he left office. I should have been agog but I wasn't. I was learning about career politicians.

Shortly afterwards Emily O'Reilly, then at the *Sunday Tribune*, contacted me for a follow-up article which she wrote for the paper.

Janelle

The possible development of the Janelle site by Monarch Properties was in the offing and we supported any new restructuring of that empty site abutting Finglas South. Jim Tunney and Fianna Fail were opposed and a public battle ensued.

I was asked by Councillor Paddy Dunne and a number of Labour branches to write to the *Irish Times* on the subject. 'The Labour Party, through the action of Councillor Paddy Dunne and colleagues in facilitating the development of the Janelle site in Finglas, is very pleased to bring new jobs and life to a site that had lain idle for a number of years.

The specious criticisms of Fianna Fail conservatives in opposing new jobs and increased competition in the local commercial services, are wholly predictable. Maximising profits in business is obviously much easier in a monopoly situation. Services deteriorate and become more expensive. I am sure that Fergal Quinn and the other Finglas traders will survive any new challenge, very nicely thank you. The people of Finglas and environs will be the main beneficiaries of the new £4 million development.

We do not consider the rezoning of this site to be any industrial loss. There is ample local industrial real estate in Poppintree and elsewhere awaiting new projects.

Employment in service industries has been replacing manufacturing jobs continually since the Victorian era, and with robots and micro-electronics will continue to do so into the next century. Therefore Labour supports the provision of service jobs and recreational facilities in an area with a great need for both.

Where are Mr Tunney's alternative jobs? Why does he oppose an overall net job gain for Finglas? The local Finglas traders and people will not thank him for calling the village shopping environment 'unsightly and derelict'. He should forget to appeal to An Bord Pleanala to avoid bringing himself into further disrepute.' Janelle was one battle that we won.

Local Branches

Stephen Dowds, as organiser, arranged a leaflet drop in Finglas South and also tried to get branches to buy and distribute copies of *Labour News* produced by the Party centrally. It is worth commenting that the Workers' Party were selling and distributing their paper *The Irish People* around the pubs and houses, and the Labour Party was a frequent target for criticism.

Some of the branches were very weak and Wadelai in particular had only seven members registered. Seorse Dearle ran that branch and needed extra members quickly and I recruited them for him. The branch had previously been a vehicle to support Brendan Halligan but when Brendan withdrew, Seorse met me and decided to help out. This did not please the Carbins or the Dowds. They wrote to Marion Boushell in Head Office to get a current list of members and kicked up a row afterwards. In April '84, there were ten branches with a total of 114 registered members of whom 91 lived in the constituency. How much of this was real is another question altogether. Just look at the number of workers in the Euro election in June.

Stephen Dowds and Shay Carbin wrote to lapsed and former members of the Party in Ballymun to try to reform the Ballymun branch at a meeting on Ballymun Road. Many branches in the Party seem to be built around strong characters and become dependent upon them. When the principal goes, the branch often folds. Where could you go after Barney Hartnett? A meeting arranged for the Slipper Pub on Ballymun on 18th April was abortive. Nobody showed but I went along to keep watch. Halligan's withdrawal from elections on the following night finished the Ballymun effort because it sapped the morale of the movers. In the autumn, Peter Daly and I tried again to get a reconstructed Ballymun Branch going and we met with Ben Ivory who was enthusiastic, but, yet again, the Ballymun people never followed up on our efforts possibly because the Labour tag was progressively developing a bad odour particularly in working class areas. On 26th September, a public meeting was held in the Holy Spirit School on Silloge Road to protest at the closure of the Bank of Ireland branch in the town centre. Ina Gould and I attended and spoke in support of the community. Local TDs Michael Barrett, Mary Flaherty, and Proinsias de Rossa all condemned the bank's move. This blow to Ballymun galvanised the people into action and directly led to the formation of the Community Coalition. In November, Ina Gould and I met Des O'Malley, Paddy Dunbar and Tony O'Brien in the Penthouse pub to help them with the setting up of the Ballymun Action Group as part of the movement towards the Ballymun Community Coalition.

CIE man, Denis Dennihy, died in Finglas after a long illness and I never forgot his contribution to the Dublin Housing Action Committee during the height of the housing protests in the late '60s. A motion of sympathy was passed and we wrote to his relatives. There was also support for the Divorce Action Group and we helped them drop leaflets in Poppintree.

Constituency reorganisation was in the air with Colm O'Briain in the General Secretary's hot seat. The North-West organiser, Stephen Dowds, and I met Colm in his office in July to discuss the issue. Colm's intended policy was that people could only remain members of a branch in their own area of constituency. It was not clear what were to be the grounds for an exception to this ruling. This created much angst amongst the old guard in some of the Finglas branches. I thought the ruling seriously flawed because it ignored the social basis of politics. Where would it leave TDs such as Barry Desmond or Frank Cluskey who lived in one area and represented another?

Shock Cut in Food Subsidies

Then, over the August holiday weekend, the food subsidies introduced in the 1970s were reduced by 50%. Organic material hit the fan in a big way. Labour members were outraged and Labour backbench TDs were shocked. Following the constituency meeting in August, a statement was issued: 'The members of the Dublin NW constituency Labour Party have been horrified by the recent decision, announced and defended by Dick Spring, the leader of the Party, to cut the food subsidies which are basic items in the housewife's shopping basket. This decision can only be seen as a penal price increase on the most basic necessities of life and a direct contradiction of Labour Party policy.

Statements from other government ministers on the need for more cuts in public spending have only served to strengthen our worst fears about the present Coalition. There can be no doubt as to what sectors of our community will suffer at their hands. Already the majority of social welfare recipients in this constituency have been refused assistance for school uniforms and clothing by the community welfare officers, although they had received assistance in similar circumstances last year.

In view of these developments and the further erosion of the Party's position in Coalition and the damage this will do nationally, this constituency calls for a special conference to discuss our continued participation in Coalition with Fine Gael. This conference should be held within the calendar year of 1984.'

As you can imagine, this latter call was wholly unrealistic. Food subsidies are an inefficient way to protect people on low incomes. Social welfare increases and tax reductions for low pay would have been better targeting of this form of expenditure. Some of the annoyance was in fact caused by the sly timing of the cut. It said something about the style of government. I met Michael Bell TD and Ita McAuliffe. Everyone in Leinster House clearly realised the extent of the public abreaction to the food subsidy cuts.

Within weeks, the more militant members of Finglas East wanted every local branch to boycott the proposed Labour Party lottery until a Special Conference was called. They wanted this action to be taken in all other constituencies also. Feelings were running very high in the Party and the leader was very unpopular among local members. I was verbally abused when I asked them for their alternatives and the abuse only heightened when I pointed out that Dick Spring's speech in Cork on 5th September showed that the Leader had guts and was not going to slink away from his responsibilities. The local Labour Party wanted to go into public opposition to the parliamentary Labour Party in government. Shay Hackett of the Deanstown-Kilshane Branch which included Councillor Diana Robertson and Angie Mulroy, a Head Office employee, among its membership, passed a resolution calling for the Party to withdraw from Government immediately because of the failure of the Parliamentary Labour Party to implement Labour policy.

Marion Boushell wrote on 19th September to inform the constituency that the Administrative Council had 'noted' the demand for a special conference. On the following night, Liam Pyke resigned as Chairman of the Constituency Council. He cited the imposition of water rates, the food subsidy cut, the butchery of the National Development Corporation and the threatened Nealon Radio Bill. He considered that when he joined the Party, 'them' were Fianna Fail and Fine Gael and 'us' was Labour. Now he saw 'them' as the leadership and the Parliamentary Labour Party and 'us' as the rank and file membership. Colm O'Briain was in attendance and Brendan Halligan finally bowed out of the constituency that night. Unfortunately, I finally lost my patience with Stephen Dowds and foolishly gave him a verbal stuffing, not a good way to win friends and influence people. What a mess!

Another bizarre incident was the witch hunt against Barney Hartnett when he left the Party. He was wrongly accused of using Labour Party notepaper when writing to Dublin Corporation and was threatened by the constituency council. Shay Carbin was obliged to issue a formal apology to Barney through his solicitor by the year's end. Many of the goings-on here were certainly strange.

General Secretary O'Briain Strikes

Stephen Dowds, as the new constituency organiser, wrote on 5th April that 'with the exception of election campaigns, virtually no work of either a political or organisational nature has been undertaken by the constituency council in years. Inevitably three successive elections did not leave much time or energy for other activities.' Mind you, it was not as simple as that. Those, like myself, willing to get stuck in to the hard graft were usually blocked by others who preferred talk, plans and good intentions to action. There was also much jockeying for position among possible election candidates, and Gerry Doyle and I were quite surprised at the extent of this when we read the files many years later. It explained some of the strange happenings at the time. I was given these files by Shay Carbin when he left the area in 1986 to migrate to Donegal. For example, to block me, the Poppintree branch was approached to try to have our advice centre closed because Ina Gould and I were providing the service. This caused a lot of strife in that branch for about two months. Branch meetings there were being held virtually every week and the constituency tried to interfere. But Ina Gould persisted and because she had the overwhelming numbers, the conflict died down and then our 'opposition' changed sides yet again!

Shay Carbin, as constituency secretary, wrote to Colm O'Briain also in August in response to the anxiety of key people in what had been Brendan Halligan's camp. He complained that 'very little information was available on what is happening apart from letters to several members who are being transferred to other constituencies and various rumours, etc., about other moves.'

The following questions were put: 'What precisely is being undertaken in the Dublin area? What is involved and what is the objective? Why has there been no consultation with the Dublin Regional Council, the North-West constituency, the branches concerned or the individuals? Is the same reorganisation being carried out in rural areas?'

Branch reorganisation and finance were discussed at a constituency EGM on 18th October attended by 22 members. In line with the direction from Head Office, it was decided to slim down the number of branches and require registered members to live in the constituency and if possible in the designated branch areas. Four people each from Deanstown and the Finglas Billy Rigney branches had received letters from Head Office telling them they were being moved, yet the branch officers had received no communication. Labour was becoming a centrally organised dictatorship. Raising money was a perennial item on which much hot air was expended and very little ever happened. It was agreed that the annual branch affiliation fee would be replaced by a monthly fee of £5 per branch and that branches would lose their voting rights if they were in arrears. This was also never enforced. The constituency wrote to Colm O'Briain and asked that a proportion of the Oireachtas envelopes issued to parliamentary party members should be redirected to constituencies without an elected member. The constituency secretary, Shay Carbin, arranged a police permit for a door to door collection over two weeks in October, but the response from the membership was minimal. Irrespective, the national collection target was set at £600. Fortunately when he announced his withdrawal from the area, Brendan Halligan donated a four figure sum to largely clear the constituency bank debt of £3,500.

Militants

At the Dublin Regional Council's Special Conference on 25th February at Liberty Hall, most of the speakers were either Militants or members of Labour Left. The speakers were very critical of the Party's performance in power and of inaction on many of the proposals in the agreed Programme for Government. Derek McDowell gave a timely warning of what was the likely result in the forthcoming local elections. He called for radical initiatives to restore the Party's socialist credibility. He was real enough to suggest that there is a relationship between tax and spending. For local taxes to be acceptable, he pointed out that they must be related to property values, or income or the use of services or a combination. The impact on the 30% least well off must be minimised. The Militants, on the other hand, were concerned about their possible expulsion and about their right to sell *Militant Irish Monthly*. Ciaran O'Mara spoke of the dangers to civil liberties implicit in some of the provisions of the Criminal Justice Bill. He wanted to retain the right to silence, to require the tape recording of police interrogations, the establishment of an independent police complaints' tribunal and to insist that the renewal of the period of detention should be authorised by District Justices .

The 'Militants' in the constituency were in a minority in Labour Youth and they upset Niall Mac Suibhne and his group because the National Labour Youth Officers had organised a public meeting in Patrician College in Finglas West in September in support of the UK Miners' strike. Niall wrote a pointed protest note which was futile because Labour Youth at the time was the definition of a party within a party. I often wondered, was Labour Left just the grown up version of the Milis. They also ran their own meetings, published their own literature and ran their own candidates at administrative council and constituency elections. Facile solutions are no solutions when facing the reality and the economic consequences of real decisions. Niall, Shay and Maeve Carbin and the people in Labour Left assumed an air of political superiority. They were the holders of the pure socialist Holy Grail and the rest of us were at best misguided and at worst despicable opportunists. Colm O'Briain in Issue 2 of *Labour Left* invited that group to produce their magazine within the Party structure, futiley pointing out that 'working together is a precondition for a healthy, dynamic party.'

'Building on Reality'

This plan was launched in October and was criticised at the Dublin Regional Council for lacking in vision, for having no real strategy, for not offering hope and that it would alienate many more Labour supporters. The NDC was watered down, tax equity was effectively ignored and health would see 3,000 job losses.

The Social Employment Scheme was intended to provide a year's break from long term unemployment for about 12,500 people. This was a good idea but people who benefited did not want to return to unemployment when their term on the scheme finished; so many human problems were being stored up inadvertently. Participants were paid £70 per week for part-time work and they were free subsequently to do other work. Paying people for work worth doing, which otherwise would be left undone, was a good idea. The scheme was officially launched in February 1985 and Ruairi Quinn wrote to all branch secretaries with the details. Under the Enterprise Allowance Scheme, 11,000 were expected to become self-employed. The ITGWU predictably opposed the plan and regretted Labour's support for a 'policy based on book balancing expediency'.

Dick Spring in his Party Leader's newsletter made a spirited defence of his position, citing the new housing grants, an extra £420 million on roads, changes in taxation and child allowance and also he detailed the bad news list.

I took great interest in discussing the plan in Baggot St hostelries and with Paul Tansey and Colm McCarthy on a few occasions. Both are expert economists and also concise and understandable debaters on these issues. They were insistent that public spending just had to be cut or national economic disaster beckoned. I agreed thoroughly. How and for what purpose the government should spend money were the important questions. Try detailing that together with the hard choices involved to a Labour Party meeting. You would want to be wearing your hard hat.

Panel for '85 Local Election

A selection convention with forty in attendance was held on November 22nd to select a panel of possible candidates to contest the local elections scheduled for June '85. I was nominated by Seorse and Fergal Dearle of the Wadelai branch and by Finglas East. The rest of the selected panel was Shay Carbin, Dermot Timmins, Ina Gould, Gerry Maher and Councillors Paddy Dunne and Diana Robertson. Shay Hackett was elected to succeed Liam Pyke who had resigned as director of elections.

A.O.B.

Ruairi Quinn arranged a briefing for me on youth employment and community services from Niall Greene who headed up the Youth Employment Agency. Niall detailed the schemes and personnel in Finglas and Ballymun involved in trying to implement the Social Guarantee as a form of affirmative action for disadvantaged youths. This was part of the response to the Ministerial Task Force on Drug Abuse. Niall also attended the opening of the Ballark Community Workshop on Shanowen Road in Santry in November. The enterprise was given the philosophical three cheers by local bishop, James Kavanagh and Tim Killeen, formerly of McCairns Motors, was the new manager. Tim was a local Fianna Fail Councillor who moved to the PDs for a while.

Bye-bye Billy Rigney

The reorganisation was felt immediately and interfered with some long established social patterns. The Finglas village branch was named in honour of Billy Rigney, a deceased stalward from Mellowes Road. Their final notice, signed by Frank Butler, said it all: 'Due to reorganisation in Dublin North-West, the Finglas/Billy Rigney branch has become redundant – after some 35 years of working for the one 'employer'.

We feel that, having given such long service, this redundancy should be "celebrated" and a "Bye-bye Billy Rigney branch" party will be held in the MPGWU Hall on Sunday 16th December commencing at 8pm. At the request of the redundant branch there will be no presentation, so admission is free. Entertainment will be provided by the guests – and of course, in keeping with tradition, there will be a licenced bar. As a friend of the branch over the years we know you would wish to attend and we look forward to seeing you on the night.'

6
LABOUR'S LOCAL ELECTION DISASTER 1985 - O'BRIAIN QUITS

A clinics' advisory service was set up by Colm O'Briain in January to give professional support to Labour Party advice clinics about family law, taxation, planning permissions etc. Our efforts continued in Ballymun. However, we could never be sure whether the building would be open when we came to do clinics and they started charging us £5 per week per session for the use of a room. Then the Poppintree Community Sports Complex was handed back to the County Council by the management committee and was in need of £25,000 worth of repairs due to general vandalism. The complex was temporarily closed and the Council then employed a manager who used the Youth Employment Scheme to carry out repairs. Meanwhile, our clinic ceased.

At the AGM of the Finglas East Branch in February, Seorse Dearle and I were elected branch chairman and secretary. The position of branch secretary is the key to control of the local political unit. Some of the membership of the now defunct Wadelai and Beneavin branches had joined Finglas East due to the O'Briain reorganisation and a combination of Labour Left and Militants were now a majority in the branch. I got agreement that a 'Clean Air Act' should be an urgent priority because of the level of toxic air pollution in the city, and we decided to campaign on that issue. Ina Gould, Noel Wheatley, Paul Maguire, Paddy Dunne and myself met regularly to keep clinic work and literature drops going. The branch was also distributing *Labour News* wherever editions were available. Henry Haughton did a fair job in getting that publication together. Paddy Dunne and I met Ruairi Quinn to lobby for a Community Hall for Whitehall, a project that Paddy had been pursuing for some time. The effort ultimately collapsed for lack of support and the land now forms part of the DCU campus. Des O'Malley TD was expelled from Fianna Fail due to his 'I stand by the Republic' speech. That was an extraordinary action against a potential Party Leader and I thought FF must have been crazy.

Local Election 1985 – Finglas

Preparations finally got underway for the local elections at a meeting in Tolka House on 12th February. Shay Hackett was Director of Elections and Ina Gould, Diana Robertson, Stephen Dowds, Peter Bermingham and myself attended. I also met Paul Mulhern and Colm O'Briain from the Party's Organisation Committee to review both the constituency branches and also the local election campaigns on 14th March. Afterwards I contacted Liam Pyke and Frank Butler to try to keep the constituency old guard together.

On 9th April, Councillor Paddy Dunne spoke to me and threatened to join Fianna Fail and said he would phone Mr Haughey in the morning. I was not surprised at this because Paddy had become progressively more bitter and angry at being unemployed since 'Portion Foods' Coolock, where he had been personnel manager, closed a year earlier. He felt that he should have been fixed up in a job by the Party. He was one of four local Labour members made redundant by that closure. As a former Lord Mayor, Paddy's plight was even featured in the *Evening Herald.* Ageism was a real difficulty to overcome in Paddy's situation and competing for jobs with young highly qualified but inexperienced candidates was demoralising. Politically, Paddy, being an old experienced head, could also see the electoral writing on the wall. He felt strongly that Liam Kavanagh, Minister for the Environment, should again postpone the local election date. However, you can't keep running for ever. In the end Paddy finished up standing for Labour in Drumcondra and was only narrowly defeated.

The Finglas East branch met to select their candidate to contest the Local Election and the Dowds brothers nominated Shay Carbin. I was nominated by John Whelan and the vote was tied. Gerry Doyle put both names into a hat and I won the night. In the bar after the meeting, I was told that the names in the hat were the same so I couldn't have lost. The name left in the hat is supposed to be the winner. The perpetrator of this political skulduggery was a close supporter of mine and told me that there was no way he would risk an accident. It was no night for fools! I drove home smiling! On Tuesday 7th May, the selection conference for the Finglas ward was held in Beneavin College and Shay Carbin and I were chosen. Gerry Maher decided not to run and told me so at the function in the WFTA hall for the 21st anniversary of the 'Finglas Old Folks' charity. Gerry's branch in Finglas North-West backed me on the night. Greg Sparks replaced Shay Hackett as Director of Elections. Shay was upset at the plight of Diana Robertson who had lost. On the following Sunday there was a Labour candidates meeting in the Mansion House which I attended and on the following morning, Colm O'Briain phoned to ask me, in the best interests of the Party, to stand down in favour of the sitting Councillor, Diana Robertson. I agreed.

There must have been animated discussions in smoke-filled rooms because three days later I was phoned by Greg to tell me that I was back on a three candidate ticket. So I said OK and we got on with the business.

Other Candidates Pre-Election Activities

Shay Carbin made representations to the Corporation for Valeview in Finglas South regarding tarmacadam for footpaths and railings on Glasanaon Road. Shay worked on the issue of drugs awareness with the local parents' action and prevention group in Finglas South under the auspices of the Coolmine Centre and sought a £400 grant-in-aid from the Department of Health for their community education programme. Local woman Bridie O'Reilly, had set the ball rolling on this by directly approaching the Minister, Barry Desmond. Councillor Diana Robertson lobbied successfully to have pedestrian traffic lights and footpath improvements at Casement Road/Plunkett Road/North Road junction in Finglas where the actor Danny Cummins had been knocked down and killed. She also tried to have the unused land on Dunsink Lane developed as an amenity park for local youth.

'Labour Is Working For You'

The fellow holding up a bar counter could easily rejoin, 'Oh Yeah, How?' to the above slogan we used during the campaign. The continuing recession had made the Government Parties more unpopular than a year earlier and it was probably a mistake to have postponed the election. As a result of a mail shot, we received £300 in campaign contributions and Greg Sparks quickly arranged for the printing of posters and canvass cards which included photobiogs of all three candidates.

The posters were 17.5 x 25 ins, red/green and black with an angular modern design and the rose in fist logo with the three names in descending order. Shay Carbin cut the centre from the poster to have himself writ large on his car and house – an exercise in futility. I thought it said something about candidate cooperation.

The Labour manifesto promised to allow local councils to decide on local charges. On jobs, we had the £200 million for the National Development Corporation, the Social Employment Scheme with 100 new project organisers, the Enterprise Allowance Scheme and State support for workers' cooperatives in buying or leasing business premises. Crime prevention was to be extended into the community with community gardai, mandatory community service orders for young first offenders and the establishment of a Garda Reserve of trained civilians to help in routine duties which were inappropriately occupying Garda time. Young criminals must be brought into contact with the suffering and damage caused by their actions. Simply locking up young offenders with other offenders solves nothing. More money must be spent on the probation services. Elected local education authorities were proposed to devolve managerial power back to local areas. The funny bit came last, just as it did on the ITN television news. Organised car racing (stock cars??) should be provided to divert potential young car thieves away from 'joy riding'. What next?

In the run in to the election kick-off, the National Union of Journalists urged their members to, 'withdraw cooperation from candidates who participate in illegal radio except where NUJ members or applicants for membership are employed.'

Patsy McGarry of Sunshine Radio News wrote to make sure that candidates knew that any boycott did not apply to his station.

Dick Spring launched the general campaign in Iona Airways at the Boot Inn on 5th June. They were nearly blown away in the breeze. I could not attend because of work commitments.

The Finglas Campaign

The first leaflet drop started on Saturday 25th May and continued for a week. This was three days after the nomination audience with Frank Feeley and nearly four weeks before polling day. Almost immediately, it was very obvious that the tag Labour was a real 'No-No' with the punters. Trying to win was like running up a down spout. Political survival was well nigh impossible but we would fight. Labour's opinion poll ratings were at 6 to 7%. The weather was a help and there were many long evenings and scorching afternoons with absolutely nowhere to hide. The Whelan, Mulroy and Costello families and Derek Keogh were a great help. On a blazingly hot Saturday afternoon in Finglas South, the canvass started with Dick Slevin, Peter and Alan Daly and Brendan Mulroy. There was nothing personal against any of us but Labour was just not popular to say the least. Fianna Fail and the WP propaganda had worked well. At some houses, we were verbally abused for being Labour and at others, doors were slammed in our faces. That, together with the searing heat and blinding glare, was not good for morale. On the June Bank Holiday Monday, we put in a ten hour day. I must have been very determined but in truth I always am in elections. Jenny Owens joined the canvass for her own area around Fairlawn/Cloonlara and over into the Gortmores. We kept up the pace day after day including outside the masses on Sundays. On Sunday afternoon, we managed to have ten people, including the Brennan's who were related to the footballer Ronnie Whelan, hitting the trail down to the Griffith Road – Tolka Estate area where it was wall to wall Jim Tunney. Pauline Cregan, originally from Tolka Estate, introduced me around and I was also grateful to Dr Catherine Hayes for her support. Between 2.00 and 3.00 in the afternoons, we visited the mothers collecting the kids at St Brigid's in Welmount Road, St Finian's, and St Canice's Bingo in WFTA and at Patrician College it was also worth canvassing because of the large number of people, mainly women, arriving in a short space of time. The good things that the Party did in City Hall such as the Dublin Street Carnival and the improvement in access to buildings for the disabled, were largely irrelevant to the Finglas voter. A cynic would conclude that good City Councillors like Mary Freehill may as well not have bothered. The flavour of the month is important in elections. As polling day approached, we had Gerry Doyle, Brendan Mulroy, Dick Slevin, Gerry and Una Brennan, Paschal O'Reilly, Josephine Gorman and Jenny Owens out regularly. It was very difficult to get Gerry Maher's group interested because Gerry wasn't running. Kieran Halford,

Kevin Raythorn, Peter McGowan were too busy! The local party had a serious motivation problem. We also visited the Drake or the Village Inn or the Shamrock after canvassing to try to drum up support, any support. Dick Spring's final message to each candidate on 13th June recognised the reality that it 'has been a tough few weeks for us all. .....Whatever the outcome, I know it won't be for the want of effort!'

There were in reality three separate Labour campaigns in the area and each had personal literature. For the duration of the election, there was no meeting of the three Labour candidates other than casual jousts outside churches on Sunday mornings. Diana Robertson did not cover the whole area and largely confined her efforts to the west and northwest of Finglas. Diana was regarded locally as a very decent woman and a good neighbour; she had six children. Shay Carbin was a CIE busdriver and had lived in South Finglas for nine years. He knew a large proportion of the hundreds of CIE men who lived locally. Shay ran for office in the NBU and following his defeat, he switched to the ITGWU. Whether that decision was related to the political fund in the ITGWU was debatable, but his former union colleagues were displeased and told me so plainly. Shay was small and thin and sported a Wyatt Earp moustache. As a young adult, he had a short spell as a clerical student. Politically, he got a lot of push at home where his wife was very ambitious for both of them. Shay Carbin styled himself 'The Vocal Local' and his interest in Janelle and a community centre was stressed in his campaign. With Labour voters, he targeted me in particular and was determined to come in ahead of me. Stephen Dowds was a close supporter, as was Dermot Timmins, and they helped him out. We met Shay Carbin and Stephen Dowds on Hazelcroft Road and you would have had to be brain dead not to have noticed the negative vibes. Dick Slevin was vastly amused but I did not think it was too funny. When it was a case of anyone except a colleague at some doorsteps, where do you go from there?

It is only fair to comment that I had one advantage in that I had more personal resources. As well as the generic drop, I also had two other small A5 leaflets, one specifically targeting each side of the Finglas Road. All three Labour candidates were against the water rates which the Party had imposed and we all supported the Janelle development. I also supported the neighbourhood watch schemes, an issue that I picked up on doorsteps and mentioned the £20 million drug company profiteering and also the problem of appropriate sentences for drug pushers. I used three pieces of literature. Initially we used the official three candidate canvass card. Later as that became overused, we produced a personal canvassing card and also used a Dick Spring generic A4 foldover during the last ten days. A double sided A3 black and white folded sheet tailored for each electoral area was produced by Greg Sparks and dropped into every house also in the last ten days. It had the candidates photographs and pen pictures on one side backed by short pieces on tenants associations, crime, transport, toxic waste and Dunsink dump (Finglas politics' version of draining the Shannon), transport where we undertook to press for a bus service from Finglas to Blanchardstown, crime and health.

Posters were put up early along the main roads and replaced infrequently because the weather was good. Only the actions of rival parties when the lamp posts were crowded led to localised repeat postering. The area was divided into five and systematically canvassed and dropped. A trade union newsletter explaining the connection of the Labour Party and the Trade Unions was circulated to explain how Fianna Fail was trying to politically neutralise the unions in order to undermine the industrial arm of Labour. It pointed out that only 10% of Labour's running costs came from unions, unlike the 90% figure in Britain.

The Griffith area community group, whose secretary Anne Kane had been in infant school with me in Booterstown, arranged a meeting in the St Kevins CBS on Ballygall Road to continue their campaign for a community hall started in the previous July. They were told that they must raise money to prove that the local people were willing to contribute to the upkeep, heating, lighting etc. This campaign was successful because the building was erected a few years later. Mr P.H. Moloney, Chief Executive of St Michael's House – the association of parents and friends of mentally handicapped children – took the opportunity to lobby all potential public representatives to impress upon them that additional funds must be provided for the association to continue their work. This tactic is common during elections and rash promises are often made by politicians desperate for the stroke on the ballot paper. Sponsorship requests for local events are also a feature of campaigns and the Cappagh Avenue sports week made sure that there would be no escape. Des Bonass of the Dublin Council of Trade Unions also sent a candidate pledge form issued jointly with ACRA, NATO, Unemployed Alliance, USI and Minceir Misli. Water rates, ground rents, travellers, college fees and construction jobs were the subjects. There were no prizes for guessing the angle in each category. As the Party pledge is signed by each party political candidate and as the DCTU know or should know this perfectly well, I wondered what was achieved by such a demand other than the massage of the egos of persons unknown? Frank Clarke, one of the independent candidates circulated photocopies of his signed DCTU pledge as part of his campaign.

Fianna Fail successfully turned the election into a type of mini referendum on the performance of central government. The Workers Party followed suit and excoriated Labour for the water rates using the brilliant slogan, 'Turn off the Water Tax!' With posters and lots of literature they rammed their points home and there was no question that they would poll very well. There was much obvious support for Proinsias de Rossa with big hoardings up on houses along main roads. Pat Quearney from Finglas West was the second Workers Party candidate. Quearney's father had been the Labour Party constituency secretary during David Thornley's time as TD. The WP produced a South Finglas Newsletter with good quality content, featuring

Janelle, Scribblestown Park amenity development, BMX clubs, maisonette points and lead in paint. Their 'Election Special' two page newspaper was a standard WP generic effort with infill slots for different electoral areas. The Workers Party also produced little staccato pieces for outside churches promising the abolition of water rates, a local council for Finglas, better bus services, youth workers, adult education and community policing. Their campaign style was aggressive and they were disdainful and dismissive of Labour. Their final flourish was a mock ballot paper with their pair of candidates names emphasised in heavy bold typeface. Something for the future I thought! I don't think we were de Rossa's favourite people. The WP women's group also managed to have their campaign for a local family planning service in Finglas featured in the *Evening Herald* ten days before polling.

Sinn Fein issued a leaflet entitled, 'The Workers Party is **not** Sinn Fein' which attacked the WP for supporting the British army, the RUC and the UDR. The WP was condemned for supporting neighbourhood watch, for compromising on water rates and the EEC, for refusing to support the Ranks workers factory occupation in Phibsboro and for refusing to condemn the regimes in Armagh and Port Laoise jails. Some of this was to the best of my knowledge, an inaccurate description of WP public policy at the time. Despite the public antagonism between SF and the WP, the voters interchanged a high proportion of preferences. Sinn Fein also targeted a women's vote with a special leaflet drop.

A widely distributed anonymous 'Rebel' newsletter supported a Sinn Fein type line and the attitude to crime was representative of a relatively common strand in deprived areas. 'Working class criminality is a clear response to the need for higher incomes and an assertion of the right to increase our value as individuals. Our young people who have been excluded from the process of wage labour, are forced to impose their will to survive. Our young are not 'mindless thugs' – they are intelligent, angry and combative and demanding of a share in the fruits of the world. Shoplifting, double claiming on the dole, nixers, lying about who we share our homes with, fraud, joyriding, robbery, sabotage, pilfering at work, occupational absenteeism and armed attacks are legitimate weapons of our class and must be defended.

Those who criminalise us, who want spies in our midst (neighbourhood watch), more prisons, police, and repression are the ones who stand to lose the most, their property, their incomes and political/social power. These apologists defend the exploitation of working class people and would make us subject to their values.'

This anarchic attitude could be easily dismissed but there is a serious lesson on the effects of alienation on a minority in places where high unemployment, bad housing, and hopelessness are endemic. The 'flog them, hang them' solution will not work but will institutionalise these types of chaotic attitudes to the despair of law abiding neighbours.

Fine Gael ran Mary Flaherty TD and Frank Barr from East and West Finglas respectively. Mary Flaherty distributed two coloured leaflets, one on child care and the other on crime, jobs and local facilities. She also sent around a very basic information sheet and wrote to residents in Finglas South from her Dail office about road bollards. She is a good door to door performer and got out the substantial Fine Gael vote. She also distributed a note in support of Eddie Nolan, another Fine Gael candidate in the neighbouring Drumcondra ward. Fine Gael also competed in the Fianna Fail pseudo referendum with a foolscap sheet urging 'Don't let him away with it.' Fine Gael is making everybody pay a fair share. Why won't Fianna Fail?' This referred to Fianna Fail's opposition to the new farm tax. Fine Gael also promised to bring PAYE down. Frank Barr, the other Fine Gael candidate, ran as a 'local man for local issues.' His personal literature did not mention his party affiliation at all. The nastiest A4 of that election in Northwest came through my own door. It was a photocopied distortion of a Fine Gael leaflet addressed to all PAYE and PRSI payers with the FG candidates faces replaced by effigies and the slogan changed to 'Pay your water rates now or else. Vote Fine Gael and get screwed!!'

Fianna Fail fielded three candidates and we knew from our canvass that they were clearly going to do well. I met PJ Mara in passing on Baggot St and he said that they were going after their traditional Dublin vote and were letting the South Dublin middle class vote do what it would. At their convention, Pat Carey was selected first, Jim Tunney second and Noel Cloake beat Cecelia Larkin by sixteen votes to one. Fianna Fail imposed Cecelia Larkin as the third candidate. The selection story was featured in the *Finglas Free Press* and in the *Evening Press.* Cecelia was from Finglas East and was Bertie Ahern's secretary. She ran a campaign as Fianna Fail's woman candidate and had her own literature. She also had good back-up services and was able to send personalised notes to voters from her home in Clancy Road. That area was solid for Fianna Fail and a preservation order should have been placed on any declared Labour voter.

Frank Carroll, another independent who polled 315 votes was supported by his family and by members of his former cumann in Fianna Fail. He ran a brisk campaign and ate into Diana Robertson's vote because they lived in such close proximity.

The *Finglas Free Press* was established as a community newspaper in 1983 and was edited by Mary McCamley, the candidate of the Democratic Socialist Party in Finglas. Jim Kemmy was their Party President and Mary McCamley was an excellent candidate. Her husband Billy, was an active trade unionist in CIE and has a great interest in transport history. The *Finglas Free Press* election edition was the best quality publication of the campaign even with the benefit of hindsight. The DSP's band of supporters canvassed hard in a group of six or eight but unfortunately Mary polled 204 votes which was not at all a reflection on her ability. She pointed out that Fianna Fail finally came out against the water rates only four weeks before the local elections! Despite this, Fianna Fail's referendum style campaign went tabloid on 'Vote Fianna Fail and end coalition and water rates'. They also highlighted other national issues such as 'Borrowing – highest ever; taxation – highest ever; prices – highest ever, law and order – weakest ever; hope and confidence – nil. They must go!' So the Corpo Councillors were going to usurp the TDs!!

There was really no contest for the prize for the most dishonest leaflet. The Fianna Fail leaflet on the Janelle development read: Promises were made. Now they are broken. Fine Gael/Labour and the Workers Party with their friends, the property speculators, promised you a Community Centre, sports pavilion, new football pitch, scouts den and, more importantly, jobs for the area. Unfortunately, none of these promises have or will be kept. Don't be fooled again. Vote Fianna Fail – Carey, Larkin, Tunney.' They must now blush whenever they drive into or around Janelle. They got that scene so completely wrong. However, the leaflet did its job effectively at the time.

The Result

The quota was 2,418 on a turnout of 43.9%. Jim Tunney (FF) headed the poll on 3,175; Proinsias de Rossa (WP) was second on 2,266; Pat Carey (FF) was third on 1,218 and Mary Flaherty (FG) fourth on 1,056. These four were elected. The party percentages were FF 42.3%, FG 12.35%, WP 23%, Lab 6.7%, SF 6.6%, DSP 1.68%, others 7.2%. Within the Labour vote, Councillor Robertson got 298, Tormey got 265 and Shay Carbin 250.

In the Drumcondra ward, Labour polled 7.2%. Ina Gould got 148 votes which was very disappointing considering her work in advice centres and in the Ballymun community. Paddy Dunne polled 720 and unfortunately lost out. Four former Labour Party members ran as Independents in Drumcondra. Barney Hartnett, Molly Bracken, and Lilly and Billy Keegan and received 751 votes between them. Labour was in disarray in the constituency.

The Aftermath

Michael O'Halloran and Sean Kenny were the only Labour Party candidates returned to City Hall. For the party, the '85 Local Government Election in Dublin was a disaster. Labour's vote nationally was 7.9% and it was 10.5% in Dublin. In North-West, both Council seats had been lost and the vote was about 6.9%. The Dublin Regional Council met in July and said that unless Labour gets a minimum programme of action on unemployment, taxation, and the restoration of cuts in food subsidies, health and education within the next Dail session, Labour must withdraw from Coalition.

'Say Goodnight Dick' warned *Magill* magazine in June after the Locals. Labour's decline was putting nearly all seats at risk except in Kildare and Carlow-Kilkenny.

7
STRUGGLING FOR POLITICAL SURVIVAL

After that whooping, heads were down and the crisis could not be ignored. I met Don Buckley and Ray Kavanagh in Mary Freehill's house in Ringsend in July. There was no avoiding the reality. Ray Kavanagh was shortly to take over as General Secretary on the resignation of Colm O'Briain. Following the job interviews for the post, one of the candidates, Bernard Browne, gave an interesting interview in the *Sunday Tribune* to Maureen de Burca in which the reader could only presume that he was to take over in Head Office. That piece must have ruffled a few feathers because shortly afterwards Kavanagh was appointed.

During the summer, I made it my business to visit or meet all our supporters at one time or another. To try to forget the 265, I played golf in various places from Skerries to Portmarnock and from Mullingar to Cill Dara. Croke Park was also visited and the Dublin-Mayo drawn All-Ireland semi-final was a cracker as was the Cork and Galway hurling semi. The games are great, pity about the organisation.

Only six people turned up to a constituency meeting at the Tolka House in September, yet at the Finglas East branch meeting in October on the day after the one day public sector strike, there were eleven in attendance because the agenda was potentially contentious. We were able to vote down any spleen by eight to three. I also spoke at branch meetings in Santry and Poppintree about the delay in the opening of Beaumont Hospital. The Anglo-Irish Agreement was signed on 15th November and meetings were arranged to discuss the implications particularly in relation to the Unionists' exclusion and their subsequent abreaction. Dick Spring circulated the details in a question and answer fashion and we went through his circular in detail.

Struggling for Political Survival

In December, it was rumoured that the Organisation Committee intended to ensure that Dr Alan Matthews, a member of my branch and a TCD agricultural economist would be the Labour candidate in the next General Election. He was, I believe, supported by Labour Left but was not seen locally on the ground. On the following day, I went in to Leinster House to discuss the issue with Senator Pat Magner. However, at the constituency council on January 30th in '86, Dr Matthews announced that he was no longer interested in seeking selection. Paddy Dunne gave a valedictory address and said that he joined the Labour Party in 1964 and was now so disgusted with the leadership that he was resigning. He was also due to meet C.J. Haughey on the following morning. The other big shock among my friends in January was the defection of Helena McAuliffe-Ennis to the newly launched Progressive Democrats. That sort of thing was a bit like a death in the family.

The Beaumont Hospital Delay

Disinformation was rife concerning the reasons for the delay in the opening of Beaumont Hospital. I wrote in the *Irish Times* on 16th November that the version of events which regularly appeared in the press following any meeting that I attended had always outlined one side of the story while ignoring the other. This resulted in a consistent impression being created that a majority of consultants wanted a private hospital on the site of the Beaumont complex as a prerequisite to obtaining their cooperation in moving the Richmond and Jervis Street to the new site. In fact, it was agreed, following a vote, that the Minister's offer of a site for an out-patients clinic built by the consultants themselves, with no private hospital provision, was acceptable provided a mutually agreed lease was negotiated.

It was also pertinent to state that the disgraceful delay in commissioning the hospital was a consequence of pigheaded stupidity on both sides. The State should not be in the business of building or financing private hospitals. Such an action is inequitable socially and may in fact be unconstitutional under Article 40 Section 1. Therefore any such demand by one side was disingenuous to say the least.

Barry Desmond's original position regarding consultant practice in Beaumont was obviously untenable in both legal and practical terms. Within the terms of Sections 9 and 12 of the Consultants' Common Contract, private practice within a general hospital is incorporated within the agreed terms of remuneration. Therefore, the initial political statements were merely time wasting, ineffectual posturings.

In the absence of my own preferred option of an NHS-type system, which would include merit awards for medical excellence and patient access on the basis of clinical need only, the present dual system would have ensured a very undesirable outcome had the Minister's earlier proposal been implemented.

A two-tier system would have evolved on Dublin's Northside, with private practice and manpower expertise gravitating towards the Mater's Eccles St site and other private institutions. The consequent effect on clinical supervision in Beaumont is obvious. Both sides should have quickly agreed an equitable lease and facilitated the urgent equipping and opening of the hospital.

Councillor Pat McCartan of the Workers Party pointed out in an answering letter to the *Irish Times* on 13th December that the equipping could take from nine to twelve months, so he demanded an immediate halt to the charade with an opening date to be set immediately.

Family Planning

Professor Billy O'Dwyer suggested that the IMO was playing politics with the issue of family planning when trying to limit public information on services and I agreed. The medical trade unions had always interfered politically when their members' vested interests were at stake. Dr Noel Browne had just been interviewed on 'Today, Tonight' where he had described some of his problems with the Irish Medical Association when he was trying to introduce the 'Mother and Child Scheme'. It is also obvious that 'Well Woman Clinics' and other female medical services would not have been successfully launched in the private sector if family practitioners were providing an appropriate service in their surgeries.

The very low number of family doctors providing a comprehensive service – one or more in some counties – was a sound reason to disseminate information publicly about where and when such services were available. It is a spurious kind of restrictive practice that would dream up 'ethics' to prevent this information being freely available to the public.

The IMO is a trade union, not an altruistic public watchdog. Union newsletters are inappropriate media to debate matters of wide public interest. Local ethical practice is properly a function of the Medical Council.

A Dole Office and an Action Group for Ballymun

The conversion of the old Bank of Ireland branch offices in Ballymun Town Centre into an Employment Office by the Department of Social Welfare, as proposed by Barry Desmond, was completed quickly and the offices opened for the public in February '86. That was a considerable advance for those in Ballymun in receipt of benefits because the convenience saved time and busfares.

The Ballymun Action Group was creaking into action in late February and former Labour local election candidate, Des O'Malley, chaired a meeting in the Junior Comprehensive School on Ballymun Road to try to coordinate a response to the transit camp atmosphere that had arisen in Ballymun. People were queuing up to get a housing transfer out of the estate and community morale was low. Many of the men were jobless and relied totally on social welfare. Unmarried mothers and single parent families were very common. Hanging around the shopping centre and the pubs, it was so easy to develop a kind of nihilism. Empty flats, vandalism and dereliction were obvious. The bleak plain concrete and treeless landscape with rubbish strewn across the often flooded, open parking lots in front of the six or eight storey blocks was enough to undermine the toughest psyche. All those activists who participated in the Ballymun Community Coalition, which led the fight back and raised the people's morale, were, in my opinion, true Dublin heroes. That kind of spirit is now needed in parts of Tallaght and Blanchardstown. Communal self respect can change the outsiders view of an area and its people.

Barry Desmond Avoids Justice

The apparent fact that in mid February Barry Desmond refused to be moved from the Department of Health into another portfolio when the Taoiseach Garret FitzGerald, and the Tanaiste, Dick Spring, agreed a reshuffle showed great determination on his part but raised the question: what was his important agenda in health that required his unique personal attention? If there was no specific programme, and I believe that there is not a lot of evidence that there was one, then why did his superiors not simply move him, or else? Barry clearly did identify himself with his portfolio to an unusual extent and I know he worked extremely hard as an administrator alongside Liam Flanagan, the Secretary of the Department of Health.

On page 66 of *'Irish Politics Now'* Barry Desmond is quoted thus: 'My refusal to go to Justice completely upset the apple-cart. That day we came within half an hour of leaving Government. I decided I wasn't caving in. I might have considered the approach until I heard that a crowd of Fine Gael backbenchers were out for my scalp. Once I heard that crowd were on the warpath the knives were out and there was no way I was going to be moved." Barry also claimed to have been 'fully supported by his party leader Dick Spring'.

By contrast, Garret in *All in a Life*, page 623, states that Dick Spring first agreed with the Taoiseach on the Desmond move but then felt he and his colleagues would have to leave the Government altogether when Barry declined. About a half hour after telling Garret this, Dick returned with the compromise – Barry keeps Health but relinquishes Social Welfare. It was very much a case of things appearing different depending on your angle of vision.

Constituency Blues

Within the constituency, I had a series of meetings with Paddy Donegan, Maura Doolan, Gerry Doyle, Shay Carbin and Greg Sparks and it was clear that the number of branches was unsustainable. As I told our stalwards, the Party was heading downhill so fast that it might soon come to a situation in the constituency where the last person leaving could simply turn off the lights! The AGM of the Constituency Council in February agreed that there should be only two branches. Labour Left, the Militants and Paschal O'Reilly were in one and everyone else was in the other. I was now the secretary of the constituency council. At the March meeting, there were three obvious and distinct camps present. I was told by Ray Kavanagh and later by Terry Quinn on 13th March that Shay Carbin was seeking a nomination for the general election and was lobbying the members on the Organisation Committee and Administrative Council for support. Six days later, I was interviewed by the Organisation Committee. Pat Magner was in the chair and Ray Kavanagh, Marian Boushell, Ann Byrne, Ita MacAuliffe and Brian FitzGerald were around the table. That same day, despite the windy weather and even with our falling numbers, I joined Paddy Donegan, Maura Doolan, Michael Purdue, Noel Wheatley and Seorse Dearle to drop *Labour News* in Larkhill. With the Party in trouble, a club-like atmosphere was developing and the members were happy to get together. Local politics had become pleasant and we held branch meetings in my house. This was the camaraderie of a membership under political siege. The opinion polls confirmed what we already knew. There were a lot of voters out there who did not care very much for us.

Open Beaumont Hospital

Two years after the contractors had finished, Beaumont Hospital still remained unopened. Fianna Fail Ministers for Health Charles Haughey and Michael Woods, had given an undertaking that consultants could build a private hospital on site. In the dying days of the Haughey Government in 1982, Health Minister Dr Woods could have signed a binding lease for a new private hospital but did not do so despite being asked by the consultants. Barry Desmond reversed this decision, but later made a compromise offer of 70 private beds within the hospital plus 20 consulting rooms which was rejected by the consultants in 1985.

Attempts were made by myself and other doctors in the Richmond in early '86 to arrange a speedy resolution to the private clinic row and to have Beaumont Hospital opened. I circulated a letter to the consultants in the Richmond suggesting that they get on with direct negotiations with the Department. On 3rd March, the Richmond Medical Board which comprised all of the hospital's consultants, passed a resolution calling for the Joint Richmond/Jervis St Staff Association to enter into separate negotiations with the Department. In order to speed the opening of Beaumont, I wrote to Barry Desmond advising him that this new resolution had been passed. To my surprise, I found myself being censured at the next Medical Board meeting for reputedly entering into negotiations with the Department on behalf of the hospital when I was not entitled to do so. I then received a letter from Mr J.D. Kenny the Secretary/Manager warning me that the Board of Governors would take action if a similar occurrence was repeated. I replied to Mr Kenny on July 24th and refuted the accusation that I had purported to be acting for the hospital. I simply stated the truth of the matter, that at no time had I claimed to represent anyone other than myself.

At that time, the Richmond was being run by a small six man finance committee which was a subcommittee of the Board that in fact rarely met. The political temperature at medical staff meetings was very high, especially among some of the surgeons. The left of centre viewpoint was not overly represented or respected or appreciated, to say the least. Either the Richmond must move or be refurbished. Argument and discussion continued for months, yet many doctors just wanted to get up and go. Not many were displeased when Health Minister Barry Desmond changed the Board of Governors of the Richmond Hospital in July.

Senator Flor O'Mahony, who was the Labour candidate in North-Central was very interested in trying to expedite the opening of the hospital and I met himself and Denis Larkin for lunch in Leinster House on 25th July. I told them that the doctors had cleared the way for the immediate opening of the hospital and it was no longer at all valid for anyone in the Department of Health to blame a medical third party for obstructing the opening. I don't think that Flor quite believed what I was telling him, but I heard subsequently that there was a lot of heat generated about Beaumont at the Parliamentary Party meetings. Authentic Dublin trade unionists like Denis Larkin are different in cultural attitude to the middle class socialists in the Party who are much slicker verbally but often lack the essential heart and soul. Even at 78 years of age, Denis was aware of the issues and was very astute.

Over the last weekend in August, confirmation of what I had told Flor O'Mahony and Denis Larkin appeared in the three Middle Abbey Street papers, the *Evening Herald* and the *Irish* and *Sunday Independents.* The headings were 'Beaumont "go it alone" move', 'Consultants to go it alone on Beaumont', 'Hospital move row: IMO attacks doctor' and 'Medic body deceiving public'.

Consultants from Jervis Street and the Richmond told the IMO: 'We'll go it alone' and a group that did not include me went to negotiate with the Department of Health for an early opening of the hospital. The IMO had accused Barry Desmond of reneging on the agreement to allow consultants to build a private clinic on 1.3 acres of leased land within the grounds. I was quoted as saying 'Following a vote amongst the consultants themselves the majority of consultants and the Minister for Health, now want the same compromise deal on private practice at Beaumont.' The compromise would allow the consultants to provide private medical consulting rooms for outpatients. I also said 'For the IMO to be still seeming to be negotiating for a private hospital in defiance of the people involved defies belief.'

The IMO's Michael McCann accused me of acting from political motives and of running a 'politically orchestrated campaign'. My statements were allegedly 'wholly inaccurate'. I added 'on the contrary it is Mr McCann and the IMO who are deceiving the public and bringing the consultants of the two involved hospitals into disrepute.' The joint medical staffs of the Richmond and Jervis Street hospitals held a meeting at the Royal College of Surgeons on July 24th and decided to send a representative group of eight doctors (excluding me) led by Dr Shane O'Neill to finalise details on a lease for a private clinic and to try to have Beaumont opened as soon as possible with the IMO acting in an advisory capacity only.

Furthermore, a subsidiary group had a meeting with two Department of Health officials on the previous Wednesday, and the full group met the Department on the following week with the IMO present as observers. I also called for 'Mr McCann to withdraw his statement that I am running a politically orchestrated campaign and that my statements were inaccurate'. The IMO council also passed a resolution preventing the IMO secretariat from representing the consultants of the Richmond and Jervis Street in relation to the Beaumont issue. I pointed out that 'Mr McCann was probably acting against the current policy of his own council', a statement Mr McCann later contested.

There were continuing major differences of opinion within the medical staffs which were reported by Fintan Cronin in *Magill* magazine in September 1986. In that article, Professor John Fielding from Jervis Street accused the consultants in the Richmond of acting out of pure self-interest in their willingness to settle for a private clinic rather than a private hospital. He said that most of the Richmond consultants had private patients in other hospitals throughout the city in contrast to the Jervis Street consultants whose private patients were in private beds within Jervis Street itself.

To avoid jeopardising a meeting with the Department of Health on 5th September, I was asked in the Richmond to decline to debate the issues with the IMO on RTE and the Richmond group met Sean Trant from the Department of Health in the State Solicitor's Office, but the representatives from Jervis Street did not appear. This was a major step in the opening of the hospital. Only in late '86 did the Department enter into negotiations with the other unions representing various skills essential to the running of the new hospital.

There was no doubt that many consultants expected that the private hospital would be provided when Fianna Fail were returned to power as looked increasingly inevitable. This factor was important in the delaying process. Barry Desmond's opposition to the building of a nurses' home was also significant. (I believe that he was wrong. Nurses' homes are like student residences in colleges and are good for hospital morale, which is very important.) I was also suspicious that the Government was really quite happy to see the opening delayed because the payments for equipment and other start-up costs were also postponed.

By November '86, Ray Carroll from the Department of Health was getting co-operation from the doctors in trying to manage the Richmond. The Beaumont Private Clinic Company began and the new hospital was at last appearing on the horizon.

PDs and FG

In the first six months of 1986, the Progressive Democrats' opinion poll ratings went from about 20% down to 11% and then to 9% in October, which would still leave them making a large impact in many constituencies in any election. In February, *Magill* magazine reported 53% of Fine Gael TDs saying that they had no policy differences with the PDs, with only 13% of their TDs claiming that there was a difference. John Kelly TD said that 80% of Irish people wanted a right-wing government and that Fine Gael's failure to provide them with this was the cause of the rise of the PDs. Fine Gael backbenchers favoured coalition with the PDs rather than Labour.

In the *Irish Press* on February 27th, I wrote: 'The more Mr Des O'Malley is reported in the press, the more difficult it is to see any difference between the PDs and FG in policy aspirations. Liberal social and Northern Ireland policy, however desirable, is one thing, but 19th century liberal economics is quite another. Even a cursory glance at budgetary arithmetic would show that reducing taxes and Government spending to encourage 'initiative and enterprise' in the private sector would require large cutbacks in the main spending areas of health, education and welfare.

Even with the present low level of capital taxation and subsidised incentive schemes, indigenous private industry has not given objective reason to believe that private enterprise alone will be the answer to the fundamental socio-economic problem of unemployment.

Did the UK monetarist experiment never take place between 1979 and 1982? Did unemployment in Britain soar during this period? Did the gap between rich and poor widen? Were there no riots in the streets? Of course not! Some people never learn. Mr O'Malley's conditions (of low taxes etc) to allow and encourage people to get up and help themselves existed, or so Mrs Thatcher said.

So what happens now in Britain? Do economic forecasts predict a fall in unemployment? Can the unemployed afford a bike to search for work in the expanding economy ? Why waste a 1.1% rise on social welfare recipients? The large mass of people paid directly by the state should think of their real interests before voting PD. What good is low taxation if you have no job and low welfare? Now that a public service pensions cut is suggested what is the next PD rabbit out of the hat?'

The PDs received a big boost with the defection of Michael Keating from FG in April and they were flying high in the polls. It was certain that they would do very well in the next election.

The Workers Party

The Workers Party, in a letter to the *Evening Herald* on 19th February castigated the Government for a 'standstill budget' in relation to social welfare payments. On behalf of the constituency council, I refuted that statement in the *Evening Herald.* 'Such criticisms were unfair and ignored the unique achievements of Barry Desmond in ensuring inflation parity for social welfare recipients in the face of trans European governmental cutbacks. Despite over 80% of the population supporting parties pledged to severe cutbacks in Government spending, Labour managed to buck the trend and ensure a modicum of protection for the weakest lobby in society.'

Divorce Referendum

Polling was fixed for 26th June. The proposal on divorce was restrictive. The marriage must have failed for periods amounting to at least five years; there must be no possibility of reconciliation, and the court must be satisfied that proper provision was made for a dependent spouse according to individual circumstances and for any child dependent on either spouse. A Bill, announced to coincide with the referendum, also proposed that divorce would have to be preceded by a judicial separation of at least two years. Before the campaign started, the polls showed 57% were in favour and 36% against. The Catholic bishops opposed it by pastoral letter. Inheritance and property rights became issues and Fianna Fail mobilised against it.

At our branch meeting on 10th June, it was clear that Noel Wheatley and Paddy Donegan were opposed to the divorce proposal and would not participate in the campaign. So I met Maura Doolan, Stephen Dowds and Shay and Anne Carbin later in the Fingal pub to arrange the campaign. We started the campaign on 16th June and I was quite surprised to find John Rogers, the Attorney General, in Shay Carbin's house in Berryfield Road, Finglas South that night when I called there. Head Office supplied us with literature and posters and we set about dropping the whole of the Finglas area initially. I spent the solstice postering in Ballymun up to midnight when it was still not quite dark. Such was the level of my mad dedication. The polls were open for thirteen hours from 9am and in Dublin North-West, on a long fine day, there was a 60.22% turnout. The proposal was defeated by 16,344 to 14,849. On polling day, I was astonished to see the Fianna Fail party machine, supposedly neutral, orchestrate the anti-divorce campaign, driving nuns to the polling stations and campaigning outside. Jim Tunney TD was very active in pressing home his point right up to the school door at St Canices' at Ballygall Road West. Nationally, there was a 60.84% poll with 935,843 against and 538,279 for divorce. On the day of the count in Bolton Street, there were many very upset people who had a vested interest in the 'Yes' vote. That night, the local Divorce Action Group met in the 'Penthouse' in Ballymun and many of the women especially were distraught. The experience of dealing with brutal husbands and families in crisis who had been to the 'Aoibhneas' refuge, had radicalised these women. There was a feeling of betrayal by a selfish, uncaring electorate and some were very bitter. There would be no respite for many years. The irony in North-West was that many of the women in the Divorce Action Group were amongst the most caring and charitable that I had ever met. They were graduates of the university of life.

The Aftermath

I thought, at the time, as I expressed in a letter to the *Irish Times* that 'the defeat of the government's modest proposals on divorce was the most serious reversal for social and political progress since the notorious 'Mother and Child Scheme' of Dr

Noel Browne. A report that the Catholic bishops were trying to tackle the incongruity of Church nullity and State marriage, seeking a widening of the grounds for legal nullity, was further evidence of their disregard for the concept of equal rights for Catholics, Protestants and dissenters.

Will the present State laws be enforced? Are the bishops co-conspirators in the crime of bigamy? What chance now of a show trial? Surely if the bishops expect the State's laws to be bent to accommodate them in their philosophical gymnastics at ecclesiastical courts then they ought to have had more tolerance for the views of those in other churches and none.

While the Catholic Hierarchy's behaviour was predictable, however, the neutral (sotto voce vote no) position of Fianna Fail could not have fooled anyone who spent any time on the campaign. Their New Ireland Forum preferred option of a unitary State has been rendered absurd by the denial of minority rights to a significant section of the Southern population. Having implicitly recognised this, Mr Haughey is now pushing the Forum's second option, the federal/confederal state. Some Republican Party! By failing to magnanimously rise above religious intolerance we have buttressed partition, torpedoed the constitutional crusade, and given a major victory to Ian Paisley.

Though defeated and depressed, those of us who were seeking a liberal tolerant and non-sectarian society will fight on'.

Selection

Again on the 2nd July, I attended a meeting of the Organisation Committee with Paddy Donegan, Maura Doolan, Alan Matthews and Ina Gould. Later on 21st July, I attended a Directors of Elections meeting in Head Office with the General Secretary Raymond Kavanagh.

The selection convention for Dublin North-West for the forthcoming election was chaired in Head Office by the General Secretary on Tuesday 5th August. Paddy Donegan, Gerry Doyle, Paschal O'Reilly, Maura Doolin, Seorse Dearle and myself were the only delegates. To represent the Labour Party was a great honour for me because I always considered that Labour was on the side of the dispossessed and the downtrodden and that we stood for the brotherhood of man in the wider sense. I felt that man could either survive and prosper by cooperation and respect because we are interdependent or we could sink in the mire of exploitation, greed and rampant individualism. I recognised the human foibles of Labour's public figures. Winning in North-West was a long shot because we received about 6% in 1982 and 7% in the '85 local elections with six candidates sweeping their personal as well as the party votes. Now the Party had sunk even lower and the nominal manpower in the constituency was very small. Unperturbed but under no illusions, we headed for a celebratory drink in the Dergvale and decided to give it a real lash.

The Tormey Brothers

Helen and Tommy (1981)

Mary, Aoibhinn and Tommy

With Aoibhinn at Glasnevin Church

With Seamus Shiels and Bill Attley

With Rover's defensive rock, Peter Eccles

Outside Beaumont Hospital

8
CAMPAIGN FOR ELECTION '87

On 18th August, we started a leaflet drop in Finglas South and we regarded the election campaign as off the ground. On 7th October '86, 14,000 copies of our candidate introductory leaflet in two colours were printed and distributed within three weeks. Getting six people out to drop from an active pool of about twenty people was easy, despite there being only an attendance of thirteen or fewer at the constituency meetings in the last four months of 1986. We also ran some fund-raising events and morale was relatively high, but thirteen was the maximum number of members attending any single meeting. Ina Gould in Poppintree told me in August that she was thinking of quitting the Party and the cuts in social welfare in November were the final straw. Ina was a serious loss and was never replaced and it left us high and dry in Ballymun, which was an accurate reflection on the state of the Party at that time.

In October, the Fine Gael Ard Fheis signalled a go-it-alone time even though they were on 27% in the polls and it was obvious that an election was imminent. The Government won a motion of confidence on 23rd October and an election was staved off for another short while. The Report of the Commission on Electoral Strategy was discussed and debated on 28th October at our meeting following a summary by Alan Matthews. There was general approval for its analysis and recommendations. The Party was to stay out of Coalition and rebuild for ten years unless the national interest dictated etc, etc. Coalition had been bad for the party. About 4,000 copies of *Labour News* were also being distributed in North-West every few weeks, concentrating on Finglas West and South and Ballymun and I wrote little pieces for it. Henry Haughton did a good job as editor. These drops went on relentlessly up to Christmas often in biting cold conditions and Noel Wheatley and Paddy and Padraig Donegan were tremendous in support. On the Sunday before Christmas, Mary Chambers and I spent five hours completing a drop in West Finglas. Determination often means that you have to lead from the front. We were certainly letting any Labour voters know that we still existed. The Cork Conference scheduled for 7th to 9th November was cancelled due to a trade union dispute. This got a lot of people off a few political meat hooks.

Stephen Collins, in a constituency review in the *Evening Press* on 6th November wrote that 'for Labour, Dublin North-West has been an unmitigated disaster over the past three elections. It was the area selected by Brendan Halligan to make his bid for a seat but he came nowhere near a quota. The Labour vote here dropped

In the Lab, at Beaumont Hospital with Maria Ennis and Reighnall Glasgow

The Independent Labour in North-West, 1993

from 12% in 1981 to 6% in the second general election of 1982. Their candidate next time out will be Bill Tormey, a clinical pathologist in the Richmond Hospital, but his chances are slim to say the least.' I was under no illusions of just where we stood electorally. Labour was down at between 4 and 6% in the polls and political oblivion beckoned.

Social Welfare Cuts

In November, the Minister for Social Welfare, Gemma Hussey, implemented the EEC equality directive which deprived 17,000 mostly low income families of up to one-third of their incomes. Working wives of men on the dole lost their automatic dependent status and the family income was cut by up to £40 per week. For example, those claiming invalidity pensions stood to lose £30.60 per week by the removal of their wives' dependent status, while a man on retirement and old age pensions would lose £39.50 per week when his wife was earning over £50 per week. The child dependency allowance was also cut by 50% if the wife was working while the husband was on social welfare. The Christmas Social welfare bonus was also cut to 64% of what was expected. On 21st November, I met Frank Cluskey, phoned Mervyn Taylor and Senator Flor O'Mahony and sent messages to Dick Spring and Barry Desmond to protest. Five days later, Billy Attlee then General Secretary of the FWUI and later Joint General President of SIPTU and David Grafton joined Seamus Shiels from the ITGWU and myself in a picket by the Dublin North-West Labour Party on the Dail on a damp afternoon in protest against these cuts. On a mild overcast Saturday, 29th November, I joined the Dublin Trades Council march from Parnell Square to the GPO against the cuts. This was surprisingly well attended and, among Labour Party people, there was a feeling of despondency over our Party's participation in this mess. This remained even after the compromise secured by the intervention of Deputies Cluskey and Taylor which still meant that some families' incomes were reduced by up to £16.60 per week.

I felt strongly that families should not be penalised for mothers working because many women were receiving very low wages in cleaning and other part-time jobs. When the basic rate of £50 to £60 per week for all social welfare recipients was introduced then and only then should the equality directive be introduced. The St Vincent de Paul Society and the Commission on Social Welfare reported that 80% of people fully dependent on social welfare were living on the margins of poverty. Many could not buy sufficient food or fuel or afford school books or busfares for their children. Rent and mortgage arrears, ESB bills, first communions, forced people to attend the community welfare officer. It was no wonder that money lenders remain a scourge.

I wrote about Labour and income cuts in the *Irish Press* on 18th December. 'Being clear in what you believe and knowing why, is the basic ingredient in defining limits beyond which one does not go in rational decision-making. The Labour members in Cabinet should examine their consciences in relation to the above process and consider the effects of the mean-spirited cuts in income suffered mainly by families with mothers working in low paid jobs to supplement household income.

Is the chosen method of implementing the EEC directive not a blatent invitation to join the black economy as quickly as possible?

If our lads in the Cabinet need a mental laxative to unmuddle their minds I suggest they consider the tone and content of what Connolly and Larkin would have to say on the matter and remember who they represent and where the socialist soul is located.

If the 'poor' were a bank or an insurance company, Fine Gael would have no difficulty in 'finding' the money to equalise upwards to preserve their liquidity. The £3 million cut in the Christmas bonus can only be considered a gratuitous insult. Sops such as mortgage and rent reliefs merely add to administrative chaos and increase the number who do not receive their entitlements.

The selfish righteousness of the well-organised interest groups in building up an apparent public consensus equating public spending with the devil and tax cuts with the gods should not fog the minds of Labour ministers. It is well to remember that personal greed and maximum profits are polar opposites to social justice and dignity for all. Profit not jobs is the objective of capitalism and the record of indigenous Irish private industry is poor. It is ironic that industry complains of State interference while expecting grant aid, tax incentives and subsidised workers from Government.

Irish industrial policy has been all carrot and no stick. Corporation tax at a nominal 10% is a write-offable joke. Wasteful economic activity such as currency and building speculation should be penalised heavily and industrial policy restructured along the lines of the Telesis Report with a cutback in the massive capital re-equipment grants by the IDA.

The National Economic and Social Council recognised the necessity of a long timescale for their suggested cut of £500 million in public spending and had useful suggestions on changes in State support for industry. As socialists, we must be committed to value for money and good quality services in the public sector and be prepared to defend them.

Public spending savings should not be at the expense of the weakest in society, but should start by clawing back money from Allied Irish Banks in relation to the ICI affair, and collecting all health and youth employment levies from the self-employed and the farmers.'

News by North-West

We decided to issue a local Labour newsletter – double A3 folded over and Seamus Shiels wrote most of it. As editor of *Liberty News* in the ITGWU, he was an accomplished editor and propagandist. We got the first issue out before Christmas and we delivered to every house in the constituency in less than four weeks. It featured the welfare cuts with the picture of Bill Attlee, Seamus and myself on the picket line – a collector's item! The lack of local employment on the Janelle redevelopment and the preponderance of workers from the Dundalk and cross border area was also noted. This was an area of some local controversy in Finglas. Privatisation of State companies would not serve the public interest and we were concerned even then about the fate of Aer Lingus. Public sector commercial companies should be developed to create jobs which would not readily transfer to cheaper labour countries. AIDS and the heterosexual was also featured because of the African experience. Sex tourism is a potential problem, usually unreported, and sexual contacts in Central Africa are particularly dangerous because AIDS there was mainly found among the heterosexual population. The need for a comprehensive approach to drug abuse was stressed because of its strong association with unemployment, the lack of community facilities and family problems such as unemployment.

We also supported the Shelbourne Hotel strikers who were at least £12 per week worse off than their colleagues in other Dublin hotels.

At the Labour Christmas party in the Dail and at our constituency drinks party in the Fingal Pub, we all knew that we were in the blocks under starters orders.

Ballymun Fire Danger

On 28th December, I was contacted about a fire in Thomas Clarke Tower and the local Gardai, the fire brigade and the priest were there immediately dealing with the consequences. Fortunately a major fire has not occurred due to the concrete construction of the buildings and the speedy response of the local fire brigade based about two miles away in Finglas Fire Station. Lift shafts, refuse chutes and lock-up basements are common sites of attack over many years. Smoke inhalation and plain terror have been the main consequences of these arson attacks.

John Stalker

When a man stands out against the establishment on a point of principle, then he should be supported by the fair-minded. John Stalker's quick removal from the investigation of RUC's 'shoot to kill' policy was just such a situation. So we passed a motion at our branch and in January we sent a small contribution to his defence fund administered by Michael Unger at the *Manchester Evening News.* He sent us a personal acknowledgement which impressed us greatly.

Bailing Out

Despite the political impossibility of agreeing massive cuts in public spending which was clear before the Christmas recess, Barry Desmond is quoted by Shane Kenny and Fergal Keane in *Irish politics Now* as giving this tactical reason for hanging on – 'the Labour ministers had taken a decision to go all the way with them, right up to the book of estimates. We wanted it on paper, out in the open so people would see the estimates and know why we were quitting. We were determined that the differences between the parties on the estimates would be written into the public record. We were very bitter against those who said we should come out in mid-'86. We had to come out on specifics and not on generalities or some piece of individual opportunism.' I could hear the orchestra playing the soft soap in the background but I suppose that's just my cynicism!

There was a Directors of Elections and candidates meeting in the Department of Energy in Clare Street on 7th January. Seamus Shiels, who was our Director of Elections, and I attended for North-West. Frankie McLaughlin TD from Meath was in ebullient form and gave us all a peptalk. Little did he know what was coming! Three days later the latest record unemployment figure of 250,178 was published. Politically, it was another shout of Fire! in the theatre.

On 20th January, attempting to make a virtue out of necessity, Labour ended their agony and left the Government to Fine Gael. The ostensible reason was an unbridgable gap in balancing the budget. To keep within a budget deficit target of 7.4% of GNP which was the Fine Gael bottom line, there would have had to be substantial cuts in health and social welfare. The scale of retrenchment was simply politically impossible.

Liveline

Coincidentally, on the same afternoon of the 20th, I was on the Marian Finucane programme on RTE radio talking about medical incomes and competition. I pointed out that in all monopolies and restraints of trade, fees always tend to be high. The level of appropriate incomes in medicine is a matter of opinion just as the very high fees in law are also controversial. Health and access to medical services can be determined by income. Two cardiologists or orthopaedic surgeons or urologists or pathologists or gastroenterologists at £ X each is better for the public than one at £2X. Once the income level is high enough to reward excellence, it is sufficient. I was asked if there were specialists earning six figure incomes and I said Yes! Some practitioners in some of the above areas were likely to be in that income bracket. Under successive governments, the health sector has been underfinanced and this has helped to create a two tier system where the patient's bank balance – rather than the patient's condition – determines the standard of health care he or she receives. 'The notion of people making vast profits out of the pain and suffering of others is particularly repulsive'. I heard that my comments caused consternation at the Richmond because some doctors mistakenly thought that I had been virtually naming them. Some people are very sensitive about their earnings.

A Four Week Marathon

On Wednesday evening of the 21st January, Fergus Egan and I kicked off the four week campaign by postering in Finglas Village. Polling day was fixed for Tuesday 17th February. We had collected the posters earlier in the Glasnevin Industrial Estate where they had been printed by arrangement with Head Office. By the end of the first week, all the main roads in the constituency were postered. We then filled in the spaces on our poster map and later we repostered the sites where our first posters had been removed by the weather or otherwise. The poster of Dick Spring in an open necked white shirt, was also used and we in no way dissociated ourselves from the Party leader. This was certainly not the case elsewhere in the city.

Fine Gael were now in office alone and they released their proposed Budget containing extensive cutbacks. These were about £140 million in health and social welfare and they included a £10 out-patients hospital charge, £1 prescription charge, increases in the health contribution PRSI ceiling, a 50% cut in pay related benefit for new claimants, and more restrictions on disability benefits. Dick Spring condemned these cuts as unjust and unsupportable.

Fianna Fail released their manifesto, the 'Programme for National Recovery' on 29th January in a tactical move to effectively shorten the campaign to three weeks. Charles Haughey had described the four weeks as 'outrageous, just prolonging the agony'. Fianna Fail promised to curtail public borrowing at 1986 levels as a proportion on GNP and to progressively reduce public spending and to achieve economic growth of 2.5% per year over five years. They carefully avoided specifying where the knife would slice. Typical Haughey!

When I went to hand in my nomination papers on 29th January to the City Sheriff, Michael Hayes, in Fownes Street, I was delayed by the arrival of the Taoiseach, Dr Garret FitzGerald, and his two running mates in Dublin South-East, Joe Doyle and Willie Egan. I had no idea that an appointment was usual and I certainly wished to avoid a totally unnecessary return visit. The whole incident was quite funny at the time and was featured in the *Evening Herald* later that day.

'People Matter Most'

On the following day, Dick Spring launched the Labour manifesto under the slogan 'People matter most'. It stressed that the sacrifices necessary to get the country's finances in order must be shared in accordance with the ability to pay. The tax system must be fair and just and farmers and the self-employed must be fully in the net as must business and capital taxes. 'More enterprise and effective co-operation between the public, private and co-operative sectors is the key to economic recovery.... Risks and benefits must be shared.' Labour is committed to redistribution of income, wealth and power in Irish society, to give genuine equality of opportunity to all our children. A new constitution was also proposed. Labour's main achievements were in keeping social welfare payments ahead of inflation, in increasing pensions and children's allowances, in establishing the National Development Corporation, in almost eliminating housing waiting lists, in helping the unemployed through the Social Employment Scheme and the Enterprise Allowance Scheme, in extending the national gas grid, in helping the development of the Anglo-Irish Agreement and in holding the divorce referendum. Opposition in cabinet to the sale of state companies including the Great Southern Hotels, Nitrogen Eireann Teo, Aer Lingus and Irish Steel was also important.

A 4% economic growth rate was proposed and the National Development Corporation was to be an economic engine. A wealth tax, an increase by 25% in corporation taxes, an extension of PRSI to farmers and the self-employed, disclosure of salaries and fees from public bodies to the revenue commissioners, tax relief on life assurance and VHI premiums at standard rate only, tax collection to be overhauled radically, tax certs required for state grants, and a widening of the 35% tax band were all proposed. In education, funds were to be reallocated towards the primary level and to the disadvantaged away from subsidising exclusive fee paying schools. In health, a comprehensive national health system was to be phased in and two tier care in public hospitals was to be abolished. Primary care was to be developed and there should be democratic management and full accountability for the voluntary hospital sector and other care agencies. There was to be a law change to end compensation claims in planning appeals.

We also stood for a Freedom of information Bill, the implementation of the O'Briain Report on the treatment of prisoners in custody, the abolition of the death penalty, prison reform, new family courts and easier judicial separation. Labour also opposed commercial interests having any role in local radio.

On The Hustlings

We started canvassing on January 28th and kept going relentlessly for the three final weeks. Small canvass cards were produced and we used the party literature. The campaign thrust was against the proposed health charges and the cuts in health and social welfare implicit in the commitments of Fine Gael, the PDs and Fianna Fail. We had an A5 leaflet on these issues

The opinion polls showed labour at 5% with Fianna Fail on 52% and Fine Gael on 23%. The presence of Proinsias de Rossa distorted these figures locally but they still gave a very credible message.

An election version of *'News by North-West'* was produced and we set about using it as a drop and while canvassing. We covered 90% of the constituency. The Fine Gael health cuts, Ballymun fire safety, toxic waste dumping and Irish Sea pollution; the Ballymun SUSS centre report '*A block of Facts*' on the maintenance situation and on the necessity for a social mix in Ballymun was highlighted and 'Tormey's Stormer!' on the Liveline programme was summarised. The Government's decision to reject the proposal for a National Sports Centre in Dublin in favour of a number of regional centres was condemned by the major sporting bodies. We pointed out that one of the sites in Athlone was in Minister Pat Cooney's constituency, yet Tullamore Harriers, with their fine facilities, was nearby and could have been usefully further developed. For the weekend after masses, we used a coloured A5 'Finglas/Ballymun says NO to Health and Social Welfare Cuts! Put people before profits! Put People before privilege! Put people before private interest!'

Later in the campaign, we produced a large A4 with 'Which future will you choose?' We contrasted our policies on jobs, pay, taxes, cuts and general state resources with those of FF, FG and the PDs. From the last weekend, we distributed a facsimile of the ballot paper with the Number 1 placed in the wishful thinking spot.

Seamus Sheils was ill for part of the campaign and that certainly slowed down our literature production. The canvass was difficult because of the length of the campaign and the bad weather. It was very cold. Our small bunch of canvassers included Gerry Doyle, Paschal O'Reilly, Noel Wheatley, Bob Slater, Ed Kearns, Bernadette Doyle, Syd and Peter Sutton, Maura Doolan, Paddy and Padraig Donegan, Billy Kelly, Josephine Gorman, Madge Guthrie, Dick Slevin, Jenny Owens, Gerry Brennan, John Whelan, Barbara Reid, Mick Purdue, Christy Sands, Olive Morgan, Seorse Dearle, Colette Coleman, Brendan Tyrrell, Vinnie Reddin and Tom O'Keeffe. Many of these were not party members and we were grateful for their help. Most nights there were only about five or six of us. Gerry Doyle and Noel Wheatley were everpresent stalwards. We did not get around every house because of the weather, but virtually all of the Finglas, Ballygall, Santry and Ballymun houses were visited.

The general doorstep attitude was very anti-Labour but personally we were doing all right, or so we thought. Proinsias de Rossa was doing very well and many of his voters were very antagonistic towards us. The Workers Party 'Fight Back' slogan was a real cracker and was very effective on huge posters on empty sites and nailed to the front of houses in Finglas. They also used another slogan 'Tax the greedy not the needy' and their campaign was pithy and effective. They regularly cited East Germany as a role model for Ireland and I, on more than one occasion, pointed out that the guns on the Berlin Wall and the wall itself were aimed at the East German people to keep them in and not to keep West Germans out. Ignoring facts which get in the way of ideology is an old human trait and we're all human. In the Election '87 special issue of the *In Dublin* magazine, it was reported that the PDs in Dublin North-West decided not to contest that election because of a local deal with Fine Gael to save Mary Flaherty's seat. We heard that rumour at the time but discounted it because it was only six years since Fine Gael had two seats in the constituency and it was extremely unlikely that their seat was in any real danger. However, some of the local Fine Gael activists had joined the PDs and Fine Gael were nervous of them. Garret FitzGerald suggested Fine Gael transfers should go to the PDs but there was no reciprocity.

Because of the time of year and the weather, television and radio played a large part in the campaigns and Fine Gael and Labour, for different reasons, distanced themselves from the last four years as much as possible. Fine Gael tried to GUBU Charles Haughey on television and on the issue of the Anglo-Irish Agreement, they succeeded. On the leaders debate on RTE, Dr FitzGerald forced Mr Haughey to deny his own words about 'taking political and diplomatic action' in relation to changing the constitutional implications of the Anglo Irish agreement to which he took exception. Garret FitzGerald was widely considered to have scored a win over his rival that night and it probably put a Fianna Fail majority out of reach. Dick Spring was interviewed separately and I thought that he performed well as also did Des O'Malley and Tomas MacGiolla, both of whom I respect.

The most abiding memory was not the hostility to Labour at some doors but the smoke pollution from open coal fires which descended like clockwork every evening just after 4 o'clock. A Clean Air Act was obviously needed and Mary Harney's clean-up some three years later was long overdue. Madge Guthrie berated anyone she knew from the Oliver Bond area originally who would not vote for us. Madge was reared in Oliver Bond flats and was a dark, round faced, curly haired jolly woman with four children. She thought Dick Springs (always plural for Madge) was lovely and would tell anyone prepared to listen. Canvassing with her was like participating in a street pantomime. Madge was naturally funny. She was not averse to giving a few youths a clip around the ear for lighting fires and carrying-on at her gable end in Finglas South. I could not believe it when on polling day she disappeared from canvassing outside St Fergal's school to go to a part-time cleaning job in town. We would have reimbursed her for any lost earnings but she never told us. Another funny incident was the expression of disbelief on Gerry Doyle's face when a young lady opened her door in a negligee and Gerry handed her the literature. She politely remarked on the coldness of the night but Gerry could only mumble, such was his surprise at this apparition. Dick Slevin remarked that it never happened to any of the rest of us! Barry Desmond and Dick Spring were unpopular in particular in areas where the Workers Party had concentrated. Cuts and an image of chaos in government were hard to shake off but if the ministers had not left the Cabinet, Labour votes on the ground would be rare enough for a preservation order to ensure survival. Some of the officers and crew members of Irish Shipping, which had been liquidated in 1983, lived in Santry and were rightly very bitter at their treatment which contrasted badly with the fate of the Insurance Corporation of Ireland. For legal reasons, they were paid only statutory redundancy payments. Dr Garret FitzGerald in *All in a Life* claims that there was no sensible alternative because by supplementing their redundancy payments, the State would have put itself at risk of another £140 million of liabilities. The Irish Shipping crews would not be voting for either Coalition party.

On the last week of the campaign Fine Gael moved Tom Farrell, a local councillor for Clontarf in the neighbouring North-Central constituency, and Mary Flaherty into my best area. Tom Farrell ran a very personalised campaign giving out free sloganised biros and other gimmicks. He was formerly a member of the Labour Party in Dublin Central and he left with Michael O'Leary. He produced a Farrell plan for Finglas and hired two large poster sites. One faced the bottom of Ballygall Road and left the image of Farrell staring down at all comers all day. We thought it was funny at the time but it was effective. This site was right next door to the Fianna Fail headquarters. The second Farrell poster was on Cardiffsbridge Road facing the Dunsink dump direction! Tom had a Hiace van with a public address speaker blaring at everyone that he stood for 'Jobs, jobs, and more jobs for Dublin North-West'. Farrell added innovative spice to the scene much to the particular and obvious annoyance of the Flaherty camp. Gerry Doyle was told that a Fine Gael private poll showed us running well at over 2,000 votes, with one week to go but the Fine Gael final push ate considerably into this vote. Mary Flaherty's personal last throw was effective and it was a double A4 which featured her wedding photographs taken in an ornate city carriage when her husband Alexis FitzGerald was Lord Mayor.

Our election address was the most detailed such prescription I have ever seen. It was full of ernest intentions. Seamus Shiels designed the address and called it the 'Tormey file'. The big problem was that we were swimming against the tide. There were separate sections on each issue and these included unemployment, job creation, tax reform, social welfare, health, education, women's rights, childcare facilities, status of children, divorce, recreation and social amenities, privatisation, the public sector, law and order, Northern Ireland, neutrality, community action, the environment and political philosophy. The envelopes were addressed and organised by the Donegan family with help from my mother and Maura Doolan.

The most astonishing piece of election literature was the '*Pat Carey newsletter*'. It was published as 'a non-party publication'. This was Pat Carey's first General Election for Fianna Fail. This tabloid paper contained pictures galore with Pat taking local kids to Coolure House in Co. Westmeath, Pat in Rivermount and West Finglas community workshops and listed his appointments due to his membership of Dublin Corporation. There was also what was to become a Carey trade mark – an extensive list of grants which he was reputed to have delivered for what appeared to be every football, athletic, karate, swimming, angling and bowling club in the area and not forgetting active retirement associations. There were a total of forty-five different clubs listed. All we could say was Wow! and sigh ! What a player!

Jim Tunney was supremely confident and with good reason. He always had his own entourage and was quietly effective. He had an uncanny knack for putting names on faces outside the churches. Michael Barrett had many Fianna Failers of rural origin supporting him and he was popular on the ground in Ballymun where local woman Agnes Cox was the community candidate in an area where people's political consciousness was quickly rising. Agnes Cox was well supported locally and I was in no way surprised by her vote. Proinsias de Rossa's supporters were aggressively confident and were absolutely dismissive of Labour. Their claim that they could take two of the four seats was quite hollow. Stephen Collins in his constituency profile in the *Evening Press* summed up each candidate most accurately and predicted the unlikely possibility of Pat Carey displacing Mary Flaherty for a third Fianna Fail seat. He knew we were in reality building a base for the future.

Both Seamus Martin in the *Irish Times* and Mairtin Mac Cormaic correctly predicted the result and my claim that we would increase the vote over the 2,054 which Brendan Halligan polled in 1982 was wrong.

The final opinion poll in the *Sunday Independent* just before the election gave Fianna Fail 38%, Fine Gael 25%, Labour 5%, PDs 11% with don't knows at 15%. We knew what was coming.

Polling Day

It was cold, very cold and the dedicated few stuck to their task outside the voting schools. Gerry Doyle, Sylvia Byrne and Paschal O'Reilly covered St Canice's Girls on Ballygall Road West. Gerry and Betty Maher, the Mulroys, Dick Slevin, Maura Doolan, Olive Morgan, Paul Brien, Jenny Owens, Mary Llewellyn, Frank Kennedy, Gerry Juhel, Richie Harte, Pauline Cregan, Philip Gifford, the Dearles, the Purdues, the Donegans, the Costellos families all came out to help in various places. Sally Shiels organised a little party afterwards and we went home happy thinking that we had done better than the disastrous low figure the next day would reveal at St Vincent's School in Glasnevin.

The Result

With 1,370 first preferences, I finished only seventh in the list of candidates. Proinsias de Rossa headed the poll on 6,866, with Michael Barrett 6,698, Jim Tunney 6,591, and Mary Flaherty 4,662 following. Pat Carey polled 3,448 and Tom Farrell 1,831. Harry Fleming and Niall Donnelly for Sinn Fein got 1,065 between them and Alison Larkin for the Greens got 504. The Ballymun woman, Agnes Cox, got 844 which was a very good return on very meagre resources. We were eliminated on 1,983 after the tenth count just 45 behind Tom Farrell, the second

Fine Gael candidate. There were 3,279 votes between Pat Carey and Mary Flaherty when she took the fourth seat.

I did not hang about at the count and the tally volunteers were so demoralised that they also left. Gerry Doyle visited the count centre and kept me updated and we headed for the television to watch Brian Farrell and company. Gerry Doyle and I were not too pleased but what could we do?

Fianna Fail polled 48.34% (+8.17%), the Workers Party 21.61% (+1.83%), Fine Gael 18.75% (-11.58%), Labour 3.96% (-2.49%), Sinn Fein 3.08%.

In Dublin, Labour was now in fifth place only winning 7.1% of the popular vote compared to 7.5% for the Workers Party, 13.6% for the PDs, 23.7% for Fine Gael and 40.5% for Fianna Fail. This was the first time Labour had been outflanked on the Left and was a serious setback continuing a long slow decline in the capital. Nationally the Labour vote was a small 6.4% down from 9.4% in 1982.

Dick Spring had the dreadful experience of keeping his seat by a four vote margin and it was sickening in Dublin to see and hear some people who have been on the Administrative Council cheer when it was wrongly suggested that he was going to lose. The plural of a certain organ would be an apt description of that gang. Labour returned with 12 TDs, Workers Party 4, Fianna Fail 81, Fine Gael 51, Progressive Democrats 14 and others 4. Labour also had 3 Senators.

9

LABOUR GETS OFF THE FLOOR FROM 1987 -1989

Following the defeat in the General Election, which was in reality a fair old hammering, Gerry Doyle and I met Paddy Tierney in the Grand Hotel in Malahide to sort out where to go from here.

There was more to life than losing with Labour. On the plus side of February, Shamrock Rovers won the League of Ireland for the fourth successive year. Rovers is another opium for the smitten! Ireland beat England 17-0 at Lansdowne.

'That The Health Service is Sick'

That was the title of a major debate at the Annual Conference of the Medical Students Association in the Royal College of Surgeons on 6th March. I spoke in the debate as did Dr James Sheehan an orthopaedic surgeon and a director of the Blackrock Clinic, Professor James McCormick, former Dean and now Head of the Community Medicine Department at Trinity College Medical School, and Mr Tom Ryan the General Manager of the VHI.

James Sheehan said that the Irish medical system was in need of an overhaul. Our hospitals were too old and were poorly equipped. A whole range of vital services were not being provided. Sheehan said that the time had come to seriously develop the idea of independently funded private medical services. In future we should discourage hospitalisation and improve outpatient services with more emphasis on day care and day surgery. Grants to hospitals should be related to actual turnover and not to the number of beds. He also criticised the VHI's monopoly of private health insurance in Ireland as the VHI is answerable to the Minister of Health and his department. Some of the most modern equipment available in other European countries was not present in many of our hospitals and the only way forward for the Health Services was through the development of independent funding.

Professor James McCormick is an iconoclast on many issues. He is a rational exponent of fairness and has an international reputation as a debunker of medical mythology. He has questioned the accepted conventional view that there is a direct relationship between diet, cholesterol and coronary heart disease. Two years later, he and his colleague Dr Peter Skrabanek produced the iconoclasts guide to clinical medicine entitled *'Follies and Fallacies in Medicine'* published by the Terragon Press, Glasgow. Tom Ryan defended the VHI and maintained that his company was the backbone of the health services and allowed patients more choice which was what the public clearly wanted. The numbers subscribing to VHI had continuously risen year by year. The company was set up to give health cover to the upper income group but had grown to such an extent that it now covered many who really could not afford the other clinical costs of private medicine. I argued in favour of a national health service free at the point of usage similar to the Aneurin Bevan National Health Service Act in Britain and I said that the state should play a greater role in developing the health services. In relation to general practice, I pointed out that only those on very low incomes were in receipt of medical cards. I also pointed out, apparently much to the surprise of the man himself that James Sheehan had acted most honourably regarding his position in the Blackrock Clinic because he had resigned his public post at St Vincent's Hospital, Elm Park to pursue his private interests. This I believed, made him unique in this country. Funnily enough, there were telephone enquiries made to some medical acquaintances of mine before the meeting to find out if I had horns. Run for Labour and stand by to be branded. Amazing how quickly times change!

When the new Dail met, Charles Haughey was elected Taoiseach on the casting vote of the Ceann Comhairle Sean Treacy and on the following day, Dr Garret FitzGerald resigned as Leader of Fine Gael.

The constituency council met in the Willows in mid-March following the election and twelve attended. They were Paddy and Padraig Donegan, John Whelan, Noel Wheatley, Paul Foran, Tom and Madge Guthrie, Josephine Gorman, Maura Doolan, Bob Slater, Seamus Shiels, and myself plus two militant supporters Sean Rea and Gerard Murphy. We were determined to fight on and increase our vote now that the Party was in opposition. The Ray McSharry budget was very stringent and would make oppositionism much easier. Shouting foul quickly became a national sport but there was no doubt that something had to be done to curtail the public sector borrowing requirement and whatever it was would have to be politically painful. The U-turn in the Fianna Fail attitude was total. It certainly put into context the cynicism of their tactics and statements in the Dail while in Opposition. Later that month the General Secretary, Ray Kavanagh, chaired a wide ranging directors of elections meeting in Head Office which included Seamus Shiels, Paul Mulhern, Caroline Hussey, Grey Sparks, Frank Buckley, Padraig Turley and Pat Fox. The Party had escaped the predicted fate of returning to Dail Eireann with all members arriving in one Mini car but it was a tight squeeze. Dave Grafton suffered the same fate in the NUI Senate constituency as I did nearly six years later and on the day Dave and I did the obvious. We headed for Nesbitts and downed a few pints.

Dublin 'A City of Cultural Vandalism'

We had Hume Street, the ESB in Fitzwilliam Street, Wood Quay, Frescati House – the list of destruction in Dublin is very long. The destruction of Glenmalure Park, Milltown was for me another cultural outrage. Shamrock Rovers' last game there was in the FAI Cup semi-final against Sligo Rovers and as Max Boyce succinctly put it 'I was there'.

Shamrock Rovers may be a company like any other whose owners may do what they wish with its assets. However, it is part of the culture and tradition of generations of Dubliners with the owners/directors acting as effective trustees and thus it is much more than a mere possession. Therefore, I viewed the move away from Glenmalure Park as a form of cultural vandalism and as a betrayal of those supporters who organised fund raising for flood lighting and other ground improvements over the years of the Kilcoyne regime.

Domestic football will never again get really large regular attendances because of the modern emphasis on participation and the ever widening choice of sporting and other leisure activities available to the public. Thus some direct linkage of player remuneration with club receipts is inevitable.

I readily acknowledged the considerable financial sacrifice made by the Kilcoyne brothers since 1972, but the present move will demolish loyalties built up over decades. Rovers will no longer be Rovers! Senior soccer will be on its knees in Dublin.

If it was a question of money then they should move over and sell their shares to a large commercial concern and also directly to the supporters who would then have a real stake in what could develop into a true club. Why the stealth and the speed of the flight from Milltown? It would have been better if the Kilcoynes had closed down altogether rather than go through the charade of 'moving' to Tolka or Dalymount Park.

I joined the Keep Rovers At Milltown (KRAM) committee at their June meeting in the Tara Tower Hotel and we organised a boycott of Tolka Park in Drumcondra and a picket on Richmond Road which reduced attendances dramatically and persuaded the owners to sell the club at the end of the season. Brian Murphy was in the Chair, and also present were Jimmy Keane, Gerry Mackey, Ronan Boyle, Eddie Cowzer, Ed Kenny, and a number of others.

'Health Cuts Hurt The Old, The Poor and The Handicapped'

'It is now 10 years since the World Health Organisation adopted a resolution that the main social target of governments should be to attain a level of health for all by the year 2000 which will permit them to lead a socially and economically productive life. The 1978 Declaration of Alma-Ata included the concept of universal accessibility to appropriate primary care and medical technology.

FF, FG and the PDs were insisting that Department of Health spending was too high for our means. This fallacy should be refuted immediately in the interests of that well advertised group 'The old, the sick and the handicapped'. Ireland spends about 7.1% of GNP on health, the US spends 10.75 % and Canada 8.4%. The British figure is less than the Irish figure after three terms of Thatcher government and the *Guardian* in May '87 described the British health authorities as 'impoverished' and health research morale as devastated – certainly not a resource model to be aped.

A major effect of the present round of cuts would be to boost private practice (a prediction that was a correct in hindsight) because access is increasingly restricted in the public general hospitals. The extension of VHI schemes is further evidence of this. Geriatric and psychiatric services will suffer most. The effect of falling morale in all health services employees has been largely ignored. Standards of patient care will undoubtedly fall.

It was interesting that on the occasion of the '87 radiographers strike, a lesser threat to the lives and well-being of patients should have elicited a public warning from the joint medical boards of the Dublin teaching hospitals. Why the silence now when public representatives elect to reduce services to a dangerous level ? It is a moral imperative for doctors to say No!

The increasing number of beds and the degree of complexity of services being provided in new private hospitals in Dublin is surely proof positive of the public perception of inadequacy in our public health services and the desire to ensure personal access to care if ever required. The state acquiesces through the tax deductible subsidy to VHI subscribers. There are obvious benefits to the public as a whole in unifying our dual health service because the rich and powerful would demand and get a top class service for all. As it is at present, once the upper income groups perceive themselves adequately provided for, pressure on politicians becomes in reality much less because the voice of the poor is dissipated by their voting in the main for 'catch-all' parties.

Waste in our system was obvious. Why eight health boards? Why underdeveloped cost accounting in our hospitals? Why such costly drugs? Is it merely because we have never had a consistent, coherent policy for the provision of universal health care? Why not collect taxes levied for health purposes?

As they warned in the billboard advertising, Fianna Fail has found a better way to hurt ...

Fine Gael wanted prescription charges to raise £16 million but show no concern for the unfortunate consumer of the second most expensive pharmaceutics in Europe. The PDs with Fine Gael abstained on the Dail vote on the £10 charge.

Ironically, Barry Desmond and Labour are now seen to have done a much better job in 1982-87 that they were given credit for.

These comments were published in the *Irish Independent* and *Press* in May/June.

Could there have been a political element to these collective medical actions? Dr Bryan Alton of the Mater hospital was a well-known Fianna Fail supporter and appeared on a Fianna Fail Party Political broadcast on RTE television stating his position as a former President of the Royal College of Physicians of Ireland. Another consultant, a Dublin urologist has also batted publicly on television for Fianna Fail. Medical supporters of political parties must always be careful to put the patient first.

Brendan Howlin was Labour's Health Spokesman and I tried to offer him as much factually based advice and information as possible. This issue was to grow and grow to become a crucial element in the 1989 general election when Taoiseach Charles Haughey's comments on radio that he did not realise the extent of the public reaction on the health services issue was to cost him dearly.

We printed 14,000 hand leaflets with details of the crisis in the health service. Bed closures in St Mary's in the Phoenix Park and Blanchardstown, hot breakfasts in St Ita's Portrane restricted to two per week, 15 temporary community welfare officers laid off by the Eastern Health Board, dependent persons allowance effectively discontinued, bone marrow transplants curtailed, £10 charges for hospital services, discontinuation of prosthetic services for the disabled and restriction of casualty services in Blanchardstown hospital to one day in four were listed. A total of 116 hospital staff were dismissed in the area and we gave the details. About 40 beds were also at risk of closure at Cappagh Orthopaedic hospital.

News by North-West

The May Day celebration in the Zoo was a great success and Mary Coghlan sang a small number to enthusiastic applause. The third issue of *News by North-West* was published. The featured issues were the Cappagh Hospital story and gas leaks worrying residents in Coultry flats in Ballymun because of the disastrous consequences of two gas explosions in Dublin earlier in the year. We demanded better street lighting because of violent attacks in dark laneways around the Casement area of Finglas West. Loose horses were a serious problem in the area and were the cause of injuries to children and adults from kicks and bites. Cruelty to many of the unfortunate animals was also common and the need for local stabling and a change in the law was obvious. We spent many long evenings in May stuffing our message into hall doors all over Finglas and Ballymun. Noel Wheatley and Andy Earley were out most nights and gave tremendous help.

Finglas Heritage – The Barn Church

The Finglas Barn Church is an unobtrusive building perched over the end of Ballygall Road West. It was the Catholic Church for the area from 1820 until St Canices' was built in 1922. It was then used as a community hall for many years and later as a Scouts Hall. Since the mid '80s it has lain vacant and unused and has been subjected to vandalism and general destruction. In an area where the physical features of the past have largely been obliterated, this is an important landmark. 1988 was a good year to try to save that part of Finglas's heritage. I was elected Chairman of the Barn Church Restoration Committee and we set about trying to raise funds to restore the building for a community hall. Local businessman Terence Christie, Una Polion from the Credit Union, Angela McGrath, Pat Grant of Fianna Fail and Paddy Cromwell of Fine Gael were involved. Buy-a-brick campaigns, race nights in pubs, contributions from local businesses, and contact with FAS and with St Laurences Trust through the local parish priest were all organised and the project started. It was actively supported by John Haughton of the Corporation Planning Department.

Tom Murphy, the property company manager sponsored a scale model of a fully restored building and our committee was very angry in March when there was an attempt by vandals to burn it down. However, the fire brigade acted quickly and saved the structure. The newly painted walls had been scrawled with graffiti and the newly replaced windows smashed. It is difficult and disheartening to continue voluntary work to provide a village hall when this sort of thing happens.

Lord Mayor Ben Briscoe came to Finglas the next May to launch the buy-a-brick campaign at a reception in Premier Dairies who started the ball rolling by donating the first £2,000 of the £150,000 target. Despite help from a security company, vandalism has dogged the project and there were at least four attempts to set the building ablaze.

Finglas Writers Group

This group has been active since 1985. Aine O'Kelly, Marie Kenny, and Betty Cloake organise a short story and poetry reading session linked with the Finglas Arts festival. These are very well attended and interesting. Guests are nearly always invited and produce a good show. The group runs a class and workshop every Monday morning in a room beside the library. The visual Arts are well served locally with Mary McDermott organising regular exhibitions by local and other artists. Michael Johnstone in the Finglas Camera Club exhibits in the library and organises exchange exhibitions with groups in other countries in the town centre with the compliments of space provided by Tom Murphy of Chatham Management who owns the building. The area's best-known writers are Dermot Bolger and Patricia Scanlon.

Civic Pride

In June, the Finglas Enlivenment Project was sponsored jointly by Dublin Corporation and the local Chamber of Commerce. John Haughton, the town planner, organised a 'shopfront, buildings and amenities' competition to improve the village environment and it was a resounding success. Finglas greatly improved its image in the following two years.

Janelle Shopping Centre completed

This development was certain to provide an overall increase in the level of local employment even if many of the jobs were low paid. The construction phase had resulted in very little local employment as we had predicted. But Fianna Fail managed their classical bi-location act on the Janelle scheme. When the development was first proposed, it was Fianna Fail alone of all the local political parties who had staunchly opposed it. Former Lord Mayor Jim Tunney was particularly vociferous on the issue. Ironically, another Fianna Fail Lord Mayor, Bertie Ahern performed the official opening of the centre on a fine summer's evening in front of all the local chieftains.

The Single European Act

Our campaign on the issue started in early May with polling day on Tuesday 26th. There was a 'minor' complication for the campaign. Seamus Shiels, our propagandist was decidedly antipathetic to the whole treaty whereas I agreed with the economic side of the issue but the possible ceding of Ireland's independence in foreign policy, security and defence worried me. Issues like radiation leaks from the British Nuclear Fuels reprocessing plant at Sellafield, apartheid and sanctions, human rights, world hunger, the arms race and necessary support for NATO made Title 111 of the Act very difficult to support. Only months earlier while in opposition in the previous December, Charles Haughey said, 'It is dishonest and misleading of the Taoiseach, Government Ministers or anyone else to attempt to put the ratification of this Single European Act across as something of a great benefit to the people of this country because that is not in fact the case.'

Irish neutrality may be a very anaemic animal when compared to the versions in Sweden, Switzerland or Austria but it sometimes serves a useful purpose. We have been in reality neutral on the side of the US. We also have a border agreement with Britain regarding the landing of non EC nationals, so-called aliens and our defence budget is inadequate to guard our coastlines.

The Anti-SEA campaign held a meeting in the Holy Spirit School in Ballymun and local post master, Noel Wheatley, and I went along. Noel did not want any diminution of Irish sovereignty and was in good company at the meeting. The worries about Sellafield were frequently expressed as was a definite opposition to any common European army. Others argued that there would be a large increase in unemployment because we needed tariff walls to survive. The fear of being swamped by an alien culture was also expressed. The little Irelanders were out in force. We combined local, national and SEA issues in *'News by North-West'* and dropped the whole area systematically. This also gave us a chance to meet many people out and about chatting to neighbours and walking about in the bright evenings. Changes in the physical feel of streets were quickly happening because people had purchased houses from the Corporation and were adding extensions, porches, dormer bedrooms, etc. Many small gardens had mature plants and shrubs although garden trees in West Finglas were still a rarity. In the courts in Poppintree, the open plan fronts were being walled off as people appropriated gardens and the area settled in. Where there was an obvious interest in the local environment, the level of vandalism was quite low.

The Single European Act was overwhelmingly carried.

Non Consultant Hospital Doctors Strike

The non consultant hospital doctors in the Irish Medical Organisation were in a pay and conditions dispute which lead to an all-out strike in May which dragged on into the middle of June. There were a number of consultant meetings in the Richmond and it was a case of all hands on board. A rota was drawn up and we covered casualty and the medical side of the house with the surgeons covering their own patients on a similar rota. Strangely, the nurses were able to tell us that we were lucky because the patient numbers were well down on normal. Morale was very good. John Horgan was elected to deal with the chest pains and I organised the electrolyte problems in Intensive Care and around the house. Mick Farrell, normally a neuropathologist was very funny dealing with boisterous old men with too much alcohol on board. There was very little tension among the working doctors because there was so much cross consultation and people were not pretending that they knew everything about everyone else's specialty. It was interesting and informative to see the entirely logical approach to patients problems taken by Hugh Staunton. There was an ironic side to all this. The queue to see a neurologist was about three months but you could find one in casualty during the strike. Frank Walker, senior registrar, stayed around when he was asked to help deal with some unstable, very ill patients. There were quite a few 'where's Frank' comments around the house. I enjoyed the strike and the effects on the relationships between consultants was very positive.

There was a lot of discussion about how doctors should pursue a pay claim and most consultants thought that a 'strike' was not ethical as it placed individual patients at great potential risk irrespective of the nominal claims of emergency cover and other such escape clauses. I left the IMO as a consequence of this action and I believe that the whole experience was fundamental to the setting up of the Irish Hospital Consultants Association. It came as quite a surprise to me when, years later, one of the leading lights in that NCHD action, Dr Collins, was appointed a special adviser to Brendan Howlin as Minister for Health in February 1993.

Constituency Business

Seamus Shiels was in the Chair for the June '87 constituency meeting held at the Willows. Also present were Paddy and Padraig Donegan, Paschal O'Reilly, Maura Doolan, Gerard Murphy, Josephine Gorman, Dermot Doolan, Mary Chambers, Paul Foran, Paul Brien and myself. This was the sort of typical attendance with another eight people also involved at times. Weakness would be a fair description of the condition of the constituency with one branch and thirty-five nominal members of which about seventeen were for real. Yet we battled onwards. A week later, I was invited to speak at the Constituency Council in Dublin North-Central at the Artane/Beaumont Centre and there was a much bigger attendance with Paddy Bourke, Big Jim Murphy and Michael O'Halloran present. There was no joy earlier that week watching Margaret Thatcher win a landslide victory and also virtually wipe out the SDP in Britain.

Garden fêtes in Oakwood, charity football games in West Finglas, Pub Quizes for any number of causes, fund raising discos in Ballymun, and working hard made the summer pass quickly.

I also visited every registered Labour Party member in the constituency during July and August to give them a pep-talk and to try to galvanise them into action for the autumn and winter. At the July constituency meeting there were twenty-one present with three apologies. New members were being recruited. Andy Earley arrived and stayed the course. Alan Matthews was nominated to the Labour Party policy committee on agriculture under the direction of Emmet Stagg who was the new party spokesman on agriculture. Noel Wheatley demanded that the parliamentary party should be opposing the cuts in health and education inch by inch. Fifteen and seventeen attended the next two meetings and morale was rising. In September, the officer board was Seamus Shiels as chairman, Paddy Donegan as secretary and treasurer and myself as organiser and candidate designate.

There were a few thousand leaflets still to be dropped on the cuts in health and education and out of the blue Paddy Donegan arrived with five members to finish the job. Things were looking up. We dropped 7,000 leaflets and 7,000 *Labour News* in September before the Cork Conference. An advice clinic in John Whelan's shop Spudatoes, in Finglas South was agreed and was started in the late autumn. We, or I, also had to pay £375 for the Labour Party's National Collection.

Professor Fielding and Private Medicine

I debated the ethics of private medicine with Professor John Fielding on the Pat Kenny radio Show on RTE 1 on 1st September. One rhetorical question that I put to the professor was, had he ever noticed any difference in the Pathology textbooks between public and private patients, therefore why should such patients be treated differently? While there may be socio-economic factors in the cause and persistence of disease, was this sufficient reason to perpetuate the dual two speed Irish health care system? I did not know John Fielding personally at the time but later when I got to know the man in Beaumont Hospital I came to have enormous respect for his integrity, honesty and moral courage in the face of great adversity. Many times later when I expressed my view of Fielding the man, I was reminded of that particular Pat Kenny show. I still hold my position very firmly on the equality of man but I have come to realise that everyone should be a private rather than a public patient in their own interest.

Labour National Conference in Cork on 25th-27th September 1987

City Hall in Cork is an impressive imposing building and was the site where the good ship Labour was refloated after the traumas of the period of coalition with Fine Gael. Hard decisions, even when correct, require time for people to recognise often grim unpalatable necessity. Labour barely survived the learning experience and did well in terms of Dail seats when the Party's vote dropped 32% to finish on 6.4% of the national vote.

The policy statement on Fisheries was well researched but the Health Policy 'Towards a socialist health service', was wide ranging but seriously underestimated the cost implications of a National Health Service particularly regarding Family Practice. The financial burden on taxpayers of the full implementation of the policy for the aged alone would have been enormous yet it remained uncosted. Nursing homes with adequate staffing would be increasingly necessary and should be as near as practicable to the areas of origin of their patients to maintain as much social cohesion as possible. Many of the suggestions, such as the old folks paying rent to institutions instead of having their pensions appropriated and the amending of the 1963 Health (Homes for Incapacitated Persons) Act were welcome. Loneliness was specifically identified as a major problem and a policy to encourage neighbours and relatives to keep in contact with old people was emphasised. The worst section was on medical education and there, the degree and speed of change in medical science and practice was clearly underestimated. The suggestion that Health Boards should organise medical education was touchingly naive. In the final section on cost-effectiveness, the comment that 'health administrators must be trained to evaluate different alternative technologies' would prove disastrous to health service morale. Academic units constantly publish their findings in relation to the usefulness of specific treatments and often the conclusions are controversial and are contradicted elsewhere. Thus there is a constant dynamic in medical research and evaluation unrecognised by the authors of the policy document.

The final sentence is interesting because it is a frank recognition that rationing of health resources might be happening. It reads 'If available health resources must be rationed in any way it must be in proportion to medical need, not by price or ability to pay.' The truth is that waiting lists are a form of rationing and the VHI is a state subsidised queue skipping mechanism for the benefit of those who can pay but the public does not want to overtly recognise these facts.

The Conference agenda had a plethora of earnest motions. The Anglo-Irish Agreement provoked strong motions against it from some branches noting the upsurge of violence since its introduction and the fact that it had really changed nothing. Other branches including Dick Spring's in Rock Street, Tralee were fully in support of it. The debate on employment was full of commitment to a 'socialist economy' and to halting the spending cuts in the social services. The big question of how utopia was to be achieved was left for another day. Clontarf East submitted a most telling comment 'That this conference further calls on the AC to set up a sub-committee to formulate a comprehensive economic policy to be presented to the next annual conference.'

1987 was the 'International Year of Shelter for the Homeless' and the Western Regional Council appropriately wanted the implementation of the Housing Bill without delay to finally decriminalise homelessness. The compilation of a thorough register of all landlords and rented properties would make rent receipts for rent allowance payments more easily obtained and the inspection of such premises could ensure that they comply with minimum standards for health and habitation.

Kilnamanagh in Tallaght proposed a form of National Understanding subsequently agreed with the Unions twice by Fianna Fail alone and then by the FF/PD coalition. They also recognised the truth about PRSI , that it was really only a part of generalised taxation and that it was and still remains a tax on employment. They also gave full support to European union, industrial democracy, technological development, a National Health Service, the separation of church and state and to an extension of democracy in education. This was a very reasoned and constructive motion for discussion to form a framework to develop a detailed manifesto for the next General Election.

There were also the 'Laurel and Hardy' type motions. 'That the Labour Party adopt as its policy the nationalisation of supermarkets in the country because many are foreign owned and transfer their profits overseas, many treat Irish suppliers abominably, many exploit their employees, many cause higher rather than lower prices, and many continually put smaller grocers out of business'. That pretty well says it all.

The Lower Glanmire Road branch in Cork demanded that 'Any attempt to introduce the element of competition especially between provincial bus services and the railways be utterly rejected.' Other political parties also have their moments in the theatre of the absurd.

A new constitution was agreed for Labour Youth partly to try to deal with the difficulties posed by the militants. Labour Youth had virtually no impact in North-West at that time because most Labour Youth members, since Stephen Downs migrated from the area, were in fact militant supporters. I explained this to Pat Montague, the Party's Youth officer, on many occasions later, particularly in relation to Dublin City University but nothing concrete was ever done by Head Office on this subject. At that time 40% of young members left the Party within one year of their joining. This had to be saying something fairly obvious. There were Youth Sections in only 75% of constituencies where Labour was organised.

Health and education were to command major public attention in the next two years. The 1987 health budget was cut by £50 million to £1,111 million. This lead to 3,500 redundancies, to £10 hospital charges and to severe cuts in many services. Labour proposed the accelerated collection of VAT and health contribution arrears. The rescinding of the decision to abolish the Land Tax; an increased allocation from the National Lottery; increased revenue from capital taxation, the extension of retention tax to VHI payments. Implementation of these constructive proposals could have ended the acute crisis in the health services.

The education cuts were also slammed – 20% cut in money for adult education; £0.5 million cut in the allocation for community and comprehensive schools; £2 million cut in VEC second level schools; more fees in third level; less teaching jobs and an increase in casual labour within the service and cuts in school maintenance.

Section 31 of the Broadcasting Act was condemned. An interesting situation for the Labour Fianna Fail coalition. Policy documents on education were presented by Brendan Howlin TD, Shipping and the Irish language were also submitted to conference. Democratisation, accountability, access and openness were the main themes and all education sectors were addressed. The removal of sex stereotyping was underlined. However much detail was omitted and the question of streaming and the pursuit of excellence in mathematical and science subjects ignored. I remember having a row about streaming in these subjects with Councillor Frank Buckley around that time and I was taken aback at his dismissive attitude to educational research results which had been published in the *Guardian* newspaper. The shipping policy called for an enquiry into the reasons for the collapse of Irish Shipping. The officers and men made redundant were very bitter at their treatment and held the Labour Party responsible for some of their misery. A number lived in Finglas and were not shy about expressing their views. Some were left stranded for a while in the Far East when the company crashed. If I had had a similar experience I think I would have felt the same. The Irish language needs to become chic if it is to survive. For about one year in the early 80's, my branch conducted business 'as gaeilge'. Gerry Doyle, Noel Wheatley and Stephen Dowds were particularly fluent. I tried to show that my time in Marian College wasn't completely wasted. Dinger McCullagh and Peader Barrett would have cringed!

We took an afternoon away from the conference and visited Fota Park. It was a well worth while trip and I thought it was a much better concept than Dublin Zoo. The branches in North-West supported Mervyn Taylor against Ruairi Quinn in the election for Party Chairman.

Dick Spring Visits Finglas in October

We invited Dick to visit the constituency and on 16th October, Sally Clarke phoned from his office to set up the meeting for the following Tuesday night at the Willows. One of our supporters, Joe McCreanor, aged 42, had died at home in Ballymun a week earlier following a brave fight against cancer. Most of our members were at his funeral, and I told them that Dick's visit was imminent. So when he arrived we had informed as many of our loose supporters as possible and about 65 people turned up. This was a terrific response in the circumstances. Madge Guthrie, Maura Doolan, Mary Chambers, Carmel Hilliard and Michael Purdue were very keen to get into the photographs. Brendan Howlin TD accompanied the Party Leader and the atmosphere at the meeting was very positive. Dick spoke very well and was quickly at ease when he realised that there was no hostility present. Truly we were turning the corner in the constituency.

North-West members were overwhelmingly Spring supporters at that time. A situation that was not the case, to put it mildly all over the city. Those four vital voters in Kerry North could have had a pint or named their poison on us, no problem.

In Finglas, Ballymun and Santry, charity nights are sometimes arranged by friends and neighbours to help out families hit by personal tragedy. Many of those who came to Dick Springs night attended a Joe McCreanor benefit gig in the Penthouse in Ballymun and the family were very appreciative of the goodwill of all those around them. The spirit in adversity and the concern of the community for those in difficulty is a wonderful feature of local people. Charity for them truly begins at home.

News by North-West

Within weeks we produced the next edition of *'News by North-West'* with photographs of the big night at the Willows. Mickey Martin has always facilitated us in his pub and we continue to be most grateful. Minister Mary O'Rourke's famous education cuts circular which worsened the pupil/teacher ratio headed the abuse bill. Fine Gael, with their 'Tallaght Strategy' giving conditional support to the government, refused to support Labour, the Workers Party and independents in the lobbies when there was a vote on withdrawing the infamous circular. A delegation from the constituency supported the teachers demonstration outside the Dail. We also featured the chronic flooding in Virginia Drive, South Finglas due to drainage design faults. Griffith Community Centre saw the opening of a preschool playgroup run by Patsy Lindsay and Pauline Murphy and the Labour Party Advice centre in John Whelan's shop in Rivermount, South Finglas was advertised.

Medical and Other Matters

The Richmond and Jervis Street hospitals closed and moved to Beaumont over the weekend of 29 November '87. Greg Sparks' wife who is a GP and had been working in the general practice, left and set up on the Finglas Road. To minimise patients' misunderstanding, each was sent a notice that the practice was continuing with services as usual. I suggested publicly that the Richmond should be taken over by the Eastern Health Board for a public hostel shelter for the homeless. That would have been a fitting gesture for a health agency at the end of the UN year of shelter for the homeless. Ironically by 1992, the Army was being used to take homeless people to the other end of that site at Grangegorman to try to stop unfortunates dying on the streets from hypothermia.

Restrictive Practice in the General Medical Services

Solicitor Ciaran O'Mara arranged for Mary Chambers and me to meet Mary Robinson SC. to seek her advice regarding the legality of the restrictive practices which were in place to control the number of doctors who would be paid under the General Medical Services Scheme. The question was – were the Irish Health Boards in breach of the EC rules regarding the right of people to freedom of movement and the right to work in any state within the Community? In reality , the five year rule, which has since been abolished prevented people setting up in practice in poor areas of the city because there would not be enough private practice to sustain a doctor until eligible to take low income patients with medical cards. This restraint of competition is particularly felt in working class areas where the choice of doctor is restricted and therefore competition limited. It may be a factor in the complaints about poor service in areas like Ballymun. Mary Robinson told us that we might have a case but that it would take up to three years to be heard, would cost a lot of money, and Mary Chambers would have more than five years served by that time. Therefore she advised us not to proceed through the courts and we accepted her advice.

In July, I wrote to the European Commissioner for Competition Policy, Mr Peter Sutherland, asking him to investigate the five year rule restricting entry into the General Medical Services on the basis that it was a restrictive practice. The five-year rule is a breach of Article 7, section 3 of the 1986 EEC Council Directive on specific training in general medical practice. Non-GMS GPs are excluded from treating medical patients, but they are allowed to provide medical and surgical services for mothers and infants, under the 1970 Health Act. Non-GMS doctors are also permitted to issue sick certificates thus the restrictive practice only involves part of the national social security system. I asked the Commission to intervene to ensure that the new contract for the GMS, then under negotiation between the Department of Health and the Irish Medical Organisation, was in line with the principles outlined in the Commission's directives. In order to prepare for the completion of the internal market for goods and services in the European community by 1992, the Irish government should bring forward the date from which all doctors entering general practice should be formally trained from 1995 to 1990. I enclosed a copy of a letter which I had published in the *Lancet* earlier in the year in which I stated that the system of appointment of general practitioners 'creates almost insurmountable obstacles to true job mobility, resulting in national closed shops'.

GMS reform should include a basic capitation fee with a fee per item for immunisations, smear tests, out-of-hours work and house calls. GP team groups should ideally be linked into local hospitals for better liaison with radiology and laboratory services. That would improve efficiency and standards and act as a filter for unnecessary tests. GPs should also have a unique code number to link into their own patients on hospital information systems.

Irish general practice at present includes many doctors with GMS lists who would not fulfil the requirements for vocational training yet there are others fully vocationally certified who cannot accept publicly funded patients and must remain in wholly 'private' practice because of the closed entry to the scheme.

Ballymun To Be Renovated After 21 Years

In 1966, the first tenants of Ballymun received the keys to their flats. At that time the estate was the place to live but no longer. By 1987, Ballymun had hundreds of vacant, wrecked flats. Vandalism was rife. Decay, drug dealing, and crime combined to give the area a disastrous name. The flats were transit halts on the way to a better life somewhere/anywhere else.

The Ballymun Task Force was set up as a result of pressure from the ad hoc Community Coalition. Its job was to devise a housing policy for the whole estate using the wishes of the residents as a foundation. On the Task Force were Ina Gould, Dennis Kennedy, Val Langstone, Noel Martin, Marie McNamara, Pat Mooney, Fr Eugene Roe and Fr John Sweeney from the Community Coalition, Jim Crowley and Peter Whelan from the Corpo, Adrian Charles from the Health Board and Margaret Barry from Combat Poverty. All four local TDs were involved. The

Beaumont Hospital Teething Problems

Morale was high when the hospital finally opened because hope springs eternal and because the Richmond was so run down. I defended the new hospital on John Bowman's 'Day by Day' programme on RTE Radio 1. Some problems involving missing charts, patients reports getting lost and confusion in the appointment systems were inevitable. Many of the staff were new and we all had to become familiar with a large strange building full of long corridors. Beaumont has national commitments to neurology, and neurosurgery and to renal dialysis and transplantation, regional commitments to ear, nose and throat and local commitments to the biggest patient load of the northside hospitals. We were proud of our high standards and are utterly determined to be second to none in Europe.

Mary Flaherty TD criticised the hospital early in '88 and I responded. Like all Dublin hospitals Beaumont was very busy at the time. With the bed cutbacks and citywide ward closures, it is easy to appreciate that isolated incidents of unacceptable delays for patients were bound to occur. This was happening in all our public hospitals.

At Beaumont, there was a new dynamic management appointed in the past four weeks who were obviously so competent that they have already won the confidence of a wide variety of staff. Problems have been identified, options determined and appropriate action taken by this new regime.

Problems publicly identified by myself, among others since the November opening have largely been resolved. Staff morale was high and rising. The suggestion of Richmond/Jervis Street staff tensions was simply not true. Ms Flaherty needed reminding that the public spending cuts which she voted for in Dail Eireann did really have consequences on the ground. Pretending otherwise was disingenuous.

Within a short period, my view of the management of Beaumont was to undergo quite a change. New people must always be given the benefit of encouragement before any knocking. It would be instructive to compare the number of patients, doctors, nurses and administrative staff from the baseline levels found in the Richmond and Jervis Street to the numbers now present in Beaumont. The results would only surprise the naive. The potential conflict of interests between administrators and doctors was publicly outlined by me later. The doctors appointed to the Board of Management were not elected by their colleagues. This is a general problem in hospitals and industrial democracy in public institutions must be extended in the interests of morale.

I was in the main corridor at the hospital when I saw some guys wearing balaclavas and waving what looked like a sawn-off shotgun as they tried to rob the bank in the main hall. That was the oddest thing I had ever seen in any hospital. Now security video cameras would have these people on film.

The Budget Vice Grip from An Bord Snip

Ray McSharry's budget insured that the public spending vicegrip would tighten and this meant more grief for the dependent needy. The health cuts were biting further and I pointed out on local radio that Fianna Fail were still subsidising Fine Gael's coping classes in pursuit of votes and that the public hospital queues would quickly grow to crisis levels. That was fairly stating the obvious.

The Party in North-West

The new Finglas Branch elected Paul Brien as chairman, Sylvia Byrne as deputy and Paul Malone as branch secretary at its inaugural meeting on 1st March '88. The following night Finglas East restarted and there were growing signs of new life in the local party.

The constituency AGM was held on 14th March and Seamus Shiels was re-elected chairman for '88, vice chair was Paul Brien, secretary and treasurer was Paddy Donegan, organiser was Bill Tormey and the members of the executive were Paschal O'Reilly, Padraig Donegan, Paul Malone and Gerry Doyle. The real numbers participating were still in reality very small. However we did manage to have 25 teams at tables at a Pub Quiz in the Drake Inn, Finglas in late March. The May constituency meeting had fourteen in attendance. Paul Brien in the Chair, Paul Malone, Paddy and Padraig Donegan, Gerry Doyle, Andy Earley, Paul Foran, Maura Doolan, Al Callender, Vincent Kirby, Claire Daly, John Whelan, Billy Keegan and myself. That low number was an accurate reflection of our weakness. Despite this we did manage to get about six people out regularly dropping literature in Finglas West. These included Paul and Dan Malone, Paul Brien, Eddie Lynam, Andy Earley and Paschal O'Reilly. Many members were reluctant to do anything other than talk at meetings and have a few social drinks between elections. Politics for some was a form of low cost group therapy. I always envied de Rossa because of the dedication of his supporters whose zeal seemed almost to border on the Messianic at times. Outings like the FWUI reception in the Grand Hotel in May were very useful to meet friends and to swap notes and chit chat. It never ceases to amaze me how some people use those sort of social occasions to character assassinate their enemies without fear of legal redress.

Tax Breaks For Some

The influence of the ideas of Professor Lawrence Lindsey of Harvard University were reported to be the rational basis for the assertion by Nigel Lawson in the British Budget that the lowering of the top personal tax rates to 40% would result in greater, not less, tax revenues. Lawrence had made the point that if tax levels are low enough (threshold effect around 40%) then the incentive for high income earners to seek further remuneration through benefits-in-kind rather than cash income would be greatly diminished. Thus (taxable) cash replaces (non-taxable) perks as income.

The US figures in their initial 20% top rate cut in 1981 showed that the increase in hours worked was not enough to account for their huge revenue increases. In real terms the top 5% of taxpayers in Britain pay a third more now than they paid in the last year of Labour Government while the remaining 95% pay about the same. Lawson also claimed that increased economic activity fired by the £4 billion taxbreak will, through the 'Lindsey effect' further increase the relative tax revenues paid by the very wealthy by £2 billion by the end of that particular parliament.

However, Lindsey subsequently confirmed my suspicions when he wrote in the *Sunday Times* that 'the reason that the rich will be paying a higher share of taxes is that they are reporting a higher share of income.' Perhaps all we are seeing here is a tacit confirmation of the size of the very rich man's black economy. Obviously harder to hit than the working man's nixers! And of a different order of magnitude!

Like Geoffrey Howe and the money supply, this supply-side lurch will be reversed when the balance of payments deficit becomes too big. Meanwhile, God help the masses relying on the public services in health, education and welfare.

Therefore I hope we in Ireland are spared the spectacle of this policy being unwrapped here by any of the parties of the Right and sold as a mould breaker in an effort to buy votes in the next election by a facile appeal to unrestrained greed. Bribing the rich to declare their true incomes is not a new angle on revenue buoyancy, it's another version of the self-assessment carrot without the stick.

De Rossa, Leader of the Workers Party

By mid-April Proinsias de Rossa became leader of the Workers Party in succession to Tomas MacGiolla. That appointment made the task of winning a seat much more difficult because party leaders get a great degree of soft focus relatively uncritical media attention. In discussing the issue with Fergus Finlay neither of us underestimated its significance. Our members in the constituency were much less concerned and thought the appointment was neither here not there. They were so wrong.

KRAM

On the KRAM (Keep Rovers At Milltown) front, the committee met regularly with Brian Murphy in the chair and was raising money and pledges of money in an effort to try to buy both the ground and Rovers from the Kilcoynes. A well attended public meeting was held on Sunday afternoon 29th May outside the gates of Glenmalure Park at Milltown. The meeting was addressed by Tom Kitt TD, Niall

Andrews MEP and Councillor Eoin Ryan all of Fianna Fail, Councillors Eithne FitzGerald and Frank Buckley from Labour, and Tom Hand a genuine Rovers supporter and a Fine Gael councillor. There was a lot of anger and emotion and all the public speakers promised to fight the issue all the way which they did as far as was possible at local authority level. Lobbying the press and dealing with the counter lobby from supporters of the Kilcoynes who were in high places in the football world was a time consuming challenge. At Supporters club meetings, there was great insistence on the necessity for absolute self control. Rumour was rife about our chances of success.

John McNamara took over Shamrock Rovers in the summer of '88 and the Kilcoyne's put Glenmalure Park out to tender. Having taken a lot of professional advice, I joined with John McNamara in placing a £500,000 bid for the Milltown ground on Friday 18th November. We had high hopes of success for quite a while and it came as a shattering blow when the decision of 'An Bord Pleanala' to grant planning approval for a property development was made. I would have loved to have been in a position at the time to place a few Dail questions on that decision! What is the point in local democracy if the decisions of the elected councillors to preserve an area are overturned?

Disability Claims Bogus!

The headline in the *Irish Independent* in early August that '50% of Disability Claims Bogus' was itself bogus. There were 205,080 claims for benefit in 1987, 95,845 being called before the medical referee. As most illness is short-term, it was not surprising that 25% of those called did not attend. Any other result would have been amazing.

A judgement by the medical referee that a person is capable of work is not infallible. The interview by the referee is at least superficial. All patients are new and with the pressure of numbers the assessment must be cursory. Back pain, post viral fatigue syndrome, depression and neuroses are examples of notoriously difficult problems to assess clinically. Many patients are intimidated by the experience of attending a doctor who is in effect a judge and fail to present their own case properly. The recipient's own doctor may not have written any appeal detailing the case and almost certainly will not be able to be present.

There are people who abuse the disability benefit scheme but the Craig Gardner report on social welfare fraud found only 1% of payments in that category.

Harmonising VAT

Equalisation of indirect taxation across the EC is the logical consequence of the passage of the referendum and the enactment of the Single European Act by the Oireachtas. Otherwise the abolition of economic borders is impossible. The French Socialist Government actively supports this position and, in principle, so do I.

However, I believe that Mr McSharry was clearly wrong to agree to the Commission's proposal of only two VAT bands at the Crete meeting in September. A zero rated band for food and other basic necessities should have been insisted upon in the interest of all those on low incomes across Europe. It is spurious to pretend that changes can be made in social welfare benefits, etc, to compensate those most affected because it is administratively nearly impossible to cater for the diversity of circumstances of those on low incomes and small fixed pensions.

On health grounds, the proposed VAT changes were ill advised. There is a relationship between price and the consumption of alcohol and tobacco. The rising number of women and teenagers smoking is worrying and reducing the price will only make matters worse. Similarly a reduction in drink prices together with the recent extension of pub opening hours will encourage more alcoholism, absenteeism and road traffic accidents. Thus there are health and economic grounds for a special high VAT rate for addictive toxins. Furthermore under the Commission's proposals, the price of pharmaceuticals will rise.

Seeking compensation for revenue loss, i.e. production of the begging bowl, is not a valid substitute for an alternative to the Commission's recommendations. As the *Irish Times* editorial said on 19th September, 'Much of the groundwork for harmonisation remains to be done.'

Stopping Suicides in Our Prisons

The whole community has a responsibility to ensure that people found guilty of crimes and incarcerated on our behalf are treated in a dignified manner and their human rights are respected. Serious questions in relation to the assessment of the mental state of prisoners must arise when five prisoners in custody had apparently taken their own lives up to September '88.

There was, at that time, no medical director appointed to the prison service. However, the appointment of a suitably qualified person may be easier said than done because the appointee would ideally need postgraduate training in general medicine, psychiatry, and addiction studies.

If the Prison Service is unable to find such a person after a reasonable search, then a radical approach must be adopted in the interests of all. For example, the Department of Justice should approach the hospital services in Dublin to agree the inclusion of the medical care of prisoners as part of their responsibilities. The psychiatric services of the Eastern Health Board must also be involved. Such a scheme would also ensure that the doctors will put the patient, not the institution, first, should a conflict arise.

The increasing numbers of drug abusers, HIV positive and AIDS victims in prison will place heavy demands on any isolated institutional medical service and in the longer term the only solution may be to formally associate with the hospital services.

Even with hindsight, this is still the best approach.

The Bed Crisis Again

By October, the bed crisis was recurring. Over the preceding year nearly 2,000 hospital beds had been closed in Dublin alone. I said that the Dublin Fire Brigade was dictating the admission policies of the Dublin Hospitals. Public waiting lists were three months to see a neurologist, six months for ear, nose and throat and ophthalmology, and also six months for an out-patients barium enema. The people most at risk were those with asthmatic and bronchial problems, the elderly, and those waiting for cardiac bypass operations at the Mater. Mary Harney said at the time that 'No doctor or consultant is going to admit publicly that a patient died because the operation was too late, or because they did not have the operation. But its certainly happening now. The warnings are there loud and clear. It's not just the politicians who are saying them any more.'

The Courier – The Local Newspaper in Finglas

Declan Cassidy started to produce *'The Courier'* newspaper from his home on the North Road, Finglas. This was a 16 page tabloid free sheet with local advertising and coverage of all local events from talent contests and sport to law and order issues like crime and vandalism. It was published at intervals of between two and four weeks. I wrote a medicopolitical column in it and answered queries which were taken by phone or in writing. I used it primarily for public health and self help education.

I wrote pieces outlining the wide spectrum of services available in Beaumont Hospital and tried to dispel the notion that private hospitals were somehow superior. Details on some of the hospital services were provided. Exactly who did what in neurosurgery, kidney transplantation, in the professorial departments of medicine and surgery and in cardiac surgery in the Mater were named to try to put as much of a human face as possible on large often intimidating buildings. The bus services were listed and where buses stopped near the front and back entrances of Beaumont was outlined so that our people knew the score.

The first week in May was the 'Europe against Cancer week' and when the Irish Cancer Society issued a ten point plan which, if followed, promised a 15% reduction in cancer deaths in the European Community by the year 2000, I supported them and covered the whole subject over a whole page in the June issue of *The Courier.* I also highlighted the positive side with a quote from Dr Des Carney of the Mater Hospital 'Cancer is in fact the only chronic disease that is curable'. Smoking, lung cancer, colon cancer, cervical smears, testicular cancer, problems were tackled under the headings – Security by control of access; a balanced community between young and old, at work and unemployed, married and single; and the physical environment to be improved by maintenance, compartmentalisation, trees, etc. At the end of Phase 1, six years later, Ballymun has undergone huge change and there was a queue to enter the estate. The Task Force with its changing personnel, has been an undoubted success. The shopping centre is now the major remaining eyesore and something must be done there urgently because it is so dingy and depressing. Omni Park, Janelle, Northside, and Finglas village provide enormous competition so there is a real challenge to be faced. Tax incentives may be necessary to ensure an adequate renewal.

Participation was to be the by-word and on Shangan Road, the tenants association was involved in flat allocations, maintenance schedules and crime control through neighbourhood watch and liaison with the local community gardai at Ballymun Town Centre. Giving people power over their own lives is the way to progress. The flip side is that those given power then take responsibility and everyone benefits.

Local initiatives have for years addressed many of the area's problems. The Youth Action Project for drug abuse and Community Outreach were run from 1A Balcurris Road and Queenie Barnes played an important role in its success. Barney Hartnett's *'Ballymun Echo'* has been published since 1982 and is the longest running local publication. It was started by the Ballymun Branch of Labour but has been independent for about ten years. Local writers contribute and advertising and sponsorship pay the piper. I have occasionally contributed.

Dublin's Great in '88 – The Millennium

On the stroke of midnight at the new year, Taoiseach Charles Haughey and Lord Mayor Carmencita Hedderman inaugurated the Dublin Millennium near the Mansion House. It was the City Manager Frank Feeley's finest hour. 'Dee allaminyum' created a terrific buzz about town. Civic pride was being restored to a city in need. Move over Cork 800, the Dubs were back with the round grand. Slogans, stickers, street concerts and festivals, arts and theatre events even a 'Millennium' 50p coin and a special Rugby International against England at Lansdowne. The only break with tradition was that Rovers did not win the FAI Cup!

The East Link Bridge

Dublin Corporation agreed to a 5p toll increase for the Eastlink company and I thought that this was a dereliction of its duty to towards the citizens of Dublin when it is remembered that the cumulative increase in charges over three years was 50% when inflation had been only a small fraction of this. The bridge company had reported a relatively high usage of the bridge by cars which had significantly relieved inner city traffic congestion.

mammography and breast lumps were covered. There was a large response with many queries which we tried to answer. There were many worried people out there.

The Fairbrother Incident

Local man Sid Sutton often had a few pints in the Aylesbury Inn (formerly the Quarry House) on Ballygall Road East. On the 13th June, the day following an incident at the junction of the Finglas Road and Griffith Avenue involving members of the Gardai and Derek Fairbrother, Sid called to my door and asked me would I see the son of the pub owner who had allegedly been beaten by the police. I agreed to see him and I then heard the story and looked at the wounds. To check the story, I also talked to some of the girls who were in his vehicle on the night when they were stopped. Ironically, they had been in Frank Kennedy's house in Valley Park in Finglas South. I knew Frank well as he had been a supporter of mine for some years. He played and sang in 'Gypsy Lacy', the ballad group. I checked with Frank to find out whether Derek Fairbrother had been drinking alcohol at his place and he said, 'no'. Derek Fairbrother was obviously injured and seemed slow and withdrawn. I phoned Dick Spring at his home in Tralee and told him what I had been told had happened. When he returned to Dublin, he met the girls in his office in the Dail to hear what they had to say and he was convinced by their story. The Fairbrothers had by that time produced colour photographs of the incident which were given to Dick and they looked awful. Some were later reproduced on the front of the Sunday newspapers.

On 14th June, I wrote a referral note to Dick regarding Derek Fairbrother.

During that week there was a lot of talk, rumour and innuendo in the pubs in Finglas village about the incident. Details had been spread far and wide and there was little incredulity.

Dick wrote to the Minister for Justice, Gerry (Gerard) Collins, to ask him to take some action on the issue and he gave him one week. Collins did not act on this and precipitated the Dick Spring statement in the Dail about the whole incident.

I was interviewed on the Pat Kenny Radio Show on RTE 1 and on Millennium Radio in the Henry Street arcade by Mark O'Hanlon about the incident. It was interesting to feel the disbelief in the body language and attitude of some including Rory Godson, the security correspondent of the *Sunday Tribune.* I gave as much of the story as I knew and as fully as possible. During the next week, there were many calls from journalists. At the weekend I sat in the Millennium Radio studio in the Arcade in Henry Street for a discussion with Mary Harney on Law and Order and related issues with again Mark O'Hanlon in the chair. Mary took a very righteous line on the issue and I was a bit surprised that she would ignore the implications of what had happened or at least allow for the possibility that the allegations could be true. Mark O'Hanlon was anxious that no slander went over the airwaves so some circumlocution went on.

The newspapers were full of the story. Dr Damian McCormack, a surgical senior house officer in the Mater was reported in the *Irish Times* to have found 'four superficial lacerations to the scalp ... with possible loss of consciousness as a result of head injuries... with definite amnesia for the immediate events and otherwise well'. In the same report, Neurologist Dr Sean Murphy stated that 'he (Fairbrother) was involved in an altercation with the Gardai in which he claimed he was struck on the back of the head on a number of occasions. Following immediately on this, he claimed that his memory was hazy but he did not lose consciousness. He was taken to the casualty department.... where sutures were inserted into a laceration or lacerations in his left occipital area.... when I saw him (on 14th June) he complained of headache and stiffness, but there were no other complaints whatsoever'. Dr Murphy said that he had been informed by Professor FitzPatrick's house staff that the patient was fully orientated in place and person at the time of admission but could not name the day of the month. Skull X-ray failed to reveal a fracture. It was stated that he 'smelt' of alcohol and said he had had 'two pints'.

He (Dr Murphy) stated that he found 'no evidence' of any neurological abnormality whatsoever. 'He had some tenderness over the left occipital area but there was no laceration visible on his face, no bruising and so forth.... I found no evidence of any damage to Mr Fairbrother's brain or nervous system in general. Furthermore, I don't think there is likely to be any sequel whatsoever to this, at least from a medical point of view'.

I also heard the neurologist express these views separately that as far as he was concerned Fairbrother had suffered no nervous system damage. However I was personally not at all impressed with that particular attitude without the results of detailed psychometric testing to confirm or refute the case. When the pressure was at its height, Jim Kemmy phoned to offer me any support that he could give.

The *Irish Times* editorial on 23rd June wrote 'it is surely improbable that any group of Gardai would act as Mr Dick Spring has alleged in the Dail. Yet it seems clear from the evidence so far presented that Mr Derek Fairbrother received a terrible beating in some circumstances involving members of the force....it could not be justified by any act or word of provocation....

Under the editorial heading 'Brutality' on 23rd June. the Irish Independent wrote..... 'we must take issue with the Garda Representative Association general - secretary Jack Marrinan, who suggested that Mr Spring was wrong to have raised this matter in the Dail, acting as 'prosecutor, judge and executioner'. Mr Spring was perfectly right to have done so.'

In 'Guarding the guardians', the *Sunday Tribune* said 'Gardai are entitled to use only the degree of force necessary to effect an arrest or to put an alleged offender into safe custody. No more. Without prejudging the present case it would need the most strenuous resistance to warrant assaults on the head with a baton'.

On 8th July, Superintendents Jordan and Hickie met Derek Fairbrother in the Aylesbury Inn to begin the Garda Complaints procedure. Meanwhile, I received anonymous letters and telephone calls from people purporting to be members of the Gardai and relatives of members of the Gardai accusing both Dick Spring and me of being everything from liars to apologists for criminals. There were also all sorts of rumours about the Fairbrothers and a squad car was frequently parked outside the Aylesbury pub. Over the next few years, the attitude of many members of the Gardai locally was cool to say the least. I believe that it is most important that acts of violence by police are within the context of the minimum use of force. I know full well that there are increasing numbers of thugs terrorising people both young and old on our streets and in their own homes. It is most important that the community should have full confidence in the Gardai. The vast majority of Gardai are embarrassed by such incidents. On 31st August in the *Irish Times*, Sean Flynn and Joe Joyce gave a detailed summary of the conflicts of evidence contrasting the story of the Fairbrothers and witnesses with that of the police as outlined in the Garda Complaints Board's report.

Myles Dungan on 'Drive at five' on RTE Radio 1, December 1st, interviewed me about the refusal of the DPP to proceed with criminal charges against the police. I was not surprised because of the potential implications of such a move for the police and for the individuals involved and I guessed that the authorities would wait until a civil case was decided before acting. This, of course, lays the onus on the family of the complainant and this fact was much commented upon around Finglas. Access to justice for low income families has always been a problem and there was a general feeling, whether true or not, that if Derek Fairbrother's father had no money then little or nothing would have come of the whole affair.

Before the case went to court, I was told quietly by many higher ranking serving and retired gardai that while I might have been correct, the force will close ranks and admit nothing good, bad or indifferent about the records of the officers involved. I was uncertain that the case was really proceeding as I had no further role to play when the psychiatrists and clinical psychologists became involved. (See appendix p. 220)

Finglas Millennium Festival

Bunting, balloons and flags were everywhere. There was an air of anticipation and excitement around the area. A festival committee had been meeting for months arranging events. The committee had members from the Chamber of Commerce and from many local groups. It was said to be a Fianna Fail set-up but it really was not. Shop fronts and pubs had been renovated and repainted and all rubble cleared. An all around effort was obvious.

Every community group in the district was involved in putting on some event from treasure hunts, puppet shows, fortune tellers, street parties to childrens plays, poetry readings to rock bands, cabaret acts in pubs to the beauty of the Miss Finglas and glamorous granny contests. A colour brochure was produced and I placed an add on behalf of the Finglas Labour Party. All the other main parties did the same.

On 3rd July, Finglas village was closed off and a covered platform and bandstand was erected in the carpark in front of the Shopping Precinct. The Lord Mayor, Carmencita Hedderman, arrived by helicopter to open the two week long Festival. There were bands playing, lead by the Guinness Jazz band and majorettes marched around to the swirl of battons. Traditional ceili dancing was held outdoors in the grounds of St Canice's Church. There was an American Jazz Night in the Village Inn and the house was packed out. The days were long and warm. The crowds were very big. Every age group in the district from kids to old folks was involved with specific targetted events. Most shows were sold out and there was no aggravation on the streets. Nine-a-side GAA matches were run as was a seven-a-side soccer tournament. The Drake Inn ran a fancy dress 'Good Ould Days' music hall production, a separate fancy dress competition night, a fashion show, and special cabarets.

A cholesterol testing service in the village run by myself with the help of local nurse Laura Leonard was the result of pressure on me from the Festival organisers to do something positive for the community. The queues were out the door and down the street. It was much busier than a crowded hospital outpatients. The limiting factor was that we ran out of blood tubes after a few hours. The crowds were totally unexpected and I had originally intended to do the job on the spot with a 'Reflotron' but two minutes for each result would have been much too long so I got tubes and did the tests in the hospital. This was much cheaper and more efficient in any case. I sent out the results to each person and people with high values were directed to their own GPs.

There were posters up on lampposts for the campaign for Lord Mayor of Finglas. The winner was the person who raised the most money for charity during the festival. Five figure sums were achieved which were very large in the context of the local economy. We supported local Finglas man Noel Cloake despite his Fianna Fail pedigree because he was supporting the Barn Church committee and he had worked with Eithne Fitzgerald in Threshold, the voluntary agency for rents and accommodation in Church Street. There was some negative comment on that but why not ? Noel is a decent man and he asked for help. He ran sponsored pub quizzes, street collections and sold Lord Mayor of Finglas tee shirts and hats emblazoned with the Dublin Millennium crest. He was beaten by Mick Doyle backed by the big commercial interests in Janelle and also by Superquinn but the money Noel raised went to the Barn Church Restoration Fund and to Cappagh hospital. There was also a marathon organised by Cyril Chaney which had around one hundred competitors.

The Festival closing dinner was held in Erin's Isle GAA club on 15th June with an attendance of more than 200. It was great fun. The Millennium had brought civic pride to the city and Finglas was great in '88.

Cholesterol in Finglas

In late June, I gave information in *The Courier* about cholesterol and diets and gave a rundown on some of the reasons why 20,000 people die from coronary heart disease in Ireland every year. Later in September, the results of the cholesterol study done at the Finglas Millennium festival were published. How to reduce blood cholesterol conventionally was also covered. About two-thirds of those studied had levels greater than the European Atherosclerosis Society and British Cardiac Society's recommended upper limits. Finglas has a high rate of coronary artery disease and the levels of total cholesterol pumping around the body public here were an indicative marker. About 7% had levels where many doctors might use drugs as a treatment. I advised them to see their GPs and also gave them the number of the Irish Heart Foundation and of the Irish Family Heart Association run by Mrs Anne Power, a local woman from St Canice's Road.

The results of the Finglas Millennium Festival Study were presented in October to the Pathology section of the Royal Academy of Medicine. Before Christmas, the Pat Kenny Radio Show featured the study in the context of its relevance to the situation nationwide. The advantage of dropping the cholesterol levels of the population here by 10% would be seen by a drop of 20% in the coronary rate.

Army Pay

Over 200 army wives met on 2nd September in Liberty Hall to form an Eastern Command branch of the National Army Spouses Association. They vowed to fight for better pay and conditions for their husbands. Many women spoke of the differences in pay between gardai, prison officers and soldiers and they pointed out that both the gardai and the prison officers had their own unions.

Army privates were being paid £65 per week less than the average private sector wage in Ireland and as a result, wives and children of soldiers were suffering deprivation and hardship. Some women said that they had to concoct alibis to hide the fact that they were attending the meeting because they feared that their attendance would jeopardise their husbands' jobs. One woman told the meeting that she was bringing up five children on her husband's take-home pay of £139 per week. She said that she ran to the post office every week to collect £5 in state assistance and was saving this to help put her daughter through the Group Cert course. Another woman complained that she had lost a child in a fire at their army owned living quarters eight years earlier and still had not received any report from the Army about an investigation into the cause of the fire.

Carol Tiernan said that the government review on pay would take far too long and that their association wanted better living conditions for those living in barracks and improved health services. Both Pat McCartan TD and myself agreed that the levels of army pay were demeaning and we promised that Labour and the Workers Party respectively would fight the cause of the soldiers in the Dail. I was familiar with the low pay levels from my brother Peter who is an Army officer.

Drug Prices Again

Ireland's burgeoning drugs bill could be cut by 20%, about £24 million, if the Government sourced medicines at cheaper prices in other Community countries. The majority of drugs on sale here were readily available at cheaper prices throughout Europe. These are the same drugs made by the same companies at the same sites throughout the EC. If an Irish agency bought the drugs in bulk in Belgium or Italy, they could save a lot of money. In 1988, the state spent £120 million on drugs for use in hospitals and in the GMS scheme.

When a drugs buying agency had been demanded by me earlier, the Irish Pharmaceutical Union objected on the grounds that the package instruction insert would be in another language and any consequent confusion could be dangerous. I pointed out that this was nonsense because drug companies were obliged by the EC to provide instructions in the language of the country in which the products would be sold and also it is the job of the pharmacist to provide the customer or patient with instructions on the dosage of drugs dispensed.

Objections from the drug industry that the content of medicines in parallel imports could not be guaranteed were a self interested distortion. Once drugs are manufactured within the EC, the manufacturers are obliged to provide all the necessary documents about their contents.

Following a two year price freeze, the Department of Health and the Federation of the Irish Chemical Industries agreed a 6% price rise and I called for at least an interim further freeze. I felt that the Department of Health officials had been knowingly acting against the public interest in relation to proprietary drug prices for well over a decade. They had actively prevented parallel importing which would have reduced industry prices and profits by at least 15%. There was a rumour about that FICI had said that some of their members might move their manufacturing plants outside the state if parallel imports were allowed. If this were true then we were paying a very high price for any such jobs and the cost benefit was very unlikely to be in Ireland's favour.

The Gay Byrne Radio Show sent Kathy Moore to ask the Belgian Consumers Association to investigate pharmaceutical prices across Europe and their survey confirmed that we had remained in the same expensive position in the league table. Our drugs were often three, four or five times more expensive than the same drug sold in Spain, Portugal or Italy as many people had realised while on holiday. In 1984, the Belgian consumers association had shown a global price difference of 100% between the cheapest countries, France and Italy, and the dearest, Holland and West Germany. By 1988, a basket of the twelve biggest sellers in Ireland cost £241 here, £222 in the UK, £316 in Germany, £100 in Greece, £121 in France. These were identical brand named drugs only. On air in November, Gaybo agreed that my suggestion of a national drugs buying agency was the way to go. By tagging our prices to 107% of the British price, only Holland and Germany had higher prices than ours. As we all know, the average income per family is much higher in those countries and they also have drug refund schemes to compensate the sick for the cost of drugs from their social welfare budgets. Dutch and German consumers only pay a small proportion of the costs as their social security systems pay for the rest. 87.7% of Irish drug prices were higher than the European average and 19% were the highest priced in the Community. Spain, Portugal, Italy and France were the first four for cheapness. It was also worth noting that we were underwriting profit levels of 21% on capital as agreed and guaranteed by the British Government for their drug manufacturing sector and 85% of drugs sold here were imported from the UK.

The next FICI agreement had a lower profit margin most probably due to Gay Byrne and his show. I received many phone calls at home on the subject from people in the constituency and a few from outside. But translating effort on public issues into votes is a difficult trick. Since the Trident report in 1980 first reported these basic facts, the Department of Health and successive ministers have a lot to answer for in the interim.

VHI and Private Hospitals

On 14th October, Dr Joseph Ennis of the Mater Private Hospital detailed the virtues of private medicine in Ireland while commenting on recent comments from the Fine Gael Health Spokesman at the time, Deputy Ivan Yates. The subject was important and deserved a comment. I replied in a letter to the Irish Times on 20th October :

'Any analysis of a health system which does not define its objective will be seriously flawed. I believe in universal access to health care based on need and not on the ability to pay. The Beveridge-inspired National Health Service in Britain and the Canadian Hospital and Physicians 'Insurance Plan are two contrasting systems which have achieved this objective and could act as models for this country. The

Canadian system differs from the 'free' British system in that comprehensive care is provided through the private sector with payment through joint federal and provincial governments. However, the fee per item payment schedule is determined by the government.

In the US there are a wide variety of private schemes from health maintenance organisations to for-profit hospitals allied to insurance schemes. The government funded public health system is underfinanced to the extent that 30 to 40 million Americans lack adequate medical care. The administration cost of this unwieldy American system is 22% of the total health spending. This contrasts with 6% in the British NHS.

The private sector provides a financially-based mechanism for queue jumping and does not, in fact, affect overall demand for health services, which is a function of disease incidence and prevalence in the community. It is also politically expedient because one million poor are less well organised and vociferous than the rich. Mainly the same consultant staff provide services to both sectors. The tax system subsidises their costs of practising in 'high-tech' hospitals through deductions for legitimate expenses and through the allowance on VHI premiums.

There is a further rarely mentioned downside for the public sector. Private hospital facilities have until recently acted as an escape valve for the frustrations felt by consultants at the shortage of beds and equipment in our public hospitals. The pressure on all staff has now become so great as to override these factors. Witness the growing outcry. In the longer run, there will also be adverse effects on the ability of the medical schools to ensure adequate access to patients for their students. Also, supervision and training of junior doctors may be compromised.

If Dr Ennis consults the medical literature, he would probably be more reticent in his claims for the ability of the private sector to deliver health care to the people of Ireland. He should read the article 'An end to patchwork reform of health care' published in the New England Journal of Medicine 1987;317:1086-8, which concluded that for the US, 'a new national health service ought to be seriously considered.' He should follow that by reading, 'A free market in health care' published in the Lancet 1988;i:1210-4, which found 'no compelling case for changing the NHS. Its only crisis is one induced by the present government's policy of not allowing the service to grow to meet people's needs.'

The VHI is an insurance company and not an arbiter of excellence other than in the hotel sense. It would be more efficient for the 'B' and 'C' VHI subscribers to have an expanded cardiac service at the Mater Public and more prostheses for joint replacement at the Cappagh Orthopaedic Hospital than to have whole new institutions built with their attendant enormous cost. Without VHI schedule 'D' and 'E' , the cost of the existing schemes would have had to rise by more than 20%. This would have affected all subscribers, reducing the overall numbers covered.

The doctor's obligation to protect the standards of care for all patients must never be put before the legitimate activity of protection of income which is a trade union function. Constructive coherent reform and more resources are needed, not further cuts, closures, abolitions or semi-privatisations.

VHI

In late September, there were press reports that the VHI was having difficulties meeting their claims. Figures in the range of £17 million were cited as the deficit. The VHI's financial crisis could be partly attributed to its failure to take adequate underwriting precautions. The bed costs in public and private hospitals together with the introduction of new expensive private hospitals had broken the organisation.

The VHI proposed to pay consultant pathologists collectively £32 per patient irrespective of the service provided. Several consultants might have to work on an individual's case but only one fee would be paid by the VHI. The VHI rejected this criticism by saying that the tests were automated. This showed the depths of their ignorance. Chemical pathology is a relatively undertaught subject in medical schools. Of the £4.6 million paid to Pathology by VHI, the distribution of fees was very unequal. Some of the work is highly specialised and the individual specialists are entitled to be paid for that. Much of the VHI pathology payments were for technical fees in private hospitals as could be seen by the case which I highlighted where the VHI paid out £7,000 to the Blackrock Clinic for one patient's Pathology bill because of the heavy demands placed by intensive care treatment of very serious illness. This was obviously largely a charge for technical services and the figures bandied about by VHI for propaganda purposes lumped such payments into the professional fee slot on the assumption that who will believe the doctors anyway? Aren't they stinking rich and isn't it all only special pleading? Dr Michael Farrell, a Beaumont Hospital Neuropathologist said that the VHI fees were 'meaningless, insulting and irrelevant'. Professionals working their butts off were very annoyed at the VHI's gratuitous insult.

On Millennium Radio lunchtime news in 6th January, I got stuck in against Ivan Yates of Fine Gael about the issue and I reminded him that being an instant expert on many complex issues is the sign of a guess what? I don't think he enjoyed it somehow. On 17th January, the VHI recovery programme was discussed on 'Today Tonight' on RTE television, and I made a few points about automation and test interpretation. For the VHI to have arrived in a virtual bankrupt state did not inspire confidence in their management. The confusion of technical and professional issues by the VHI when making a propaganda point was very annoying to those of us working hard with patients performing detailed investigations.

I was provided with another bill from a patient who had been in Blackrock.

There were three pathology charges for £9,999, £9,999 and £3,700. I asked publicly why there were two identical segments and questioned whether the pathology bills had been artificially padded to help the institution accelerate its capital repayments. The patient's total £106,000 bill for a 90 day stay did not appear to include consultants fees, anaesthetists, intensive care therapists or surgical fees. These would have been extra. Dick Spring asked the Minister for Health Dr Rory O'Hanlon whether he was satisfied that all the bills paid by VHI to the Blackrock Clinic were justified? There was no public response to these queries.

In February 1989, the VHI agreed to a fixed fee for designated operations in the Blackrock Clinic similar to the 1987 Mater Private Hospital deal but the VHI were leaving their subscribers uncovered for pathologists' professional services in other institutions. The issue was reported by Maol Muire Tynan in the *Irish Times* on 18th March.

Review of Dr Joe Collier's 'The Health Conspiracy' on the Pat Kenny Show

On the Pat Kenny Radio Show on 27th February '89, I reviewed *The Health Conspiracy* a book by Dr Joe Collier, a clinical pharmacologist at a London Teaching Hospital who later became the editor of 'Drugs and Therapeutics Bulletin' published by the Consumer Association. This book is a must for anyone sceptical about the international drug industry and its relationship with the medical profession and what they might get up to. Collier detailed many of the restraints of trade and profiteering in the pharmaceutical industry and detailed what could be done to counter this.

The book is a bit over the top but that is no harm. Patients want health, doctors want cures and drug companies want profits. The minimum allowable profits on capital employed in the UK drug industry was 21% and some earn 30%. The Official Secrets Act is involved in the UK in keeping profits secret and the government sets the price through the Pharmaceutical Price Regulation Scheme. The financial stakes are enormous. Wellcome shares rose 260% due to the AIDS drug zidovudine. Glaxo rose 60% due to a new antidepressant in 1987. He tells of Sir James Black, a Scottish academic who discovered propranolol (Inderal) for ICI and cimetidine (Tagamet) for SKF and maintains that 'the larger multinationals have begun to realise that the best brains wither in the hothouse of the commercial environment. Collier predicted that new discoveries would slow down in university departments such as Oxford which have been effectively bought up by the industry. Squibb owned the Oxford University Department of Clinical Pharmacology until 1992. There is commercial pressure to target and restrict research and intellectual pursuit is stifled. 60% of all medical research in Universities and Teaching Hospitals is paid for by the industry.

He covers the strong placebo mind over matter effect but does caution that alternative medicine on the other hand may be dangerous if it deprives seriously ill people of life-saving drugs such as antibiotics. Sexism in medicine is suggested by the prescriptions for tranquillisers being three times more common in women than in men. In a high blood pressure trial of a ß blocker in 17,354 patients, no women were asked about a possible loss of libido. Racism is also rife. 25% of UK doctors are non-White, 17% of students at the Royal Free and 5% at the Westminster were non-White. St Georges Hospital computer had penalty points for applicants who were non caucasian.

GP's prescribe 80% of drugs and companies spend £5,000 per annum per GP on advertising. The Committee on the Safety of Medicines has no responsibility under the Medicines Act to consider 'relative efficacy'. The British National Formulary still contains notes on drugs that proclaim that 'no convincing evidence that drug X has a beneficial action'. Examples include 'vasculit' for senile dementia, opilon for poor circulation and stanozolol for leg ulcers. He slams the misadvertising of some drugs for example amiodarone and keflex. New improved pain killers with aspirin, paracetamol or codeine bases are nothing of the kind. There is no evidence of a real clinical effect for tonics and pick me ups.

Drug disasters are listed – thalidomide, osmosin (may have killed 40 people), opren (may have killed 100), surgam and phenylbutazone (may have killed 1,000 in UK only in twenty years). Dr Aileen Scott's stewardship of the National Drugs Advisory Board here in Ireland ran an independent and very professional service on our behalf for years. It should be noted that drug approvals were most carefully checked here to avoid some of the disasters abroad. Her conservatism was in the true interests of the Irish patient and she did not jump to the bark of the industry.

The Pharmaceutical industry acts as paymasters also. The Royal College of General Practitioners was given £105,000 to establish in the 1950s and the Royal College of Physicians was given £100,000 in 1985. The 'quid pro quo' for these gifts was likely to be the establishment of benign unquestioning neglect by the medical establishment of many of the hard questions about the industry and its relationships.

In 1986, the *Guardian* exposed Bayer for phoney trials of the performance of adalat. No trial data was sent back to Germany. The company was merely operating a clever marketing ploy. Doctors were given cash, gifts and tickets to foreign conferences with the drug's compliments! So-called 'post marketing surveillance' though a good idea is often a hidden means of increasing sales. Strange incidents have occurred. Three cardiologists working in St Thomas's Hospital in London accused Sterling Winthrob in a national newspaper of harassing and discrediting them for saying that their drug amiodarone was not safe or effective.

European Election 1989 – Barry Desmond Gears Up

Barry Desmond was selected as Labour's candidate for Dublin on 7th February at the Royal Marine Hotel in Dun Laoghaire and I thought he was the obvious choice even though the Dail seat in the Borough would be at maximum risk if he carried out his stated intention of standing for Europe only. The general support for his candidacy contrasted sharply with the manoeuverings before the previous election in 1984. From Deputy Leader to MEP, that was his trip. I had always voted for Barry when I lived in Trimleston. The Elder Lemon is an original. Clever, cunning and brave, he campaigns hard and gets stuck into any task he undertakes. I always had the impression that his colleagues were fearful of his flights of rhetoric lest the genii released proved impossible to contain. He was Minister of State at Finance for a while in 1982 and he put on a good show as a treasury antispending mandarin. Silas Mariner strikes again! Then in Health, he became Dr Desmond, an authority on all health matters and by God he was a class act. Belligerent and brave, some said politically reckless, Barry fought the good fight. What exactly was constructively achieved in the end? Ahem!? For all that, I like the guy but I don't have to always agree with him. His wife Stella is another brave woman and a competent politician in her own right.

I especially remember him after some of our by-election debacles on television with Brian Farrell defending the indefensible with a straight bat and the political equivalent of a Geoff Boycott forward defensive push. Barry was in many ways the Labour Party version of Brian Lenehan. He was a go-for, a warmer upper and the person to spoof himself out of a tight corner. When he was Minister for Health, I thought him unnecessarily belligerent – first pick a row and then work it out afterwards. His appetite for work was voracious but real reform would I believe require a more reflective minister. He was inclined to overly personalise his ministry. He was the Minister for Health and the doctors were somehow the opposition. Barry inspired great loyalty from those around him even in the highest reaches of the Civil Service. It was often said about him, even by some of his political colleagues that he would have made an excellent departmental secretary. At a parochial level, I was surprised that he appointed Mr Phillips, a neurosurgeon and a PD supporter as chairman of the Board of Governors of the Richmond Hospital before it closed. Barry never extended industrial democracy into voluntary hospital boards. Ministerial appointees remained exactly that. There has been no extension of industrial democracy within the health services since Erskine Childers established the Health Boards in the 1970 Health Act.

Labour Conference at Tralee in March '89

The conference at the Mount Brandon Hotel was very well attended. Dick Spring had been performing very well in the Dail overshadowing Alan Dukes and effectively assuming the mantle of Leader of the Opposition. Even his detractors in the Labour Party could see that. The Leader's speech on television live on Saturday night was the focal point and highlight, and 'Wine and Roses' were the symbols. The idea of a song to symbolise Labour's struggle and to link the old with the new worked well and was a first at an Irish political party conference. The less overt agenda was to ensure the election of Niamh Breathnach over Emmet Stagg as vicechairperson of the Party with Mervyn Taylor unopposed as Chairman. Liam Kavanagh chaired the commission on the new rules to elect the Party Leader and Deputy Leader which was set up as a result of the Rock Street amendment on the subject passed in 1987 in Cork. Their recommendations were adopted and Ruairi Quinn was then in a position to succeed Barry Desmond as Deputy Leader when Barry was elected to the European Parliament. In 1990, the membership elected Dick Spring and Ruairi Quinn unopposed to the leadership positions. The organisation in Kerry was superb and it was interesting to watch the rival busloads of personal supporters arriving, heads being counted and then registered in the lobby carefully watched over by Denise Rogers, Ita McAuliffe, Sally Clarke, and Marion Boushell. Nothing was being left to chance. If Emmet and company thought they were being watched, their suspicions were spot on.

Resolutions passed at Conference are in reality aspirational despite the theory that they should be Party policy when the Party is next in government. Some madcap intentions may be passed and much effort and hot air expended but in the end, many of the TDs elected quietly demur and when in government the loony solutions hardly surface. This is rightly a source of persisting irritation to the zealous Left who for years hated the social democrats in the Party regarding them as traitors, imposters, and power hungry opportunists. The irony is that the Left were theoretically correct because even a cursory perusal of the party's constitution would confirm that it was the social democrats who were out of step and not the Left. However, the public not the Party activists elected the Labour TDs. There is always a market for the politics of protest and this niche was occupied by the Workers Party for most of the 1980s. The easy sloganised solution when in opposition is a convenient luxury and that Party had a lot of money for campaigning in the constituencies. Their publication *The Irish People* ridiculed Labour systematically but their own sell-by date was fast approaching. They had held up the East German economy and the Soviet Union as role model solutions for the Irish working class. The progressive collapse of Communism in Eastern Europe by 1991 and the exposure of the low living standards and often dirty polluted working environments must have been an embarrassing blow to these chest-thumping Marxists.

Socialism

May Day was celebrated at the Wolfe Tone monument in St Stephens Green on Sunday with a few drinks afterwards in the Shelbourne and on the real May Day, Monday 1st, we all went to the Royal Marine in Dun Laoghaire for a party. Red roses for all and Barry Desmond was a picture as he limbered up in training for Europe. De Rossa and the WP were only a pimple on the landscape at that point. There was a real family feel to these occasions and the atmosphere was warm and friendly. Chit chat and gossip was the order of the day and our external enemies were easily identified and even more easily vilified in their obvious absence.

Drugs and Alcohol in Suicides and Other Deaths

The veil of silence hiding the serious rise in Irish people killing themselves often with lethal cocktails of prescribed drugs and drink was lifted when Anya Pierce, Helen Crosse and I reported from Beaumont Hospital that 62 out of 302 coroners deaths tested positive for drugs. The study was published in Human Toxicology in London.

All too often, the real problem is kept hidden by families of suicide victims who attempt to obscure the diagnosis for fear of embarrassment. Many people are not aware that relatives are depressed and are using drugs. Doctors are strongly urged to prescribe such drugs in limited quantities only to any patients who might be at risk of suicide.

Dr Des Corrigan of the School of Pharmacy in TCD commented in the *Herald* on our findings and said that more money should be ploughed into educating people about the danger of drugs, particularly teenagers and pupils in the last two years of primary school. AIDS has replaced drugs in the narrow public attention focus and general consciousness about drug abuse has declined but the Government should not adopt a slack attitude towards the problem.

In May, the *Sunday Tribune* ran a detailed report on the hospitals crisis where thousands of patients were waiting for routine operations. Some figures included 7,000 waiting for orthopaedic operations, 23,000 for orthodontic treatment, and 3,000 for eye operations. The Mater alone had 3,500 on its waiting list. Over 3,000 beds had been closed across the country since 1987. The government were blithely ignorant of the extent of people's anger.

The Constituency Scene

There was more life appearing at branch level only. The January constituency meeting was attended by only nine members and in February, the Santry Whitehall branch met in the Autobahn Pub with fourteen present. Leaflet drops were continuing regularly and we were at least competing on the ground. The Militants from DCU in particular were very disruptive at the constituency council meetings because they were fearful of mass expulsions following the Tralee Labour Conference. It takes much self-control, sometimes beyond me I'm afraid, just to sit there for up to 90 minutes and listen to a load of old nonsense. Most of the branch members would not attend which of course only strengthens the hand of the loony fringe.

I arranged a Euro elections campaign meeting in the Willows on Tuesday 2nd May and another in the Towers in Ballymun on the 11th to tell everyone that this outing was going to be for real. We were going to give it a lash for Barry and the Party. Later that week there was a brief meeting with Dick Spring and Fergus Finlay in Leinster House about the current political situation. Barry Desmond arrived in Finglas in mid week on the 9th and again on the 17th May and we got going immediately on his campaign. For a few successive nights Bob Slater and I spent a good few hours putting up BD Euro election posters around the area. I knew that water would have a disastrous effect on these efforts. The design and the photograph was grand but the board was like blotting paper. Enough said. We prayed for a drought. We met Hilary Tierney a social worker in Finglas South about the stray horses issue which was a big problem locally at the time and we also made preparations for the general election which was then pending.

On the weekend of 20/21 May, Paul Malone, Paul Brien, Andy Earley and myself joined Barry with his wife Stella, Sinead Bruton, Barry's son Ciaran and his wife. At Janelle, and at Superquinn in Finglas Village, Barry was well received. Recognition was no problem. Barry in action in Janelle reminded me of Bertie Ahern in Drumcondra. Hello Mrs , smile, agree with the person , thank them for their nice words and move on. He was more accomplished and self assured, with a lot more gravitas than he had when I watched him in Manor Street in the Dublin Central by-election in 1983, admittedly not the best of circumstances. Outside the Masses in Finglas on Sunday, Barry was a figure of considerable curiosity to the locals and he was very much at ease in talking to them. Some of our members were reluctant to support him because of his reputation in the locality as a cutter of the health services. However, local events were overtaking the Euro scene as Charlie struck back and dissolved the Dail on 25th May. Barry's posters were well in evidence but what was yet to come from the Workers Party in that Eurocampaign was unbelievable.

Neurodisney

Dr Pat O'Neill continued his fight against his dismissal as a neurosurgeon from Beaumont Hospital before Mr Justice Murphy in the High Court on 2nd May. Professor John Fielding, Drs Michael Farrell, Sean Murphy and myself went down to support him for a while at the Court. It was the start of an awful episode at the hospital that split the staff and led to much bad feeling which I believe will largely persist for the rest of the careers of the cohort involved. I feel that no part of the affair should have been heard in private because ultimately the public and also the other doctors in the hospital should have a right to know what the problems are. Transparency in professions is unlikely before the turn of the century. Vested interests always like official secrets. Law, medicine, insurance, accountancy and stock broking will inevitably be gradually reformed.

10

1989 GENERAL ELECTION – THE 54 VOTE GAP – SO NEAR BUT YET SO FAR

On 26th April, Fianna Fail were defeated in the Dail on the issue of additional funding for haemophiliacs infected by the HIV virus. As this was a financial matter and as the Taoiseach Mr Haughey was looking for an 'out' to try for an overall majority and free himself from Fine Gael's Tallaght strategy, he now had the perfect excuse. The European Elections, already scheduled for 15th June were ideally timed for a summer outing and the Dail was dissolved on the 25th May. Fine Gael and the Progressive Democrats agreed a pact on the 27th May and allowed Fianna Fail to start its campaign on the issue of who could form a government. The FG/PD agenda of privatisations was attacked by our side and we remained independent with Dick Spring advising Labour supporters to pass on their lower preferences to other left-wing candidates which included the Workers' Party, the Democratic Socialist Party, the Greens and Tony Gregory. Dick Spring aimed to achieve a balance of power between the two groups of right wing parties.

Now More Than Ever!

With this slogan he launched his national campaign on 1st June. The country did not need an alternative of 'Zig or Zag', between the 'ad hoc' conservatism of Fianna Fail and the Thatcherism of the alliance of Fine Gael and the Progressive Democrats. Unemployment and emigration were key issues to be tackled. There was a reespousal of the role of state companies in the economy and we were opposed to privatisation to keep jobs in the country. Privatisations would lead to massive redundancies and closures in the interests of removing competition and siting production in cheaper labour markets where economy of scale would allow the Irish operation to be a distribution business only. The National Development Corporation was to be reorganised as a central focus of industrial policy. Employee Investment Funds to invest in local industry would be encouraged through the tax system. The legal protection of part time workers was to be encouraged and Labour also supported the principle of a statutory minimum wage. Cooperation from the Trade Unions would be sought to extend the definition of work and paid employment to try to address the jobless crisis.

Tax reform rather than tax reduction was recommended as Ireland was seventh of the twelve EC countries in the tax league. The tax amnesty which had yielded

£700 millions had shown that there was considerable hidden wealth in the country. Tax avoidance and evasion were national sports. The PAYE sector should be asked to pay no more than their fair share. Tax credits rather than allowances were suggested and an increase in the child allowance to £40 per child per month payable to the mother was promised.

The worsening pupil teacher ratio of the previous two years meant that for some teachers crowd control rather than teaching had become the norm and we were pledged to reverse this. An Ethics in Government Act, a Freedom of Information Act, a register of financial interests of Oireachtas members, backup staff to help in the preparation of private members bills and Dail Committees to oversee the business of every government department were proposed. These policies are almost identical to the Programme for Partnership Government agreed with Fianna Fail three and a half years later and Labour's environment document was published on the following Monday which was World Environment day.

Fast Out Of The Blocks

The lingering death of the Dail over a four week period gave us time to prepare for the election. Photographs were organised and a printer contacted. The posters were also finalised and we ordered 3,000. They were 18 x 26 ins printed on firm cardboard and were ready to roll when the gun sounded. We set about the task as quickly and efficiently as possible and we were about the first in the field locally. The posters kick-started the campaign because of their high visibility and were a good morale booster for the troops.

A few hundred posters were already up on lamp posts when the General Secretary Raymond Kavanagh came to the Willows pub on the 31st May for a 10pm selection conference. There was to be one candidate and we were all fired up to have a real go. I gave an acceptance speech urging a big effort to increase our first preferences to get us seriously back in the race. I felt without blushing that I was carrying the flag for a party with a long proud history of real concern for the social and economic life of the underprivileged. Dr Mary Chambers was the nominal director of elections because there was nobody available to do the various jobs. These were done by myself as quickly as possible. Mary and I were absolutely determined to have a real go in the election. On Sunday 28th, I spent the afternoon with Fergus Finlay and Sally Clarke in Head Office composing press releases and some local literature. The Ireland – Malta World Cup qualifying game was on in Lansdowne and I gave my ticket to David Costello. Politics was a lot more important. Health, handicap, education costs, poverty and job creation, planning and environmental chaos were the targeted issues and the local slogan was 'Serving need not greed'.

Gerry Doyle volunteered to look after the organisation of the canvass teams for Finglas East and West in the evenings; Paul Brien, Paul Malone and Sean Rooney postered and canvassed in Finglas South; Paddy Donegan and his team did likewise for Santry and Whitehall and Eithne Costello and Gary Scully with their crew were to look after Ballymun. In Finglas South, the two Pauls had no transport yet they went out postering with one carrying a ladder and the other the posters. That was real dedication. On other nights, Sean Rooney drove over from Ballygall and collected them in his car to help them out.

This was a sharp three week campaign and the plan was to poster and canvass as much as possible and to get three leaflet deliveries into each house, approximately one per week. John Grundy was tracked down and asked to organise the leaflet drops for the whole area. He agreed but little did he realise that his butt would be run off for the three weeks. At least he is reliable and gets the job done. Declan Cassidy had been trained on the Apple Mac and was able to make up the leaflet pages to give 'camera ready' copy to the printers. The message was tabloid with a 16,000 print run. 'Three of the four TDs for Dublin Northwest have been keeping their heads well and truly down. Like the three wise monkeys, Messrs Tunney, Barrett and Ms Flaherty hear no evil, see no evil and speak no evil about the suffering of their constituents. They just go on voting quietly for cut after cut and hope that no one will notice. This election gives you the chance to elect a TD who will fight your corner – and not hide in the corner.' The voter was urged to 'Stick your neck out for a change'. A sin list of exactly why 'Enough is enough' covered the back. — sacked 4,000 health workers – closed 4,000 public hospital beds -almost bankrupted the VHI – abolished the farm tax – froze child benefit – got rid of 2,500 teachers – begun to dismantle free education – sacked 2,000 local authority workers – cut social welfare – 230,000 unemployed – 36,000 emigrating yearly – 1.3 million below the poverty line.

Ellis

Paul Brien persuaded me that in the next Finglas leaflet, we should press for the implementation of the Criminal Law Jurisdiction Act in the case of local Finglas man, Dessie Ellis, who had served a long sentence in Port Laoise jail for terrorist offences. I have always opposed the IRA and all purveyors of violent solutions to problems and I satisfied myself first in as much as was possible that the local story on Ellis's situation was true. Ellis was under threat of extradition but because of the miscarriages of justice in Britain in the Birmingham Six, the Guilford Four and the Maguire cases, at least a prima facie case should be made here first and then the validity of any new charges would be apparent. The feeling was that Ellis had served his sentence and should not be tried twice for the same crime. It was surprising how much abuse I got over that leaflet even from some people in the Workers' Party.

Army Pay

Army pay was a very simple issue and the loyalty and devotion to duty of our soldiers was being exploited. We called for a just wage and campaigned on the issue. There were many soldiers and their wives in the constituency as we quickly found at doorsteps. Most of the army men were postal voters and we had a separate list of such voters extracted from the register and we wrote to them early in an attempt to leave no stone unturned.

Fianna Fail

Fianna Fail, to my absolute amazement, selected only two candidates squeezing out Pat Carey. It was widely rumoured that this was in the interests of protecting the incumbents Jim Tunney and Michael Barrett and of avoiding a switch of personnel in the two seats that Fianna Fail were likely to take. I felt that Michael Barrett's personal electoral base was more solid than Jim Tunney's and was less likely to crumble against an onslaught from Pat Carey or de Rossa. Dr Michael Woods and the Kinsealy maestro were supposed to have approved this strategy which appeared on the surface to be savagely unjust to Pat Carey. I was very pleased because Carey had a strong base in Finglas South and many of his personal votes would be up for grabs with de Rossa being the main beneficiary but I reckoned that it would also suit us. The Carey factor was important at the count where he would have been in receipt of transfers which would not have gone to another Fianna Fail candidate. Despite seeing Jim Tunney out with a large body of supporters, including solicitor Tony Taaffe, I did not think that Fianna Fail fought the election particularly hard.

Following the previous election in 1987, I had been told by some parents in Ballymun of some promises made to them in relation to curing their asthmatic children by senior local Fianna Fail people. These were most definitely bogus and were very cynical in the context of the cuts that were subsequently introduced and passed. I was very angry and decided to exact a price at the next outing. So a 'Ballymun has had enough, Stop the cuts' leaflet had the resolution 'Barrett-definitely never again' emblazoned across the centre. The health charges were listed and cuts in social welfare were predicted. 5,000 were printed and distributed. However, I regretted that degree of personalisation later.

Fine Gael

Fine Gael again had a two candidate strategy with Tom Farrell standing with the incumbent Mary Flaherty. Farrell had his own plan for the area and ran a vigorous campaign. He had lots of personal literature and helpers and was intent on grabbing as much of the Fine Gael vote as possible. There was therefore obvious discord in the Fine Gàel camp and Mary Flaherty's people were not happy to say the least with her running mate. This festered until polling day when a notice went around East Finglas featuring Tom Farrell and Alan Dukes with a signed statement purporting to come from Dukes urging people to tactically vote No1 for Farrell before a transfer to Mary Flaherty. The card was designed and printed identically to the rest of Fine Gael's literature. I recognised it for what it was and I knew that the FG temperature and tempers would be very high for the day. Mary Flaherty's father, Tom, was visibly angry and upset and passed remarks to me about her running mate's tactics. Politics is a funny business and people do and say the most amazing things in the heat of the battle.

Campaigning – More Important Than The World Cup!

Mary Chambers and I spent the whole of Sunday afternoon of the Ireland – Hungary World Cup match on the 4th June postering around Larkhill and Santry with the car radio loud enough to hear Gabriel Egan's commentary from Lansdowne Road while on a ladder up lamp poles. Dave Costello was again pleased that the election resulted in him getting a pair of World Cup match stand tickets from a determined candidate. Now there's real dedication to the task in hand which is another way of saying that maybe my priorities were assways ! There was no way anyone can canvass when the soccer team is in action so posters were an efficient use of time. There were a number of voters pottering about in their front gardens in the sunshine who spoke to us so we were also canvassing at the same time. It was disappointing that they were nearly all Fianna Failers.

Maura Doolan, who was a union leader at the Irish Hospital Sweepstakes in Ballsbridge for many years, took Gary Scully and myself to call to Tim Killeen in Gaeltacht Park. Tim was a former Fianna Fail TD and City Councillor who had joined the PDs and he gave me a quick run down on the area. His wife Eithne is another formidable local politician in her own right. She knows virtually everybody in her district to the extent of their likely political preferences.

We visited the Bingo session at WFTA hall at 7.45 on Saturday night and also the Saturday night masses. Local Belclare Park community activist Kathleen Maher took us around Belclare in Ballymun on a Sunday afternoon and it was clear that the Workers' Party was doing very well. Michael Barrett also had a local following there as a result of some personal social work he had been doing.

Public Meetings

Public meetings to apply pressure on local representatives are a feature of election campaigns everywhere. St Aidens a popular school, has limped along in prefabs since 1982 when they were promised a new building. The head teacher Brother Cashel, a Christian Brother induced all the candidates to a meeting attended by a full assembly hall of parents interested in the school's welfare. Jim Tunney and

Michael Barrett spoke on a sticky wicket. Jim's effort was vintage Tunney-speak while Mary Flaherty always comes across as a true conservative blue rinse. I was probably too blunt and direct in pointing out that the government TDs and the Tallaght strategists could be held responsible for the lack of progress. There were a number of side issues such as whether the Christian Brothers wanted to pull out and whether there were too many local secondary schools and therefore which one would have to close. There were a plethora of speakers because the school covers an area in three adjoining constituencies. Tony Gregory spoke very well and obviously was well versed on educational issues. It is easy to oppose but it is often an entirely different matter when in government. The broader picture and scarce resources dictate that priorities have to be chosen.

On the following lunchtime, Aoibhneas – Ballymun's women's refuge, held a lobbying meeting in the Holy Spirit Girls School chaired by Sr Stanislaus Kennedy of Focus Point to try to have their funding put on a more solid footing. Again the room was full and I enthusiastically supported their efforts as I had known the women involved and the great efforts they had been making for some time. Years later despite various assurances from politicians, Aoibhneas still struggles on soft money from one short term source to another. None of this is the fault of the management committee.

'The People's Health Service'

Health and Health Care had quickly emerged as the burning issue of public concern all over the country. It was immediately obvious on the doorsteps. There was very little of the hostility to Labour from voters, quite unlike our 1987 experience. On Thursday, 8th June, the Labour Party held a press conference in Power's Hotel to launch the policy proposals to meet the crisis. It was called 'The People's Health Service'. The real cuts in health spending were outlined. When Labour was in government, health spending was 7% of GNP but this was reduced to 6.3% in 1988 and was projected at 5.8% by the end of 1989. The OECD average was 5.6% but per capita our spending was 71% of the OECD average. In Ireland, 5,000 workers were gone, 4,000 beds removed from the system, 3,000 acute beds, 300 geriatric beds, and 700 psychiatric beds. The commentary stated, 'Statistics alone convey only a cold impression of the suffering caused by health cutbacks, but it is necessary to point out that that suffering has been meted out to people who suffer from spina bifida, hydrocephalus, mental handicap, psychiatric illness, asthma, AIDS victims and a host of other particularly vulnerable people. To their suffering must be added the hardship and indignity caused to the elderly and infirm.

What all these groups have in common is that they are to a very considerable extent defenseless. It has taken a general election to bring home the reality of people suffering to the politicians who caused it. The politicians who caused this suffering are those who proposed the Health estimates of the last three years together with those who refused to oppose them.'

Fianna Fail first maintained that there was no health crisis at all and then they said that areas of particular pressure would have a reallocation of resources. That meant a removal of money from one area to relieve another. There was a guillotine hanging over Temple Street Children's Hospital and this had a great impact across the northside of Dublin where Temple Street is held in great esteem. The political fall-out for Fianna Fail was very big and they were very slow to realise this. Labour considered a proper health service as a fundamental human right and pledged that a majority Labour government would introduce a comprehensive National Health Service phased in over a six year period. (The incongruity of fielding insufficient candidates to deliver on these policies went unremarked.) Health promotion and primary care would be emphasised and an attempt would be made to get away from an overdependence on major institutional care. Health spending would be fixed at a certain percentage of national wealth and therefore would be related to economic development. Labour regarded the two tier health system as unacceptable and condemned the development of 600 private pay beds in the public health system.

Solutions offered included an extra £48 million in 1989 and an increase in health spending to reach 7.2% of GNP by 1992; £20 million for the re-opening of public beds in our larger hospitals all over the country; 24 hour Accident and Emergency cover; £5 million for community care; £3 million for 300 long stay beds; £2 million for adult mentally handicapped, £2 million for a long term illness scheme to include asthma; £2 million for the Health education Board; £3 million for the orthopaedic and cardiac services in Dublin and Cork; £1 million for an extra 60 mental handicap residential places in Cheeverstown House and £0.5 million to ensure a full intake of students nurses in '89.

The capital programme included the Tallaght Hospital, and developments in Ardkeen, Wexford and Temple Street Children's Hospital. There were major and detailed commitments to the mentally handicapped and to the care and protection of children. A reduction in the cost of drugs was suggested along the lines of my publicly stated policy position. The curtailment of tax relief on VHI plans D and E was proposed with the retention of tax relief on the other B and C plans at the standard tax rate. This last policy was more populist than ideological.

Later that day, portrait posters of Dick Spring and slogan posters 'Say No to emigration', 'Defend your Rights' and 'Health Care is a Basic Right' were put up around the whole area. The only problem with these was their tendency to bleach in the strong summer sunlight.

So, with a week to polling day the gauntlet on health care had been truly thrown down. Taoiseach Charles Haughey made a surprising admission during an interview on the Pat Kenny Radio Show that he was unaware of the hardships caused by the Health cuts. He said 'I personally wasn't aware of the full extent of the problems and difficulties and hardships it was causing.'

De Rossa's Huge Campaign

But the real cloud on the horizon was the European Parliament Campaign by the Workers Party in the city. In the middle of the General Election Campaign, de Rossa was writ high apparently everywhere. Huge posters were erected on vacant sites, and on every imaginable vantage point including billboards along the sides of roads, on bridges and in front of houses all over the city. The posters were superb. De Rossa was brilliantly portrayed in a photograph taken on Sandymount Strand as a 'breath of fresh air'. The cool clean hero had hit the town. There was a huge popular move towards de Rossa and the Workers Party in the last five days of the campaign prompted by the success of their Euro campaign and we could do nothing to counteract it. Their television commercials were also powerfully effective.

Strangely, I was talking on the phone to Fergus Finlay one night when Mr deRossa arrived at our house. I immediately thought that he was coming to talk about preferences and he was invited inside by Mary. He told Mary in the hallway that he was going to win both seats. He was then ushered into the surgery where I was speaking to Fergus Finlay on the telephone. He accused me of saying at doorsteps that he was not running in Finglas – a laughable comment when all of the posters and election paraphernalia were considered – and that he was a paramilitary – another fabrication. I had my serious doubts and misgivings about the Workers Party's connections but there were not even rumours about deRossa himself. I told deRossa that Fergus Finlay was on the phone and Fergus overheard the whole exchange and was as surprised as I was myself.

Despite the power of the Workers Party campaign, we were also being well received on the streets. The canvass continued at a furious pace with John Elliott and Andy Earley out in each session. Gerry Doyle was like Erwin Rommel on Sycamore Road in the evenings directing up to twenty people exactly where to go and the time to get going was now, not at pub closing time. Gerry went out with the local known Militants himself to make sure that they were not 'storming the commanding heights of the capitalist economies' at the doorsteps of Finglas East and they created no problems at all. There was a great buzz in the campaign as we headed into the last week and morale was very high. Gary Scully and Mark Costello were given five hundred posters and told to have a go at Ballymun estate. Gerry Doyle and I drove down Shangan Road in front of the Ballymun flats and could not believe our eyes. Most of the lamp posts were festooned with double Tormey-Labour posters, six high. The impact was huge. Gary and Mark met us with broad grins – 'what do yis think of that! Ye have to come to the Mun to see how it should be really done!' That was great but what does Scully then do? He disappears for four days to take up an offer he couldn't refuse from a friend leaving the remaining pile of posters in his flat. He won the 'Wally of the Week' award and we were not impressed. Meanwhile going door to door in Coultry and Shangan was a pleasure. I know many of the people there and with the fine weather everyone was in a good mood. Somehow, the small area of Sandyhill Gardens in Ballymun was not canvassed but I only found out after the close of the polls when a Labour supporter living there approached us in the Autobahn Pub to complain that his house had not been canvassed. He said that he was so annoyed he nearly voted for de Rossa instead! Obviously another close shave! We called to the SUSS centre, Women's Aid and the other voluntary agencies in Ballymun and also visited pubs at night in a fairly systematic manner. Big Jim Murphy from Artane had a television rental round in Ballymun and he systematically canvassed for us. He was a great help and he thought Flor O'Mahony was crazy to leave Northcentral. Publicity for Joan Byrne, the local Ballymun community candidate was being helped by well placed priests and she had an active and well organised team in Ballymun. I felt that with a similar effort, they might very well win the next local election. As it was she got 897 first preferences. Noel Martin, formerly of the CPI was her campaign director and they were relatively friendly towards us given that we were in competition.

Paddy Donegan and his family were busy in Santry with Jack McCarthy, Sean Costello, Tom Dunne and Maura Doolan. They organised themselves and got on with the job in a no fuss manner. Paddy Dunne's wife Marie put the word around for us also but she was in an awkward position because Paddy had joined the Soldiers of Destiny in Northcentral. At least the Dunne family could still throw us the No 1.

Dick Spring was given a much harder time by Una Claffey in his leaders interview on RTE television which was recorded in Tralee than either Des O'Malley or Proinsias de Rossa who were in contrast given the political massage treatment. I remarked on the disparity to Ms Claffey as an aside at the next Labour conference but she was not impressed and felt that he deserved it!

Car and Ladder Take Off

The funniest incident happened about two days before the election. Mary Chambers finished her GP surgery at 8 pm and decided to put up some posters by herself. She headed out to the top of Cappagh Road and got on with the job. Gerry Doyle, Andy Earley, Bob Slater and the rest of us were canvassing down in Valley Park in the far southwest of the constituency when Mary arrived on foot. 'Where is your car Mary?' It was stolen, she said and the ladder too. She was up the ladder stapleing posters together with the car open below when two teenagers jumped into the car and started to drive off. She rushed down the ladder and ran up the road after them when two other kids grabbed the ladder and hared direction leaving her careless and ladderless. You can't win.

We headed up to the roads around Dunsink dump and about but no sign of the car. The police in Finglas were i Dessie Ellis's sister Martha to tell her that if the word was abo whereabouts of the car, I wanted to be phoned. An hour later in t Jimmy Spence told me that the car was seen in Mellowes Park and that I sho and collect it. When I got there, the car had already been retrieved by the police and was in their compound in the Garda Station on the Finglas Road. Gerry Doyle and Mary called up but were told that the car was been impounded because it was English registered. It was the farm car from Mary's father's farm in Somerset and had been used to move her possessions by car ferry. As we watched from across the road a Garda came out and 'inspected' the car under the bonnet! He did not notice us observing him. The Fairbrother incident was still fresh in everyone's mind. Anyway, Mary 'arranged' to remove the car from the jurisdiction by the following week-end due to the reasonable intervention of a friendly civil servant. The ladder went permanently AWOL. The whole incident greatly amused the rest of the team. Mary did not think it was so funny.

Many people with police connections were very antagonistic and felt that my purpose had been to destroy the Gardai. There was simply no talking to them because their perceptions were fixed. I was surprised at the high number of police personnel living in East Finglas/Glasnevin North. There are moral issues in life that are more important than votes, even 54 votes at that election.

The final campaign leaflet was entitled 'The Tormey Challenge'. The tabloid format was continued and we reiterated the Fianna Fail cuts in health and education with 18,000 copies. The issues around redundancy were also highlighted. The potential 'Zig and Zag' coalition of Fine Gael and the Progressive Democrats was held up to ridicule in relation to solutions to the problems of our area because of their proven support in the Dail for the outgoing government's economic policies. What effect would their policy of privatising semistate companies have in Santry and Finglas? Would unemployment soar in Aer Lingus, Aer Rianta or Dublin Bus?

We also featured the drug refund scheme from the Eastern Health Board which had slowed down to a four to six months wait for your money. This had impacted greatly on the hundreds of local families where asthma, high blood pressure and other longterm illnesses were problems and the issue was very big on the canvass. Brevity and no preaching in our literature was the advice from Dave Grafton and Fergus Finlay.

The question of an election address did not arise because we would have insufficient manpower to address and make ready the bundles. That was a mistake.

ould have done a limited mailshot targeted at the higher voting areas in West East Finglas, Glasnevin North and East Ballymun.

Caroline Hussey and Ciaran O'Mara from Dublin Southeast contacted us to offer help if needed and we asked them to canvass the southeast corner of the constituency where we were unlikely to be able to cover. They arrived on the Saturday with Mary Freehill and a few others, took some literature and finished the area. That was a great lift and a big help.

The Workers Party and Fine Gael peaked late in the campaign and I believe that this had an important bearing on the result. Fine Gael produced a double sided A3 with the FG manifesto and a warning that 'A vote for the left is a wasted vote'. Fine Gael weaved local issues and the local girl image around Mary Flaherty. That she was now living in Rathmines was somehow conveniently ignored.

Opinion Polls

With six days to polling the last *Irish Times*/MRBI poll gave FF 47%, FG 28%, Lab 8%, PD 6%, WP6%, others 5%. The final *Irish Independent*/IMS poll taken four days before the vote gave FF 44%, FG 28%, Lab 12%, PD 7%, WP 5%, others 4%. The actual vote was FF 44%, FG 29% Lab 10%, PD 6%, WP 5% and others 6%. These figures underscore my belief that the quality of work reported by the pollsters in this country is of a very high standard and it is a foolish politico who ignores their findings.

Dirty Tricks

Years later, I was told by some of their own members that Fianna Fail had a dirty tricks department which was rolled out and dusted down for elections. In 1989, it was rumoured that a stamp was ordered from a shop in Capel Street with a message to the effect that the X was the best Fine Gael Candidate and that Fine Gaelers should do the obvious. This was calculated to cause discord in the FG camp.

Another trick was to arrange a bank of ten 'sterile' phones in an office in Finglas Village from a supporter in the right job. These phones are supposedly untraceable. Then the group would start at 3 or 4 a.m. and telephone local 34 and 42 numbers asking the barely awake and bemused householders to vote for a certain candidate in the election. You can just imagine the reaction! The mind boggles with these guys.

Polling Day

On polling day, David Costello had a crew out before 6 a.m. to poster the polling stations but the Workers Party had beaten him to the best spots. During the day, we had the entrances well manned. Mick Purdue and Jack McCarthy were in Larkhill,

Maura Doolan and Tommy Dunne in Gaeltacht Park, Garry Scully, Eithne Costello, Noreen Lynch, Rachel Rooney, John Byrne and others were in Ballymun, Paddy and Padraig Donegan and Mick Hopper were at the Ballymun Road, Peter O'Reilly and Mary O'Halloran were at Griffith Avenue, Philip Gifford and Jenny Owens were at Oliver Plunketts in Rivermount, Paul Brien, Sean Rooney, Frank Keogh, Madge Guthrie and Frank Hilliard at Cappagh Road, Eddie Riordan, Eddie Lynam, Gerry Juhel and Mick Doyle were at St Finians in Finglas South, Gerry Maher, Jack FitzWilliam, Richie Harte, Paul Malone, John Elliott and Dave Tormey were at Barry Road and Gerry Doyle, Sylvia Byrne, Andy Earley, Mary Chambers, Paschal O' Reilly, Josephine Gorman and any casual volunteers were in East Finglas and Ballygall.

The Result

Fianna Fail got 10,592 (35.39%) first preferences, down by 6,145 from 1987 whereas the Workers Party increased from 21.61% to 29.5% and Proinsias de Rossa topped the poll with 7,976. Fine Gael dropped from 18.75% to 14.83% but despite the conflict in their camp 1,177 of Tom Farrell's 1,454 votes transferred to Mary Flaherty. The Labour vote moved from 4.0% to 8.2% with the final effective count being 22.7% after the full transfer of votes. The Green vote is a constant feature and we were not surprised when local woman Alison Larkin received 1,327 first preferences (4.4%) up from 504 in the '87 election. Harry Fleming of Sinn Fein polled 4.2% up from 3.1% in '87.

We finished 54 votes short of a seat and 47% of WP votes transferred to Labour but 32% were non transferable. The gap was still about 48 votes after a recount and we were defeated. At the polling stations, the Workers Party canvassers were instructing their hard core voters to go one, two and stop. So we knew we were in transfer trouble because it was obvious that Proinsias de Rossa would poll more than a quota. There were a few pale sweaty faces in the Fine Gael camp but I would much rather have had pale perspiration and a winning ticket than another moral victory. No amount of juggling of figures by Dave Grafton could alter the situation. I kept a few count tickets for my family in the off chance that we might win but really I felt that my big chance of success had gone because Fianna Fail's treatment of Pat Carey had left an opening which was unlikely to recur. Tactically, we should have tried harder for WP transfers but the retrospectoscope is always 20-20.

In Dublin overall, the Worker's Party won 11.4% of the vote and again beat Labour's 9.5% as the main Left of Centre party.

Barry Desmond into Europe

Barry Desmond had to fight hard for the Euro seat because of the size and power of the final onslaught of the de Rossa campaign which was obviously very well funded. Neil Andrews headed the poll on 72,057 with Proinsias de Rossa closely behind on 71,041. Desmond polled 57,225 and won a seat still more than 7,000 short of a quota. The total left vote in Dublin was huge and as was the case in '79 with Michael O'Leary and John O'Connell, half the Dublin seats were won by the left. The WP were triumphant as they sang and waved their way around the RDS count centre. Ita McAuliffe, Marian Boushell, Sally Clarke, Aiden McNamara and the rest of Barry's team were exultant yet relieved. We were envious at the size of de Rossa's victory. The Workers Party Euro campaign had been a major factor in holding down my first preference vote in North-West in the General Election but I was not envious because I recognised a brilliant campaign when I saw one. I had often marvelled at how the hard questions aimed at the WP were deflected. Questions such as their paramilitary connections and an economic policy which held up the East German state as a role model for the Republic of Ireland left me cold. I often wondered how intelligent people like John McManus, Pat McCartan and Pat Rabbitte could remain members of a Marxist party.

Senate Nominations

Following an election reversal, the question of a Labour Party Oireachtas nomination always arises for recently defeated and for future prospective candidates. I was no different and I looked at the quotas for the different panels and also at the potential candidates. I heard that Dr Pat Upton was interested in the Agricultural Panel and I looked at the Industrial and Commercial because it was winnable. The quota was about 74.5 but there had been a Senate by-election in which Niamh Breathnach had been a candidate and she wanted to try again. John Ryan of Tipperary North was also a runner. Ironically Henry Haughton of Labour Left proposed me and Ciaran O'Mara, who was a classmate of my brothers at school in Marian College in Lansdowne Road seconded me at the Administrative Council meeting. However, John Ryan was selected and won the seat. On the night before the meeting at the end of June, I had been phoned by Ruairi Quinn to ask me to run on the Administrative Panel but I refused telling him that I believed that Joe Costello would be better than me as a votegetter because he would be more likely to get republican votes through the Prisoners Rights work that he was involved in for some years. My opposition to political violence was public and well known. Quinn became angry and told me that 'the leadership' would not forget this. I was not in the slightest bit impressed, however he certainly followed up.

I should have had a go but I genuinely thought I was acting in the best interests of the Party. Again we live and learn.

11

AFTER 54 – LET'S GO FOR IT!

What's 'Left' Fine Gael?

In the new Dail, Alan Dukes in his position as leader of Fine Gael attacked the Left and I wrote a reply which was published in the *Irish Times.* – Mr Dukes' attack on 'the Left' in the Dail bore the stamp of political desperation. His distaste for the message from the recent election that the long awaited development of Left/Right politics was arriving fast is apparent. With the FG/PD pact gone and FG's overtures to Mr Haughey rejected, FG is a party of politically displaced persons looking for space on the political spectrum while awaiting their next chance to coalesce. Virtually indistinguishable in economic terms, the conservative parties differ only in their attitudes to liberal social issues.

Depicting Labour as irresponsible and extreme will not wash with the electorate. Labour has many times acted courageously in the national interest and suffered grievously for it while giving the kiss-of-life to Fine Gael. It is patronising rubbish of Mr Dukes to state that he will fight for the people the Labour Party represents. The elements of democratic socialism and social democracy are well represented within the Labour Party. De Valera was right, Labour has had to wait. However, our time has arrived now that Fianna Fail has abandoned its roots and not even Mr Dukes will be able to stem the tide.

By 1993, those comments looked inspired. Now if I knew next year's Derby winner! Seriously, it did look like Fine Gael had pulled up their centre board and lost their rudder. They were floating on top of the water but they couldn't head anywhere even if they knew where they wanted to go.

The fixed delusions of political schizophrenia were not new in Fine Gael. The simplest evidence is provided by Dr Garret FitzGerald in his autobiography *All in a Life* where two captions in the set of photographs opposite page 242 say it all. Under the first picture, he calls Tom O'Higgins, Jim Dooge and himself 'the Fine Gael Social Democrats' and later in the same series there is a photo of Garret with various middle aged gentlemen. The caption reads 'Pony-trekking politicians: the Christian Democrats in Killarney in 1979'. After that, what chance had Alan Dukes? Garret has been consistent in his inconsistency. He advocated FG transfers to the PDs in 1989 but by 1992, he had a different attitude. In his Saturday column in mid-summer in the *Irish Times*, Dr FitzGerald repeatedly examined the conflict between social morality with its concern for the common good and 'hedonistic' individualism. He came down firmly on the side of the former – social democracy in political terms, and he criticised the PD approach. Perhaps he was merely proceeding up his personal political learning curve.

New Developments in North-West

Shortly following the 1989 General Election, I had a phone call from Des O' Malley of Siloge Gardens, a previous member of the Party in Ballymun who wanted to meet me to discuss the possibility of his rejoining Labour. I informed the Ballymun Branch and he was welcomed there without any problems at all. He quickly made it clear that he wanted support to run as a candidate in the next local elections. I had heard a few years previously on the Ballymun grapevine that Des had left the Workers Party so I was pleased that he was going to return to us. Des had a driving compulsion to run and immediately set about organising his election strategy. Large turn-over flip charts were made with flow diagrams of political actions all mapped out in great detail. They looked for all the world like model war maps. Des had wild flights of fancy as to how he was going to sweep up the votes in Ballymun and put the area firmly on the political map. He was a member of the Community Coalition and worked as a job placement officer with the Job Centre in the Shopping Centre. Thus he was known throughout the whole Ballymun estate.

From late summer in '89, there was a quick progressive breakdown of the ability to conduct constituency business at the monthly meetings due to constant disruption through points of order, information or any imaginable procedural ploy. This was systematic and was conducted by the members of the Finglas East and Dublin City University branches. Paschal O' Reilly of Finglas East at the first post election meeting tried to have me censured for losing the election for Labour. Paul Brien told him to get off the stage and Paul said that we should be clapping each other on the back for nearly winning against all the predictions of the pundits and the so-called experts. I had fallen out with O' Reilly after an argument concerning the referenda introduced by the 1982-87 Fine Gael-Labour coalition when he was in favour of the Pro- life campaign wording and was also against the divorce campaign. He was supported by Militant members of DCU and Finglas East and the rest of us were bemused to say the least. Claire Daly the branch secretary in DCU who was also a member of the Party's Administrative Council was subsequently removed from membership of Labour in late October due to an affiliation with Militant. The then secretary of the Finglas East Branch, Sean O'Connor was also reported to Head Office, having been seen by Paddy and Padraig Donegan selling the *Militant* newspaper on O'Connell Bridge. This was considered as 'evidence' of Mili activity by the Administrative Council and was now incompatible with Labour Party membership since the Tralee conference in March.

If the nonsense at the constituency council wasn't pathetic, a little of it would have been funny. However, the humour wears off with constant repetition and you would need the patience of Jobe to tolerate what could only be described in the vernacular as absolute bullshit. Points of Order about a socialist way to conduct business; Points of Information which amounted to lectures about how the Labour Parliamentary Party was failing to lead the working class uprising against Fianna Fail; demands to organise support for any strike in Finglas when we had already been in contact with the workers affected; emergency motions condemning virtually every government action and offering simplistic slogans as solutions to complex issues. The whole Soviet Union and Eastern European issue was passed off as the collapse of state capitalism which in their eyes would have been avoided by the imposition of socialism. Bizarre! Understanding some of these rationalisations was way beyond my simple mind. After a while the whole tedium wears you down especially when you have raised the money, organised the posters, leaflets, canvass etc., at successive hustings. Rubbish from the DCU crowd is the hardest to tolerate because you know perfectly well that some of these heads will almost certainly be pillars of tomorrow's establishment having sewn their wild political oats in their youth. When Pat Montague was the Party's full time 'Youth Officer', I asked him to sort out the Milis on a few occasions but again nothing happened. Inviting potential new recruits from the locale into such a bizarre set-up would only bring your own sanity and perspective into disrepute and would immediately drive sensible people away.

Next Time for Sure!

We produced a number of two colour leaflets under this slogan with local and city wide news and comment and distributed about 16,000 of each which was a lot of work. We published a list of project applications, including the amounts of money involved which complied with the conditions for funding from the Amenities/ Recreational facilities grant scheme 1990 from National Lottery Funds. This caused consternation because three of the local GAA clubs Ballymun Kickhams, Na Fianna and Erin's Isle were in for £50,000 each and apparently some of their members thought that the money was already guaranteed but this was not the case. I had phone calls about the Lottery in relation to residents' associations and community halls. It struck me forceably that very many people were unaware of what was happening in their own communities.

Kinnock –Tobin and Sospan Fach

In September Neil Kinnock, the Leader of the British Labour Party was in Dublin and Dick Spring hosted a reception for him and his entourage in MSF in 15 Merrion Square where Neil Tobin performed a brilliant little vignette from his repertoire. Kinnock sings like a choirboy when in full flow and is a very likeable character. His wife, Gladys, is a formidable confidence woman. It's a pity that she never got the opportunity to be a British Hilary Clinton. The London Labour Party had no time for the Milis and were in no doubt that they were the equivalent of a political plague. The following March, Neil Kinnock was in town again supporting the Sospan Fach brigade at Lansdowne Road. On Sunday morning he led a whole crowd of Welsh supporters in full song at an impromptu session with a voicing boisterous atmosphere at Kitty O'Shea's on Grand Canal Street. Neil certainly had loads of charisma amongst his own. Dick escaped without having to counter with 'The Rose of Tralee'!

In an attempt to restore order in response to the local constituency anarchy, Paul Brien drew up a detailed 'standing orders and procedures' for the constituency council which we had passed after a lot of windy discussion at the next AGM in early 1990. Paul Brien later told me that he had purposely inserted silly pieces into the rules just to let O' Reilly and company have a victory in getting our agreement to remove the offending clauses. Some of the provocative clauses were missed by the Milis so we had to amend the document subsequently. Such trifles filled lots of time.

In October 1989, Ruairi Quinn wrote informing me that he had been given the responsibility by Dick Spring and the party officers to re-organise the Dublin Constituencies in preparation for the next election. He invited the constituency officers to meet him at 88 Merrion Square on Thursday 9th November, the day after the Leinster vs All-Blacks match, to discuss a detailed questionnaire about the constituency. The immediate question was how did we propose to fight the Local Election scheduled for the following summer but subsequently postponed for a year. There was no clear answer but I told Quinn that I intended to contest the constituency seriously in the next general election and that I was looking for a building to house a business and a constituency office. The idea agreed at the constituency council was that our members would operate a rota to run clinics in competition with the Workers Party and Fianna Fail.

We restarted constituency drops in late October and sent around 16,000 copies of a double A4 with a new slogan 'Next time for sure'. Nothing like a bit of misplaced confidence! Two close supporters died that Autumn, Seorse Dearle after a long illness and Olive Morgan suddenly. Seorse had been interned in the Curragh in the '50's with Tomas McGiolla and Proinsias de Rossa and had stood for election for Sinn Fein in 1957. He joined the Labour Party about 1963 and remained staunch for the rest of his life. At Christmas, Christy Kelly Labour's printer in Leinster House gave us 5,000 season's greetings leaflets for Ballymun and 7,000 for Finglas and we managed to distribute these even in the cold and wet. Christmas messages from local politicos have become routine. Nearly everyone does it now. Some send around little calendars with a mugshot and a message. As Garret might say, 'It's all in a life.'

Dump Granny and Run

Because of the lack of both nursing home places and respite beds for the care of the dependent aged, some families had resorted to dumping their old folks in casualty departments and literally running. There were more than 30 geriatric patients 'blocking' acute beds in Dublin general hospitals at any one time. This makes the bed crisis for acutely ill patients that much worse. At the end of November, I discussed this issue and offered some solutions in the papers and on the Emer Woodful programme on the now defunct Century Radio and on Capital Radio which was later renamed FM104. Then, at the MSc in Community Health in Trinity College in late November, I proposed a complete change in the payment system for health services in this country which would unify the dual public/private spheres through the introduction of mandatory health insurance for all, partially based upon the present Canadian system. All citizens must be covered by health insurance companies in open competition. Patients should be able to attend doctors of their own choice for services. Medical card holders would be insured by policies through the social welfare system. Doctors would be paid agreed fixed rates for seeing patients and carrying out procedures. Insurance lump sum packages would be worked out for all services such as Radiology and Pathology and doctors paid by the amount of work they did and by their experience and qualifications. Doctors pensions would be paid through their PRSI contributions and 'topped up' through private policies. Hospitals should be responsible for their own budgets with insurance companies paying them for looking after their clients. Insurance cover would be compulsory for all employees with those on social welfare automatically insured possibly using the VHI as a vehicle. Personal taxation would decrease if the State was no longer funding most of the health services through taxation. My presentation was covered by the *Irish Independent* on December 4th.

Winter of Chaos in City Casualty Departments

Shortly before Christmas '89, I also questioned the possible role of the new GMS capitation payment system to GP's as a contributory factor to the huge increase in attendance at city hospital casualty departments. Self-referral is a major problem encouraged by the Department of Health fixing hospital charges at less than the normal GP consultation rate. Life in casualty was becoming chaotic and staff, patients and relatives were under great strain.

Finbar FitzPatrick of the Irish Hospital Consultants Association had claimed that patients may die during the admissions chaos at Dublin hospitals but the Minister for Health, Dr Rory O'Hanlon, immediately refuted his claim and accused Mr FitzPatrick of causing unnecessary anxiety to patients and relatives. I pointed out in the *Irish Times* that waiting lists and queues for investigations and treatment are the most obvious manifestations of rationing of health care and said what questions should be put to establish the truth of what was happening.

The only valid way of discovering what was truly happening in Accident and Emergency Departments in Dublin was to organise a prospective survey of the reasons patients were attending. Questions relating to GP services, social and economic factors must be identified and all patients must be included. Assessment of the study findings would be the correct way to address the problem.

Beaumont Hospital Retail Pharmacy – 'One Stop Shop' for Health

Hard to believe, but by the next summer Beaumont Hospital authorities wanted to open a retail pharmacy in the hospital's main concourse. I was informed of these plans by local pharmacists who were absolutely opposed to this proposed development. Pharmacist Richard Collis of Phibsboro kept me accurately updated. Such a development would have resulted in an even greater tendency for local patients to by-pass their GP's and use the hospital as a 'One-Stop-Shop' for medicine. True accidents and emergencies would be even more buried in the throng of GP type illness which should not be attending the hospital. This would reverse the expressed policy preference for community care and lead to greatly increased hospital costs from defensive X-Rays and blood tests done on these patients. Hospital management had claimed that their policy was 'in line with the growing trend here and in the UK to increase the receipts of hospitals from income generating activities'. Both the Taoiseach Mr Haughey and Dr. Rory O'Hanlon had been persuaded of its merits.

However, through the *Sunday Tribune*, the downside of this project was pointed out in a letter on September 30th. The development of primary and community care has been the policy of successive governments for many years. In 1982, the Fianna Fail manifesto 'The Way Forward' stated that the 'emphasis in choice of priorities must be redirected ... towards... that element of demand which can be met by less costly community-based services away from expensive institutional care'. In 1984, the Report of the Working Party on the General Medical Services stated that 'one strong theme is the need for more effective collaboration between general practitioners and other health care staff whose contribution to effective primary health care is vital'. They also suggested that a planned approach to primary care should be prepared with GP's and other health professionals. In 1985, the National Health Council welcomed moves towards the provision of an integrated primary care service capable of reducing demand for hospital beds. I also pointed out that at that time the Efficiency Review Group, chaired by Mr Noel Fox and a Dublin Hospital Initiative Group under Professor David Kennedy were examining various aspects of the health services and were not likely to reach the bizarre conclusion that general hospitals should become the sites of primary, secondary and tertiary medical care. The Pharmaceutical Union was vigorously opposed to this development and all this pressure led to the project being shelved.

Reasoned pressure won the argument and nothing further was heard of the proposal. A blow struck for sanity and for the tax-payer!

Unity of the Left

The question of co-operation and unity of parties and people on the left was raised by many commentators. The result of recent history where the massive social experiments of the Eastern European communist single party dictatorships have patently failed raised huge questions for the Irish Left. Where now for Marxist Centralism and Stalinism? It was only one year since Mr de Rossa moved the Workers Party away from overt support for these failed policies. I put the following questions in letters to the *Irish Press* and *Times* in January 1. Has the mixture of democratic socialism and social democracy exemplified by the Irish Labour Party been correct all along? 2. Was the WP now redundant and should Labour and the WP take a leaf from SIPTU's book and amalgamate their members? For many years the Labour Party had been the recipient of systematic denigration and abuse in WP publications. A cursory perusal of back issues of the *Irish People* would quickly confirm this. During the previous 15 years the WP frequently changed political direction and espoused the new policies with equal vehemence. I wondered, was their latest move towards social democracy for real because the voters were entitled to know. But if it was, I welcomed them. The Democratic Left and 1992 wasn't too far away!

Also by 1990, Dr Garret Fitzgerald, in a Dail speech suggested that Fine Gael were really social democratic and had much in common with Labour and the Workers Party. This was despite Garret's 1987 call for Fine Gael voters to transfer their lower preferences to the PD's and the 1989 pre-election coalition alliance with the same grouping. Fine Gael's power-sharing offer to Fianna Fail after the '89 election probably came one election too early. A case of you win some, lose some. I did not anticipate 1992 when I made these criticisms of Fine Gael. Dick Spring's political adultery with Fianna Fail was only a twinkle in a political godfather's eye at that point. At that time I claimed that Labour stood for freedom, equality, solidarity and democracy. Later it became clear to me that the democracy in the Labour Party is far from being the equivalent of one man – one vote.

I learned about a different perception on the health services from a meeting in the Sheiling Hotel, Raheny with Sean Kenny and the Edenmore Branch. The Labour Party was definitely getting a new lease of life and the rise in morale among members was very noticeable. When Jim Kemmy, a man for whom I have the highest regard, and most of the Democratic Socialist Party joined Labour in April '90, that was a key signal of the success of Labour's new strategy. Unfortunately, the DSP in Finglas simply disbanded and we failed to persuade them to join Labour.

Glenmalure Park – Rovers Bulldozed

Despite the city council zoning Glenmalure Park, Milltown as an amenity area in the Draft Development Plan, a ground, which had cost £160,000 when bought by Shamrock Rovers 1972 Ltd in 1987 from the Jesuit Order, was sold on for about £900,000 and An Bord Pleanala granted permission in mid March 1990 for houses to be built there. It made me wonder about the rights of the small man against building speculators. KRAM (Keep Rovers at Milltown) and all the demonstrations at Tolka Park, public meetings in Liberty Hall, motions supported by all parties at City Hall and media pressure in all of the papers and RTE came to naught. A city tradition would be demolished. At least John McNamara and I did our bit and tendered more than £400,000 for the piece of land to preserve it for football and for the citizens of Dublin. For the city, Milltown was the sporting equivalent of another Wood Quay. To make the blow worse, someone in high places had phoned John the previous week to tell him that there would be no planning approval. That week was a real emotional roller coaster for all of us heavily involved in Rovers. To misquote the famous Charlie Haughey comment in his *Hot Press* interview with John Waters, Rovers fans could instance a load of f****** whose throats they'd cut and push over the nearest cliff, but there was no percentage in that! In June the League of Ireland nominated Mr Louis Kilcoyne as their candidate for Vice-President of the FAI. Their insensitivity was simply shocking.

Labour Office in Finglas

Early in 1990, No 2 Ballygall Road was bought from an office supply company. Gary Scully and Paul Brien were unemployed at the time and the idea of setting up a shop which would give them employment below our political offices would, I felt kill two birds with one stone. The lads set about cleaning up, painting and renovating the building and the yard behind. Paul Brien also arranged for a sign painter to design a Labour Party sign board which we erected in poll position across the front of the shop. The fisted rose was used which was very shortly superseded as the Labour Party logo by the social democratic red rose. The old plough and stars flag was also included. The name of the shop was vigorously debated and 'Gimme dat' was an original insisted upon by Paul Brien who reckoned it was in the Dermot Bolger class for realism. Another case of Finglas rules OK. Paul also arranged floodlighting outside to include the political sign. This was important for security reasons because the shop was right next to the Barn Church which was constantly under attack from young vandals. Next door, there was a school for juveniles with behavioural problems run by Tony Gorman and crowds of teenagers often hung around at the street corner. Cider was a favourite and some kids were sniffing glue and other solvents in the Barn Church yard or behind Rosehill House.

'Gimme dat' was registered as the company name and the shop opened in June with the shareholders Gary Scully, Paul Brien and Paul Malone in a full flush of optimism with a business plan including daily cash turnover, stock control, leasing arrangements, rules for selling Rehab and National Lottery tickets, etc. The lads had been to the 'Food and Drink' exhibition at the RDS and had lots of filched new ideas. Things went according to plan for a few months and the stock built up as the turnover was reinvested. No rent was charged, it was agreed until the stock and profit margins had risen to a reasonable income level. The sort of figure which Paul Brien and I had in mind was a weekly turnover of £3,500 which was never reached. The World Cup 'Italia 90' was on television, the nights were fine, long and bright and everything was fine. Paschal and Derek Murphy who were self-employed printers, approached us to move in upstairs having being told that they must move from the Enterprise Centre off the Main Street. They were locals living in Finglas South so we were keen to give any help we could to local industry.

Later that year, when we decided that another medical practice on that site was impractical because of the rigidity of General Medical Services rules, we invited Declan Cassidy to occupy some space rent free until his business had turned the corner. He had returned from Rhode Island in the U.S. where he had spent a year in the local newspaper business gaining vital experience. Armed with the Apple desk top publishing system, he launched the *Finglas New Paper* to follow on from *The Courier* which had closed about 18 months earlier due to excessive and unsustainable losses.

The shop had serious problems of undercapitalisation. There was a breakdown of trust between the lads because financial discipline was difficult to maintain. Commitment to the business was very uneven. Paul Malone told me that there were problems which he had difficulty pinpointing as he was at work all day. I gave the business a short-term loan through Paul Malone and asked him to try to find out what was happening. They needed to rationalise and should have restricted their opening hours to the times when business was best. Gary Scully left the shop after coming to an arrangement with the two Pauls. By the year's end, Paul Brien decided to end his interest and transferred his holding to the Brennans, another local Finglas family.

The whole shop episode was a serious mistake on my part as it affected relationships with people who were close political allies. Gary Scully virtually disappeared and I was left with a legacy of inadvertent bitterness. This was a double loss – money and support. Paul Malone kept an eye on the shop business for two months up to the night of the local elections selection convention.

The Constituency Council – or The Mad Hatter's Tea Party

The constituency council continued on its merry way oblivious to the rest of the world. My early public support, in letters to the *Irish Press* and *Irish Times* in April

1990, for the candidature of Mary Robinson for President of Ireland was also criticised by the Mili mob. The whole circus induced the Santry-Whitehall branch to threaten to take home their bats and not play at all if the Party General Secretary did not investigate the Militants. This, they effectively did, leaving the constituency chairman, Maura Doolan, controlling meetings which her own branch would not attend for a period of more than one year. There were about 20 delegates in attendance for most of this period. Three of the local branches had better attendances at their routine meetings.

The Mili Plague

By September 1990, I felt it necessary as constituency organiser to write to the national organisation committee describing the parody being played out in the Dublin North-West Constituency Labour Party. This notice was sent to Pat Magner and to Ray Kavanagh.

> Dear Pat,
>
> Since the last general election in June 1989, there has been a precipitate decline in activity and attendance at the constituency council of Dublin North-West. This has occurred, in my opinion, as a result of every meeting being systematically disrupted by procedural and organisational wrangles. Thus monthly meetings have been reduced to a replaying farce. Normal Labour Party members and supporters have been so repulsed by this that attendance at such meetings has been an unwelcome chore in which it is counterproductive for me to keep nagging them to attend.
>
> The following is a short description of what has transpired. The (NIHE) DCU branch was organised and run by Claire Daly. She stated over eighteen months ago that she was a member of Militant at the Constituency Council but later changed her mind to being in agreement with the *Militant* 'newspaper'. As you know she was a member of the AC and was expelled from the Party. Shortly before and during that period, her NIHE branch with the help of Messrs O'Reilly and O'Connor of the Finglas East Branch insisted early at a poorly attended meeting that all sorts of censure motions and protests be issued regarding her expulsion. This was subsequently easily reversed at the next meeting when all delegates were present.
>
> A public meeting was then held by the DCU branch in the Ballymun East Community Centre without informing the local Ballymun Branch. No locals attended but Des O'Malley and David Costello of the Ballymun Branch were informed by our supporters on the management committee of the centre. David Costello went to investigate and told me that Mr Halpin of the Finglas East Branch was 'displaying' a bundle of copies of the *Militant* newspaper. The Ballymun Branch protested to DCU and warned them that any further moves would force Ballymun to seek the transference of that branch to Head Office. Then early in the

new year (1990), Paddy and Padraig Donegan reported to the Constituency Council that when driving across O'Connell Bridge in Dublin, they were surprised to see Mr Sean O'Connor of the Finglas East Branch selling the *Militant* newspaper. This, having been brought to the notice of the Constituency Council was categorically denied by O'Connor leading to a major wrangle. The consequence of this was that Paddy Donegan announced his intention of refusing to attend any further Constituency Council meetings.

In the middle of this long hot Summer, Des O'Malley answered a knock on his own hall door and, believe it or not, was asked by Mr Alan Bermingham of DCU branch, also by the way the elected 'Youth Officer' of the constituency who had previously denied being a Militant, to buy the latest edition of *Militant* newspaper.

Mr Bermingham and Ms Doyle and another DCU member were active in the Militant role in the recent Gateaux strike in Finglas and were personally seen on the site by myself.

Last evening, Des O'Malley, David Costello and I met with the DCU and Finglas East Branches and we were told that as Bermingham was not there to defend himself he could not be called a Militant, and neither could O'Connor. This is clearly a total farce and we told them so. Finglas East and DCU branches should be transferred to Head Office immediately pending a thorough investigation. Otherwise............

Yours, etc.

This letter was cosigned by Des O'Malley, Chairman of the Ballymun branch; Paul Malone the Secretary of the Constituency Council, Bob Slater who was chairman of the Ballygall branch and myself as Constituency Organiser.

I was later contacted by Sally Clarke from Dick Spring's office and told that I should arrange a meeting with Dick Spring to discuss possible solutions to the problem but the meeting was repeatedly postponed, firstly because of the Presidential Campaign and later by the proximity to Christmas. Despite comments in the press that the Labour Party had rid itself of the Militant Tendency, nothing concrete was ever done about the problem in Dublin North-West. The real frustration was that well known sound local people were willing to come along to our meetings but we were too embarrassed to allow them sight of what the current situation was for fear that they would think that we were total idiots for voluntarily submitting ourselves to such nonsense on a regular basis. In my view, the Party organisation was very negligent in this regard and we were not too impressed by Head Office to say the least. Would the Chief Executive of a private company get away with such dilatory management. I doubt it but then the Labour Party is not a private corporation otherwise heads would roll.

The Late Suzanne C.

In January 1990, I was phoned by Ms Ryan, a teacher in Marino College who told me that she had a 19-year-old student who graduated in the first ten in the pre-nursing and repeat Leaving Cert class (about sixth as far as I can recall) but who uniquely had failed to be placed for training in one of the Dublin general hospitals. Of their eleven students, ten had reached the required standard and were placed. Her class-mates had been accepted in St Vincents, St James's etc., and some of these had family connections in medicine. Suzanne C. had been interviewed at Beaumont for the Nursing School and initially had not been accepted. Her teacher felt that the girl's home address which was a flat in Silloge Road, Ballymun where she lived alone with her mother, might have been a contributory factor to her lack of success. I saw the girl at a Saturday morning surgery and more or less subjected her to an interview in reasonable depth. She was a perfectly outgoing and normal girl as far as I could tell. Her enthusiasm was such that she had worked as a nurses aid. So I contacted a friend of mine in the higher echelons of the nursing administration and asked her to give me some advice on how this young lady could be helped to reapply.

The only objective was to solve this girl's problem and not to use her as a means of changing the system or in some form of cheap publicity stunt which might be easily organised. I thought that a low-key approach directly through the hospital would be the best way forward for this individual case. A parliamentary question plus publicity would have had the girl effectively blacked because the hospital authorities would probably have reacted defensively and would have ruled out Suzanne on the basis that there could be no possible way that any selection of staff would be anything other than objective. Bias, if it was present, simply could not be admitted as a factor in a public institution.

The senior nurse asked me did I personally know any bishops. I thought she was taking the mickey so I told her, Yeah, myself and a few bishops regularly went out on the gargle with Fr Brian Darcy after Rovers matches in the RDS because Brian was trying to impress his bosses! But she was deadly in earnest and said, 'C'mon Bill, stop messing'. I suddenly remembered that Ms Bartley, the Beaumont Matron, was a SPUC supporter from the time in the Richmond Hospital during the Abortion Referendum in '83 when petitions, little feet, etc. were floating about in nursing circles. Cop on was slowly dawning. So I said, Yes, I had met Bishop James Kavanagh who lived on the Swords Road in Whitehall on some formal occasions. The first time was with Tim Killeen and Paddy Dunne at the opening of the Ballark Community Workshop on Shanowen Road about five years earlier. Paddy Donegan told me that he knew the man for years and said that he was a good skin. Tom Dunne then told me that the bishop's brother was a psychiatric nurse in St. Ita's, Portrane and a member of the Labour Party. He had also been a trustee of the Workers Union of Ireland with young Jim Larkin.

I contacted the bishop and told him the girl's story in as far as I could verify and asked him to use his offices to try to see if he could help to get her placed for nurse training when she reapplied. He was very helpful and the young lady was very appreciative. Well, the young girl reapplied and was ultimately accepted after a second intervention by Bishop Kavanagh. I did not think that my personal intervention at the hospital would have helped her at that particular time. Best results are achieved when one's own ego is kept out of things. Suzanne's mother also phoned me a few times to impress upon me just how important nursing was to her daughter.

Within two years, I was asked to see a young nurse in the intensive care unit in Beaumont and I was stunned when the ward sister Liz Logan told me the patient's name. By this time she had coned and was effectively brain dead. The diagnosis was fulmanent haemophilus meningitis. Her class-mates were very shocked and lined out in a guard of honour at her funeral Mass in the Holy Spirit Church Ballymun. I found the obsequies very difficult to attend as I had seen her in her white nurses uniform in the hospital corridors and she had told me how she was getting on – always happy and good humoured. She had an excellent relationship with her mother who was simply devastated. This story is important because it possibly illustrates another reason why an Equality Ministry was considered necessary in 1993. Address, accent and pedigree are still very important factors in personal advancement in this republic. The bishop, now retired in his semi on the Swords Road will be embarrassed reading this so I'll have to avoid him for a while. He does care about people and worked quite hard on the Bishop's report on unemployment, published late in 1992.

There may be a case for affirmative action to train people from working-class backgrounds in Nursing because when trained they could do great work in their own areas in the community health sphere. A pilot study of this proposition should certainly be tried because cultural norms vary considerably between different areas of the city.

Finglas Branch Manoeuvrings

In the autumn of 1990, Odran Reid was very anxious to take the Finglas Branch from the control of the two Pauls, Malone and Brien, and to develop some political activities in the Finglas area. Branch meetings had been very irregular and political campaigning by the branch itself was virtually at a standstill. Reid had been asked to return to North-West from South-East by Ruairi Quinn to 'help' me because we were short of his type of experience. But, because he worked in Brendan Halligan's business, I was never sure of the possible background role, if any, of the former General Secretary. But suspicion still lingers to this day. I approached a pair of old Labour hands Liam Pike, the former Constituency Chairman and his wife Katie

McKenzie to convince them to rejoin the Finglas branch. Liam accepted after some equivocation because he still retained some anger and resentment over the way the Labour Party had treated his old Finglas 'Billy Rigney' branch when Colm O'Briain the former General Secretary decreed that only people living in a branch area could be members of a specific branch. That reorganisation in 1984 had decimated the constituency organisation.

Generic Drugs and Drug Pricing

The question of generic drug prescribing and the price of drugs in both the public and private sectors was debated earnestly in the *Irish Times* in May '90 following an article by Jill Kerby in which Clonmel Chemicals claimed that the substitution of their generic products for out-of-patent proprietary drugs could save a possible £28.8 million from the national drugs' bill in one year. RTE's Pat Kenny Radio Show followed up the story and I restated much of the case there. Dr Pat Keelan of the Mater Hospital reacted quickly and cited the potential quality control problems which doctors worry about with regard to generic drugs.

I pointed out that community pharmacists have little incentive to sell generics because the retail price is a percentage mark-up of the wholesale price, therefore the higher the supply price, the greater the profit. Mr E.A. Ryan of the Irish Pharmaceutical Union pointed out the fee-per-item system for dispensing in the GMS but I replied that the GMS only covered about one-third of the population. He also stated that pharmacists fill written prescriptions and must give what is ordered. I pointed out that if approved names only were prescribed, then it would be up to the Pharmacist to choose the cheapest product. I also commented on the use of 'branded generics' where a brand name is added to the packaging and a premium price is then charged. This perfectly legitimate marketing strategy is commonly used by Irish generic drug companies. In reply to further criticisms from John O'Donovan a pharmacist from Tullamore, Co Offaly, I rejected his suggestion that I was trying to make generic prescribing compulsory and I referred him to the Black report on disease in relation to social class which had been published in the UK. Black reported on the concentration of obesity, heart disease, depression, etc., among the working and unemployed classes. I also hoped that the agreement between the Department of Health and the Federation of the Irish Chemical Industries would end because I believed it acted against the public interest preventing parallel importing of licenced drugs and keeping drug prices high in Ireland because of the link to UK prices where the British government was still committed to ensuring that drug companies made profits of more than 20% on capital employed.

The whole issue of high drug prices in this republic was nothing new. Following the Trident Report on the very high prices in the late 1970's and early '80's, 'Today

Tonight' produced a programme on the subject of generic drugs and parallel imports in August 1984 and outlined a case for major savings which involved the setting up of a National Drugs Buying Agency and also not renewing a price-fixing agreement between the Department of Health and the Federation of Irish Chemical Industries. The Department of Health ignored it. The *Sunday Tribune* in January 1987, the *Evening Herald* and the *Irish Press* and the Gay Byrne Radio Show in October 1988 also reported on the subject but again the Department of Health did nothing. Why, why, why? Whose interest was being protected – and why?

Gateaux Bakery Closes in August 1990

Factory closures are a real body blow to Finglas where, in recent years, a main employer like Unidare had laid off thousands of workers most of whom lived locally, Nokia made about 30 redundant in the nappy section and Downes' Bakery closed. On July 29th, Gateaux, the wholesale cake manufacturing company owned by Lyons Irish Holdings announced that it was to close the Finglas plant with the loss of 250 full-time and 300 temporary jobs. Gateaux sold £12 million worth of cakes annually with 50% exported, but registered low profits of only £300,000 in 1989. The appreciating value of the punt against sterling also undermined profits. There was undoubtedly a need for redundancies to increase productivity but the bakery should not have been closed down.

The final row started in May when five bakers were fired. Gateaux workers were suspicious that the company had a single item hidden agenda – closure. Flying pickets were the understandable reflection of the desperation of staff attempting to save their jobs. Some people had worked there all their adult lives and many knew that closure meant permanent joblessness. I supported the workers in the press and on radio and spoke at a large demonstration in Finglas village in June which took place before the Ireland and Romania World Cup game. There was a further city centre march at the time of the closure which proved futile. George Morris and a number of others who had entered the factory to occupy it were served with court orders and some younger workers later claimed that Gateaux people's names were being blackened by many employers around the city. I felt that the workforce should have immediately accepted an interim offer by management at a general meeting earlier in July to call the company's bluff and maybe force the retention of some manufacturing in Finglas. There were all sorts of accusations that the Militant Tendency had a significant influence on the strikers. This was not true but feelings in Finglas ran high.

A closer look at the Gateaux management position raised a few questions. If, as reported, management announced its intention to close on July 23, why did the company set out a new agenda for discussion when requested by the Labour Court's conciliation officers four days later?

Gateaux's final offer was then rejected by the workers but, after further official effort, the offer was accepted after the August weekend. However, citing a major loss of orders, the company announced a closure. Gateaux told the Minister for Labour, Bertie Ahern, that their viability had been threatened over the past two years by the loss of export orders and that production costs were becoming uncompetitive. They never said which orders were lost and to what competitor.

By September, Gateaux cakes were quickly on sale in Ireland with the 'Made in Ireland' notice removed. Production was merely moved away to Barnsley, South Yorkshire and their Irish market share was to be serviced by using Finglas or the Long Mile Road depot as a distribution centre.

Unemployment in males doubles their mortality rate. Illnesses such as obesity, heart attacks, high blood pressure, alcoholism and depression are increased. When state agencies often spend £20,000 per year per new job provided, and when social welfare payments, retraining courses and increased demands on the health services are considered, the true cost of unemployment to the tax-payer is very high. By 1992, Finglas had its own monument to institutionalised joblessness in the form of a large new building on Mellowes Road which is fronted by high railings making it look tatty and forbidding. It is a new dole office.

Three-Day-Week for AIB in Ballymun

In October 1990, there was a rumour flying about in the Mun, that the local AIB was going to fold its tent and go. This was more than an issue of mere profit, it was a question of confidence in the community. The shopping centre was seriously run down and in need of refurbishment. Competition for business in the area was growing all the time. On the west side, Finglas Village was now just as convenient as Ballymun Town Centre itself to people living in Poppintree and Belclare due to the opening of the link road from Jamestown Road into the Poppintree Industrial Estate. Janelle Shopping Centre was also popular. Omni Park on the Swords Road was very much on the horizon and would soon be drawing shoppers away from Ballymun's 'Crazy Prices' supermarket.

In the mid '80s the action of the Bank of Ireland in closing its branch in Ballymun Town Centre caused much local shock. How could they do it? local people wondered. In response, various groups formed an ad hoc Community Coalition which was the catalyst for action on all sorts of issues, including a Credit Union, a Job Centre, the garbage incinerator, and the refurbishment of the estate. Marie McNamara, Des O'Malley, Jack Boyd, Ina Gould, Antoin de Roiste, Brendan Core and up to thirty others skilfully enlisted the help of local priests like Fr John Sweeney, school-teachers like Tom Hickey, public representatives and others and pressured Dublin Corporation into action. Combat Poverty played a key initial role in getting funding for the first three years. Margaret Barry from that agency and

John Heagney, an architect in the Corporation put in a huge effort with the local committee.

John Harris helped to form Tenants Associations in each area which acted as a forum for people to demand their rights. Morale improved as the whole community got together and decided that united we stand, isolated we're finished. Key Ballymun people emerged very skilled at organising locally responsive social services and have received financial aid from the America Ireland Fund, Smurfits, the EC etc. This was by any standards a tremendous fight back by a township with over 60% unemployment and has restored confidence and self-esteem to the whole area. Where until recently there had been an exit queue for housing transfer, there was now a waiting list for entry.

Money being God, the banks have never been in the vanguard of social responsibility. AIB's decision to go three days a week was very insensitive when it is recalled that Labour in the '83-87 government agreed to public money being used to bail out that particular bank when their Insurance Corporation of Ireland purchase went wrong. The fortune AIB had just spent on advertising their new logo contrasted sharply with their penny-pinching in Ballymun. Was the bank losing money in Ballymun? If so, how much? Could they not give a little to a battling community?

The Presidential Election

Mary Robinson's electoral victory was a fantastic personal tribute to the woman herself. The physical effort she put in was daunting and it certainly began to tell on her by the last week of the campaign. On the weekend of the last Cartier Million at the Phoenix Park Racecourse, Brian Lenihan, the Fianna Fail candidate was mobbed by supporters as arranged allegedly by a departmental press officer. The Robinson campaign was leafleting at the black cast-iron Victorian gates. This spurred me into action and I contacted John Dunne of the Finglas Workers Party to discuss the presidential election. My job was to collect posters and some literature from Labour Head Office and get some literature drops done. John Dunne got the Whelans and some of his other supporters to staple up the Robinson posters around the constituency. The Workers Party was to poster the Finglas side and we were to do the rest. Finding Workers Party lapel stickers stuck across the bottom of the Robinson posters was a bit of a provocation to the local Labour activists. I protested to Dunne but he put it down to youthful exuberance on their part.

The candidate herself arrived in Finglas on a wet Wednesday morning, 10th October, and she visited Janelle Shopping Centre where she showed great empathy with the shoppers, nearly all women. One woman said 'How would you like to live on £66 a week in a flat with a 17-year-old lad to feed? Once you get into the Park you'll be off around the world selling Ireland and you'll forget all about the little people.' Her reply, reported by Brenda Power in the *Sunday Press* was, 'Listen, I have a good job already. I don't need this – I have no interest in the job of President other than to use it to help people like yourself.' Brenda Power went on, 'But the glamour of it....' the worn-looking blonde woman continued half-heartedly. 'And ye all say the same thing .....we'll have Brian up here next week and he'll be promising to turn the world upside down.' 'I want the job,' said Mary 'not a retirement post.'

We also went along to the Barry Road shops where she met some local women who were former Gateaux workers and again with friendly banter she encouraged them very gently to vote for her. She also fielded a call from RTE radio on her mobile phone and was most obviously courteous to Proinsias de Rossa and Eric Byrne of the Workers Party who were accompanying her. The future President was genuinely shocked by the conditions of wet muck, poor sanitation and only one water tap for fifteen families at the Dunsink Halting Site for travellers. The people in FAS, though many of them ardent Fianna Failers (no longer a contageous disease!) treated her to lunch. Later, she visited St Aiden's School in Whitehall where new buildings had been promised for so long to replace their leaking 25-year-old prefabs. Tommy Broughan, the future Labour TD in Dublin North-East was on the staff and was there to meet her with the school boss Brother Cashel. The pace of her visit to Ballymun was whirlwind – the Ballymun Job Centre, the Save Santry Woods project and the Ballymun Community Project. The committees organising these activities were very pleased to see her and held her in high regard. She had a very special feeling with many of the downtrodden women in the area and watching their reactions to Mary was very interesting. Her good opinion poll ratings were obviously for real if Dublin North-West was in any way indicative of the rest of the country.

As President, Mary Robinson soon returned to visit St Helena's Community Action Programme in Finglas South and also to call on the Women's Refuge in Ballymun. The impact of these visits was stunning and proved a great morale booster for both projects. I both like and have a high regard for Brian Lenihan personally but I am very happy to have simply voted No. 1 for Mary Robinson on the day that counted.

Fergus Finlay phoned me in Beaumont Hospital on the 22nd October and asked me to meet him for a briefing in the basement at the MSF Union offices in Merrion Square which served as the campaign headquarters for Mary Robinson later that evening. He wanted me to go out to RTE at about 6.30 p.m. to sit in the audience of 'Questions and Answers'. He reckoned that there was something up because Fine Gael had recalled Garret FitzGerald from a visit to Venice and had substituted his name for that of Jim Mitchell. Nuala O' Faolain the *Irish Times'* columnist, Brian Lenihan and Michael D. Higgins were the other panellists. We had no idea of the existence of a Lenihan-Duffy tape before the programme. But we knew that the question of phone calls to the President, Dr Hillary, in 1982 when the coalition government was defeated would be on Fine Gael's agenda.

Four went to the programme from MSF with two tickets and we got in. Anita Geraghty and Catherine Delahunt, both solicitors and myself had prepared questions. I tried to get a comment in on the phone calls affair but John Bowman would not call me. However, I was able to put a relatively trite question regarding women priests which was relevant to happenings in the Church of Ireland at the time. But this was after the fireworks on the phone calls issue.

I thought Garret FitzGerald was a bit over the top on the events of eight years earlier but Brian Lenihan showed some mettle considering the intensity of his campaign and the physical problems he must have been encountering from the metabolic effects of prolonged liver failure and the effects of the immune suppressant steroids and cyclosporin. Following a straight question from Brian Murphy, a Fine Gaeler in the audience, Lenihan flatly denied that he had made any phone calls to the President during the 1982 crisis. The subsequent political fall-out from the playing of a tape recorded interview of Brian Lenihan by a UCD politics student, James Duffy, in which Brian claimed to have phoned the President and to have spoken to him on that fateful evening in 1982 was shattering for the Fianna Fail campaign.

Later that week on the evening news on RTE television, Brian turned away from the interviewer Sean Duignan and directly faced the camera. Lenihan claimed that much of what he had said on tape to Duffy was 'on mature recollection' untrue. The Lenihan campaign and the government in which he was Tanaiste and Minister for Defence was now on the defensive. Within ten days, the Taoiseach had to dismiss the Tanaiste from cabinet to save the governing FF/PD coalition. The whole episode focused a lot of public sympathy back on Brian Lenihan and gave his flagging campaign a boost towards the finish but it was not enough. These episodes add to the impression of Irish politics as a form of mass entertainment. A theatre of the absurd – harmless, great sport but really little enough to do with real life.

In his book, *For the Record*, Brian gives an account of the high dose steroid treatment he was receiving for the treatment of an episode of acute rejection of his transplanted liver. He was confused and euphoric and his behaviour was inappropriate at the time. He later made a good recovery and he has my sympathy. Had I known these facts at the time, I would have made a public comment. I believe that Brian's advisers got their responses wrong. They should have divulged the details that are outlined in his book. It would hardly have affected the result but would have mitigated the trauma to the Lenihan family.

We had an A4 leaflet printed with photographs of Mary Robinson, Dick Spring and myself and we covered each house in the constituency. Despite this, it was difficult to get many of the local Labour Party to take much heed of this election as they seemed to regard it as mainly a TV event. I can very well understand why. The Eoin Harris-inspired political broadcast with Mary Robinson dancing in slow motion with a west-of-Ireland old man to the background of Nessan Dorma by Luciano

Pavarotti was an absolute masterpiece. It was simply brilliant and moving television coming shortly after the Soccer World Cup which had used this Pavarotti best-selling piece as its theme tune. Eoin Harris is a communications genius. He may annoy some people but his talent is enormous. When he is convinced on a political issue-, his commitment, passion and powerful speech can be intimidating to opponents. It was the first election, in my personal experience, where there was no hostility to our candidate at doorsteps. It was a pleasure canvassing. New people like Louise McKeever, a very pretty insurance official, were attracted to participate for the first time and thoroughly enjoyed the experience. Others like Odran Reid had returned and were welcomed. Andy Earley, Gerry Doyle and Bob Slater canvassed as usual. The attraction of Mary Robinson as a candidate was underlined when young women phoned me to join the canvass and made it explicitly clear that they had no Labour or Workers Party affiliation. With this happening, I knew that the Fine Gael vote would be seriously undermined.

Brian Lenihan had come to Shamrock Rovers at the RDS early in the season. He was warmly welcomed and photographs of his visit were featured in a later match programme. When Mary Robinson visited the RDS for the Rovers and Dundalk game on November 4th, she got a huge ovation from all of the fairly large crowd except for a small republican element on the Anglesea terrace. Not a bad campaign move on a Sunday afternoon. Most of the Rovers crowd on the Grandstand side said that they intended to vote for her.

The Presidential Election count in the RDS was intoxicating. Watching the lengthening faces in the Fianna Fail camp as the day went on was truly exhilarating for me. It was so obvious that they were very unused to losing. Michael Freeman, Des St Leger, John Stafford and Noel Cloake were very subdued. Having lost so often for so long, it was a heady feeling for us to be on the winning side. Fergus Finlay and Dave Grafton were euphoric. What a woman, what a campaign! I marvelled at her stamina. There was no real tension because we were systematically tallying the second preferences on the Currie votes and it was quickly obvious that Mary Robinson would win on the transfers.

Barry Desmond's Christmas Party in the Garda Boat Club at Islandbridge was a very heady affair. All and sundry of the Labour Party were present and Mary Robinson was the hero of the hour. Paddy Donegan also ran a very well-attended and successful pub quiz in the Autobahn and morale in the branches by the year's end was very good. We also had a 'thank you' small A5 leaflet printed with Dick and me featured and this was distributed in December and January. In it we gave credit to the Workers Party for their hard work on the ground during the presidential campaign. High morale gets the troops out without any bother.

12

THE 1991 LOCAL ELECTION IN THE FINGLAS AND DRUMCONDRA WARDS

In the first months of 1991, the question of who would be the candidates for the Labour Party in the two local authority wards was still very much open. Odran Reid was a researcher working for Brendan Halligan in his 'Consultants in Public Affairs' business in North Great Georges St, which Halligan had built up following his short period as a substitute MEP. Reid had transferred to the Finglas Branch from Dublin South-East during the previous summer. He is an East-Finglas local from a northern counties Fine Gael background and is a TCD economics graduate. He was previously a strong Halligan supporter in the early '80s and had emigrated to London for a number of years. He regularly called to my home during the winter of '90-91 and he felt that Cecelia Rafferty from Phibsboro should be approached to stand in the Drumcondra Ward. This was not pursued but the lady subsequently ran a very strong campaign in the three-seater in Cabra, finishing only 90 votes behind Jim Mitchell of Fine Gael.

The Whitehall Santry Branch intended to try to have their former member and city councillor Paddy Dunne nominated in an effort to maximise the chance of taking a seat. Dunne had joined Fianna Fail following his defeat in the '85 Local Election. He had suffered personal misfortune due to the closure of Portion (Ross) Foods in Coolock where he was personnel manager and in 1990 his wife Marie died at home following a long illness. She had always been a driving force in his political campaigns and had remained a Labour supporter. Paddy was much liked by his old supporters in the Whitehall Santry branch of the Labour Party and they were keen to assist his political rebirth. In Ballymun, the whole branch was solidly behind Des O'Malley. At that time I felt that I should run in Finglas to take on Proinsias de Rossa's representative, Lucia O'Neill, who had been co-opted onto the council and Pat Carey, the very popular Fianna Fail man who is vice-principal of St Finian's national school in Finglas South. Otherwise, Labour would have no chance of winning a seat in the next general election or so I thought at the time. I considered that running in the Drumcondra end of the constituency would virtually eliminate the possibility of winning in the General Election. I also believed (wrongly) that I would be elected in Finglas. The constituency organisation was discussed with the Labour Party general secretary, Ray Kavanagh, on the 25th February. At about this time, Roisin Shortall contacted both myself and Paddy Donegan and told us that she was interested in standing in the Drumcondra Ward. I had first heard of her in the previous November but other than knowing that she was a Labour supporter from the canvass of her home in Gaeltacht Park with Maura Doolan in 1989, she was an unknown. On making enquiries, it transpired that she had been active as a supporter of Joe Costello for some time in Dublin Central, having been a Party member for about four years. The local elections were fixed for the 27th June and no one could claim that the timing of the election was in any way a surprise.

In the week prior to the selection convention for Drumcondra, Paddy Dunne withdrew his name because he had been made a job offer through the good offices of Vincent Brady, the Government Chief Whip. After contact with Roisin Shortall, Paddy Donegan and I ensured that she was selected without a vote as she had no support within the membership of the constituency. The Finglas ward selection followed. Three branches of four delegates each were eligible to vote – Finglas, Finglas East and Ballygall. The Finglas East branch with its Militant faction would support anyone other than myself. Ballygall included many of my closest supporters and the Finglas branch would also support me, or so I thought.

As no meeting of that branch had taken place, I spoke to Paul Malone by telephone at his workplace at the Ballet factory in the Glasnevin Industrial estate during the afternoon to confirm that he had four delegates. He told me that they would be along to the Finglas Inn that evening with Dan his father, Sylvia Byrne, and Paul Brien as the other Finglas branch delegates and that we would have no trouble handling Pascal O'Reilly, Noel Wheatley and the Milis from Finglas East. We discussed and Paul Malone outruled the possibility of Paul Brien getting up to any tricks that evening. The party general secretary, Raymond Kavanagh, arrived and the convention began with the delegates sitting around a table in the first floor of the recently renovated function room. We got to the number of candidates and Finglas East proposed two. My branch opposed this but much to our amazement Paul Brien spoke in favour. A vote was called and we were beaten seven to five. Sylvia Byrne, vice-chairperson of the Finglas branch leaned over and whispered to me that she had no idea what was going on and that none of this was agreed by the Finglas branch. The general secretary asked me afterwards, while we were downstairs in the bar, exactly what was going on and I told him I was as surprised as he was, considering that the issue had not been discussed at a Finglas branch meeting. Paul Brien later told myself and Gerry Doyle that he had spoken to Pascal O'Reilly to find out what Finglas East had planned. O'Reilly wanted Paul Brien to run as a second candidate but he said that his branch might only accept Paul Malone. Paul Malone apparently agreed to shaft me under pressure from Paul Brien while on his way up the stairs to the selection meeting. Brien was annoyed at the resolution of the 'Gimme dat' shop problem in Finglas Village, a few months earlier and wanted to exact some revenge for a perceived wrong. Paul Malone apparently merely did what he was asked on the night. Ironically, my Ballygall branch and the Finglas branch had agreed that we would support Paul Malone as our candidate at the following local election. Shortly afterwards, the Administrative Council referred the matter to the Party Officers who decided to ratify only one candidate 'in the interests of giving a clear message to the electorate' and that candidate was Bill Tormey. Paul Malone was informed by letter early in March and both he and Paul Brien subsequently boycotted the election and canvassed against the Party. They did not call a Finglas Branch meeting to discuss the situation and never appealed. Res ipse loquitur! Paul Brien later admitted that he would not have been surprised if he had been expelled! We heard of their negative campaign at some doors in Finglas South but we had to ignore it. It was some learning process for me.

Campaign Blueprint

Ruairi Quinn and Denise Rogers produced a generic campaign organisational manual which set out in stages the total organisation of a campaign. It included lists of various officers and organisers at constituency level and their tasks were logically set out. For example, in phase 1, tasks included obtaining the names of key groups such as residents and tenants associations, sports clubs, ladies and youth clubs, general practitioners and establishing the number of voters and housing units. There were check-lists for each phase of a campaign. These were great in theory but required suitable people to carry out the tasks. Unfortunately, we never had sufficient such people within the local organisation to devolve all those jobs.

Social Democracy – Spring for Taoiseach – Charlie in the Park?

There were a number of issues of controversy in early 1991 in which I was able to take a public position. I pointed out in the *Irish Times* that Social Democracy had always been a mainstream element in the Irish Labour Party and that this should not be confused with Liberalism with regard to personal freedoms. In Europe, Labour had joined with the great European Social Democratic Parties in the European Parliament and in the Socialist International. In the European Parliament, Fianna Fail, Fine Gael, and the Progressive Democrats sat with the Gaulist nationalists, the Christian Democrats, and the free market Liberals respectively. I also mentioned that Dick Spring might become Taoiseach, a suggestion that was nearer the bullseye at that time than any of the sceptics thought possible. In defending the decision of President Robinson to appoint her own personally-selected staff at the Aras in the *Irish Press,* I wondered was the political bruhaha about the replacement of Dr Hillery's own household staff politically inspired? I wondered about the Taoiseach, Mr Haughey's, perspective if as reported in the *Press,* he had called to the Aras to discuss this issue in the same week as the opening of his £17 million office refurbishment. The new president had started her term of office very positively and was continuing the good impression of Ireland abroad which the Taoiseach, Charlie Haughey, had succeeded in conveying during his six months presidency of the EC.

Hospital Beds and PESP

In late March, the Minister for Health, Dr Rory O'Hanlon, announced his plan to let patients opt for either public or private health care in public hospitals with separate beds and waiting lists for each under the Programme for Economic and Social Progress. With beds in public hospitals being taken out into the private sector, this plan amounted to a state-subsidised formal queue-skipping mechanism. I commented in the *Irish Independent* that 'the PESP proposal is entirely unethical and will spell disaster for Irish medicine. It will formalise a two-tier service and reward those doctors who have access to beds in private hospitals. The number of people entitled to a free hospital bed will be exactly the same after the extension of entitlement to public treatment as it was before.' This system was really a subterfuge to get the VHI to put more money into public hospitals. As long as medical and scientific research keeps coming up with new improved solutions to individual health problems then patients will demand access to whatever is possible at ever-escalating cost. The question for all health services is who decides how and what to ration? For access to be truly equitable, it must be based on clinical need. But the unanswered question has remained – is the economic value of the patient a value in the quantification of this clinical need? Irish society has tacitly agreed that money should, in fact, count because otherwise the present system would have been rejected years ago. Equality of access is a university debating society issue. It is apparently not applicable to the real world! While medical pay, morale and incentives are interlinked, puncturing pompous pretense is also very necessary but does not make for great popularity with the professional establishment.

The Finglas New Paper

Former *Courier* editor and publisher, Declan Cassidy, returned to Finglas following a one year sojourn in Rhode Island, USA and opened a new weekly local paper at the end of March. I wrote an 'Ask the doc' column, in it answering questions on many subjects. The paper ran until the mid-summer and ironically it was used effectively as an advertising vehicle by FF's Tony Taaffe in the Local Election. Local polls and candidate news were featured during the campaign and all the big parties advertised in it. The paper failed due to undercapitalisation.

Killarney Conference 1991

The Labour Party conference was held in Killarney on 5-7th April at the Great Southern Hotel and was low key compared to Cork and Tralee. There was an outline of our opposition to toll charges on major national roads for the very good reason that it would divert traffic away from the 'pay' routes and thus further erode the already battered county roads system. The composite motion on health recognised the work done by junior doctors in the hospitals but failed to mention consultants (many of whom work very hard and are totally committed to serve all) or the GP's who are the backbone of patient services. The other composite was that the Party should be more vehement in pursuit of a better Health Service for all, incorporating a free and comprehensive health service for those who need it. Did that mean that Labour had in reality abandoned its position of a unitary health service in Ireland. Clearly, yes it did. That left me out on a limb supporting the general ethical trust of the New England Journal of Medicine and not the Labour Party. There was no point in arguing as I was frequently dismissed by many a 'consultant' and, therefore, automatically suspect.

The Oxmantown Branch defined the Labour Party as a party of democratic socialism, a party of a third way between so called 'real socialism' and 'real capitalism', a party committed to bringing the best traditions of the left to the demands of the future. The practical reality of the policy proposals set out in the conference agenda contrasted starkly with many of the loony clichés of Galway, a decade earlier. Meetings about the local election campaign were interesting and the environment policy document alone would have made the trip worthwhile.

A new Party constitution was passed. I had long lobbied for some of the points listed under the sections on Freedom and on Democracy. In particular, 'Labour is committed to the freedom of the individual to pursue his or her own personal goals, and to seek to fulfil his or her potential.' 'To the Labour Party, individual freedom does not equate with an individualism that encroaches on the freedom and rights of others. Labour looks to the individual to contribute to the betterment of society as a member of the community and as a citizen of the state.' 'Democracy means the right of people to participate in the economic decisions affecting their interests at work. Democracy is undermined and weakened by excessive secrecy of government or of the state bureaucracy. Labour stands for freedom of information which is essential to preserve democracy. Labour stands for a high degree of accountability from those in government and from those formulating public policy. Those are many of the fundamentals that I have been pursuing for years.

Dick Spring's speech was again top class. To draw together the ideas within the new constitution and retain the link with the past, he employed the hurler on the ditch technique. An actor was placed in the audience to apparently interrupt his speech with a 'What about the..., etc' spoken with a broad Dublin city accent and dressed as an obvious historical Larkinite. When the interruption happened, I thought 'Oh No! what is that G......ite at and this on live TV!' for a moment until the penny dropped. I thought 'Fergus you old fox, you're at it again.' Anyway it clearly brought the many older members along with the renewal of direction and it was well received.

Another objective was to see Niamh Bhreathnach as Party Chairperson in succession to Mervyn Taylor who was retiring from the position. This would give her a better profile to try to succeed in Blackrock and in Dun Laoghaire.

Family Illness Strikes

My wife, Helen, from whom I was legally separated, phoned having been told that she had a malignant gastric ulcer and that she would need to have her stomach removed. I already knew so I had time to compose myself to try to help her. She was devastated but determined to be as brave as she could. I gave her as much support as possible and she was operated upon almost immediately in St Vincent's Hospital. Politics instantly took a back-seat and I was emotionally far too shocked and preoccupied to feel able to properly organise any campaign. She was discharged from hospital in late May still with recurring pain and discomfort and needing a lot of care and encouragement. Fergus Finlay, a decent human being, wondered whether I should contest the election at all.

May started off badly with Shamrock Rovers losing the Cup Final against Galway United to a late goal by John Glynn which stunned us all. The same John Glynn had played with the Hoops in the last season at Milltown where he was usually No. 12. Rovers played rubbish football with John Devine the only one to show his real class on the day. The numbed silence in the dressing-room below the stand after the game was nearly palpable. Some of the players were in tears and most of the others were pale and drawn. Manager, Noel King, was absolutely disgusted mostly because the team froze on the day. The Harp Lager reception before the game was one farcical episode as far as I was concerned. I came along with an invitation as a director of a participating club and was told by Donie Butler of the FAI that I could not go into the reception area because I had my thirteen-year-old son with me, dressed in Rovers replica gear complete with scarf and hat. I was incredulous and despite my remonstrations he said that these were the rules. It was a pity that the club was not informed of these restrictions before the game as we would have organised our own reception for Rovers people because we are a family club. As it was, I handed Butler the gilted reception invitation and recommended that he should stick it somewhere uncomfortable! Some hooligan so-called Rovers fans tried to cause trouble later in the evening outside the Horse Show House in Ballsbridge. So all in all, a very unsatisfactory day.

Cricket or Racing or 'Fast Forward Fine Gael'

These were the TV choices on a Saturday afternoon. Having a vested interest, I watched Fine Gael and leaving aside Twink's warm-up, the parade of recitations by the FG front-bench was cringingly embarrassing, an adult version of the 'School around the Corner' without the innocence. The *Irish Press* published my comments on 29th May.

'Highlighting the unemployment crisis and its effects on the whole social fabric by John Bruton was entirely valid, but other than a reference to the reform of the mechanics of employment, detailed solutions were simply not on offer. There was no comment on the validity of market mechanisms on job creation, no comment on the forthcoming impact on jobs of the single European market, no comment on the role of state enterprise on job creation, no comments on the effects of privatisations on jobs, no comment on tax policy which subsidises capital and relatively penalises labour, no comment on the effects of our awful transport systems on jobs, no comment on the reform of CAP on jobs, no comment on the effects of overflying Shannon on Mid-West jobs or on the overall effect of losses in the west against gains in the east etc. His attempt to wrestle the Leadership of the Opposition to the FF/PD coalition from Dick Spring has failed.'

Going in two opposing directions simultaneously may lead to dismemberment. This dangerous political disease may be caused by the leader of a self-confessed conservative party which sits with the Christian Democrats in Europe, while claiming to be a social democratic party at home trying to be everything yet nothing.

Dublin Locals Campaign Launched

The Labour Party local election campaign in Dublin was launched at a post-breakfast reception at Bewley's in Grafton St, Dublin on the 27th of May, a whole month before polling day. Photographs of candidates preening outside on the balcony were taken and some candidates of both sexes used their elbows liberally in an attempt to get themselves into the picture. It was all a little absurd. Nomination papers were handed in to City Manager, Frank Feely at City Hall that morning. What efficiency!

Dublin – A City that Works

The policy document on 'Dublin, a city that works' was a notably good effort which if implemented would transform life for most people in the city. The extension of local democracy was the main thrust, and empowering people in their own lives is sorely needed in this country. It never ceases to surprise me that people are often intimidated by 'the establishment' in their jobs in both the public and the private sector. Speaking out on issues is something to be suppressed in this country. The general lack of 'bottle' is very common in my experience. Establishments, medical and otherwise never like the simple question, Why? The public transport proposals to increase the speed, frequency and diversity of bus services and reduce the price was certainly worth implementing. Ken Livingstone's Greater London Council experience in public transport should be repeated here. The proposal to improve and develop the rail system is now almost received wisdom. There was one mad suggestion in the brochure which was to encourage car pooling by restriction of car registrations crossing the canals at peak hours. The mind boggles at that recipe for chaos and further inefficiency. There were also the usual clichés on crime prevention including 'an offensive against drugs', whatever that means! There was nothing about decriminalisation or taking note of the widening agreement within European police forces that maybe control by legalisation has a certain validity. Legalising cannabis smoking would not be a great vote-catcher even if it is the correct policy. Why should society recognise that people wish to seek comfort in alcohol and then tax their pleasure yet ban and criminalise a different tranquilliser like cannabis? If profits were removed from drug-taking then criminals would seek fresher pastures and also street crime related to addiction would also fall. Drug pushers were and are a menace to the community and current policies merely seek to contain the problem.

On the following week, I made a brief appearance on 'Today Tonight' when interviewed by Shane McElhatton about the VHI. Standard head portrait posters 25 x 18 ins were ordered and 2,000 were printed. Peter O'Reilly and I started postering on the June Public Holiday Monday and two days later, on 5th June, Labour's national campaign was officially launched by Dick Spring and Ruairi Quinn at the Shelbourne Hotel, an interesting choice considering the industrial relations disputes there between the ITGWU and Trust Houses Forte in the late '80s. The national manifesto 'A community that works' was comprehensive enough for a general election. It allowed for local authorities to raise revenue provided the local communities gave approval in a local referendum. Direct questions on local issues were also to be put to the people. Planning changes are an obvious example and, to date, there is no sign that the people will be directly consulted anywhere in the country.

Finglas

There was plenty of rain throughout the campaign and, much to our annoyance, our posters were virtually soluble in water. They quickly shrivelled up and fell or were blown down. They were also quite unsightly in their limp condition. The posters were a disaster but we were not in a position to do very much about it. I could only curse myself for not going big as intended after the Lenihan example in the Presidential Election. Meanwhile, Derek McDowell in the Artane Ward had organised the large 'Brian Lenihan' size posters. They were so striking and were a reminder of my own inefficiency and disorganisation at that particular time. The party headquarters did produce a very large poster about 7 ft by 5 ft with the Halfpenny Bridge in the background. The candidates name was pasted onto the centre. We erected eight near the top of Ballygall Road West/Glasanaon Road junction on both corners, conveniently placed in Derek Fairbrother's house and across the road in his cousins. It was a hell of a difficult job done mostly by the Ballymun Branchmen Frank Rock, Joe Doyle and Paddy Dunbar. The poster hoardings were like the rigid and fixed sails on Chinese Junks so when the June winds blew, off they went. Only a single pair lasted a week. So recognising futility, we gave up on them.

Barney Rock and Fine Gael

The intervention of Barney Rock for the PD's was a serious blow to us especially as his campaign was well funded and he was well supported by his Dublin Gaelic Football team-mates. Mary Flaherty again defied local cognoscenti who predicted her political demise. On this occasion, I thought that they might just be right but she concentrated her effort on Finglas East and retained her seat relatively easily. Miriam Wilson, a pleasant local girl, was Mary's running mate but found it difficult to struggle against the tide on her first outing. Despite the handicap of living in Rathmines, Mary Flaherty has become the 'young' old dog for the hard road. She is 'effective' at the doorsteps with all that that entails in politics. There is a residual solid silent Fine Gael conservative vote which other parties do not find even on canvass but who come out and unfailingly do the business for Mary time after time. Astonishingly, Fine Gael at 1,486 first preferences and Fianna Fail at 5,105 votes were almost identical to their previous totals in the local elections in 1985. The Fianna Fail vote was only -8 and Fine Gael was -7 on their 1985 aggregates. However, the Labour vote was + 2.4% on the combined three candidate '85 total which was a great disappointment because it was not quite good enough. Barney Rock's strong performance winning 940 first preference votes for the PD's was not surprising and if he had run for Fianna Fail, I am certain he would have been in the winners enclosure. The drawn Dublin-Meath games at Croke Park propelled him forward because public interest in the matches in the Finglas area was enormous. The valid poll was 47.07% compared to 43.17% in 1985, probably due to the presence of Barney Rock and the expensive competitive and frenetic Fianna Fail campaigns.

Fianna Fail

Fianna Fail ran four candidates and each ran a separate campaign. Taaffe, Carey and Grant appeared to be very well funded with the fourth man Noel Cloake left to flounder in their financial wake. Noel Cloake is a native of Cabra and has been living in Finglas for 30 years. He is a bubbly, dapper character always most courteous with neat backcombed grey hair who struts around in a purposeful manner and prides himself in being the Runai of the Kildonan Cumann FF, a fact always appended to his Christmas cards. He worked for the homeless in Threshold in Church St for many years and knew Eithne FitzGerald there. Cloaker knows his way around the administrative system well. He is a 'Charlie' supporter and is himself supported by Kevin Kenny, a well-known taximan from Welmount Road, who operates from the rank in Finglas village. Kevin has his extended family living in the 'West' and has a good ear for local happenings. He's also a friend of mine which can prove very useful for the odd bits of local information and 'tittle tattle'.

Pat Grant worked locally in FAS in Jamestown Road and was chairman of the Finglas Barn Church Restoration Committee, succeeding myself in that role. He is a quiet spoken conservative Donegal man living in the Glenhill estate across the Finglas Road from the redeveloped Janelle site where he is a near neighbour of the Green Party candidate, another schoolteacher Aiden Meagher. Grant had cavalcades of 4-wheel drive landcruisers blaring his name everywhere and he handed out free lollypops, hats, personalised books of matches and other gimmicks for kids to all and sundry. For the final weekend, Pat arranged a motorcycle parade all around Finglas with six specially-painted bikes followed by four white jeeps plastered with advertising and then a forty-foot flat bodied truck with a rock band. The cast and equipment for this stunt was all hired out and must have cost a right few grand. I was told by some friends in Fianna Fail that a quick look at those actors would suggest that they were unlikely to hold Equity cards! Pat Grant's son owned a shop in Rivermount, in Finglas South and he and his troops of friends both paid and voluntarily hyped the Grant Campaign with bodies on the ground, handouts, hoardings, noisy loud speakers and tapes.

Pat Carey had an exclusive edition of a local tabloid newspaper running to 8 pages entitled 'Pat Carey, councillor' dropped into every household within two days of polling, announcing grants for 75 sports clubs in Finglas from the Sports Advisory Council of the VEC. He also claimed to have 'presided' over the dishing out of lottery grants to about 40 other local organisations including Art groups, youth clubs, boy scout troops, down to 'the Finglas Fun Club'. There were pages of pictures of Carey with Jack Charlton, Nelson Mandela, Pope John Paul II, Charlie Haughey and another with President Mary Robinson. In case you missed any of those, Carey had a picture of himself with Mick McCarthy, Chris Morris and Chris Hughton so that the soccer World Cup also served its more useful local purpose! This operation was reputed to have cost his campaign more than £6,000. I freely admit to having been stunned when I saw the paper. Carey gave the impression that he would have no trouble leaving Jimmy Saville in the halfpenny place. Jim wouldn't be needed to fix it, Pat Carey would have done it already. This coup was organised by Brian Browning, a local publicist who many reckoned had political ambitions himself. He was well known for being the M.C. for many 'Race Nights' in pubs in Finglas and he had business connections in Dublin with Ronnie Whelan Junior. Browning is a larger than life, loud, good humoured character with a lot of entrepreneurial talent. He was credited, whether true or not, with having effectively decided who would appear on the Bibi Baskin TV Show talking about the Finglas Festival. He was 'Lord Mayor of Finglas' for one year and gloried in the experience. Swarthy with side combed dark hair, Brian Browning was a kind of Finglas Gerry Ryan with no shortage of self-confidence. Two years later, I was amazed to meet him at a League of Ireland Council Meeting in Merrion Square where he represented Drogheda United for a short time as he was Chairman of the club for a number of months. Brian certainly added colour to the village scene.

Tony Taaffe is a solicitor with offices in Finglas Village. He had been co-opted onto the City Council as a replacement for Jim Tunney who had resigned in the spring. Ironically, Taaffe failed to secure a nomination to stand for Fianna Fail at their convention for the local election despite having won the co-option some days earlier. He was supported by Jim Tunney and he seemed to have had a literature drop into each door every four days. No expense was spared with full-colour printing on glossy art paper featuring the Taaffe family in a tasteful portrait. Taaffe's public support for the police in relation to the 'Fairbrother Case' was noted by John Grundy in a letter to the *Finglas New Paper* in April. Otherwise his degree of political conservatism was unknown to the public at that time. For the Fianna Fail candidates to have the manpower for four separate campaigns was truly astonishing but their tactics were fully vindicated when they held their two seats and kept their vote at its 1987 high, despite being in government. Literature from 16 separate candidates was flying through letter boxes for the best part of four weeks. Taaffe alone is reputed to have had thirteen leaflets printed, four of which were in full colour. To cover the Finglas area, it is understood to have cost about £800 for each leaflet drop. Some of the voters understandably complained that they felt like taking to the hills to escape from politicians until the election was over.

Local Issues

We delivered four leaflet drops to each house, one per week for the four weeks duration and John Grundy helped out again. We had also dropped another election address type leaflet in April. The main issue was undoubtedly unemployment which had risen by 32,000 to about 19.7% of the labour force during the preceding year and was causing hardship right across the board.

The other big issue was the 6,000 on the housing lists due to a virtual cessation of local authority house building by Dublin Corporation since the return to office of Fianna Fail in 1987. The Corporation had built only 6 houses in 1989 and 35 in 1990. The demand for housing of any description in Finglas was huge with about 68 or more points necessary for placement into any vacancies which could arise. Single girls with babies, and young families were living in one room in their parents' homes often with the sitting-room turned into a bedroom at night. The worst aspect of the problem was that some candidates were promising these unfortunates that if they voted for them, they would get them a maisonette or a house. The tenant purchase scheme for council houses was a virtual give-away of the public housing stock. But it also created problems for people who bought their homes when the buildings were in need of repair and they then found that they could not afford the cost. The corporation trade-off was a saving on the maintenance costs caused by long-term neglect of their buildings against the give-away price. If houses were to be sold, then, the price should have been more realistic and the proceeds used to house those on the long waiting list. Selling rented council property to tenants who cannot afford their upkeep only creates other problems. The other argument for better social cohesion when people have a stake in their own area is perfectly valid but there has to be a sensible balance. In March 1990, the National Campaign for the Homeless and the Combat Poverty Agency produced a small compendium of four papers given at a conference 'Housing: Moving into Crisis?' on December 9th, 1988 which analysed the problems and foresaw the consequences of inaction. Facts and figures on homelessness, travellers, policy on integration and settlement strategy and the law were outlined and the papers were well referenced. Eithne FitzGerald, Mary Daly, Patricia Kelleher and Des Curley contributed and they should profitably be read by all politicians.

Crime and vandalism was a daily problem for many. Local youths often terrorised families by throwing rocks through windows and burning stolen cars in the street. Cars were often damaged in retaliation for objecting to hooliganism. Some areas around Barnamore and Kippure Park were no peaceful restplaces for their residents. A very large moat would have been necessary for many people to experience the old cliché that 'a man's home is his castle'. Examples come quickly to mind. One family living at the bottom of a steep incline with only a footpath leading to their front gate had the experience of a stolen car flying down the pathway and ramming into the side wall of their house. It was sheer luck that the vehicle did not arrive straight into the living room through the large picture window. Other people had stolen cars set ablaze outside their gates in the early hours of the morning when it was well known that only one mobile police patrol was available to cover the whole of the Finglas area at night. A supermarket manager living in a private house in the area had to receive time off work because his wife was too frightened to stay at home with her young babies during the day due to threats of burglary and arson. There was an estate agents 'For Sale' board in his garden and he likened a prospective move to an escape from prison. He showed me letters from his employer warning him against taking any more time off work. He was really desperate by being torn in two directions simultaneously. There was a widespread demand for a change in the system of justice to end the revolving door of arrest and release despite conviction and many victims felt that the wreckers must be made pay for their actions. Underage drinking and cider parties in parks and open spaces have often led to late-night brawling and general trouble for passers-by. Many parents and old people were very worried and frightened about the lawlessness of this type of behaviour and wanted something done about it.

Drug pushing along the park at St Helena's culvert was also an issue of great concern to parents in the houses facing the action. Some local Sinn Feiners had taken an active interest in the problem for some time but the dealing continued. More than a decade after the estate was built in Valeview, some rows of terraced houses had only a tar cum loose gravel footpath outside their front doors. The road space consisted of a steeply inclined, often garbage-strewn grassy bank which emptied rainwater onto the pathways causing persistent flooding. Obviously, a definite resolution to these problems was promised by virtually every candidate at every election but there certainly was no follow-up. More promises, promises! Such contempt for the ordinary decent citizen from the local authority speaks volumes for the general attitude to the people in the area. Cynicism breeds cynicism. Had I been elected, I would have given the resolution of the problems of Finglas South absolute priority as I was so moved by the daily plight of so many.

There was also a big demand for an extension of the gas grid to include every house in the Finglas area and we were very much in favour of the explosion in adult education courses organised by Mr Silk in Colaiste Ide on Cardiffsbridge Road. Because Finglas was built up from a rural village in the late1940s and early '50s, many families were now caring for disabled relatives at home and felt very angry that the £45 per week 'carers' allowance' was a sham because only about 1 in 8 of those involved qualified for payments. We also highlighted the issue of the lack of respite beds for dependent relatives which put huge strains on households, usually married daughters. Action from the Health Board, not merely sympathetic publicity on RTE radio programmes, was what was needed.

The whole village in Finglas is proud of the care and respect for the elderly which we all tried to foster. Fundraising for outings and special occasions goes on continually. The efforts of Betty Maher, Kathleen Staunton and their friends at Mellowes Court and at the Drake Inn, Cyril Chaney, Liam Brien, Sylvie Byrne, George Keogh, Molly Spence and a host of others have been examples to all of what could be done. Paddy McKiernan, the publican, must be acknowledged for his support. We have always supported formal funding for groups helping the isolated in the area.

The extension of democracy and local responsibility was also supported when we called for a directly-elected town council in both Finglas and Ballymun. These bodies should be set up under the Corporation's umbrella and would serve very useful local purposes. We wanted Light Rail for Finglas and late night buses on the hour with security for the drivers. We were also opposed to the introduction of timed local telephone call charges because of the important social uses of modern communications.

The plight of approximately 400 homeless children in the city was also highlighted and we supported Fr Peter McVerry's efforts on their behalf in Ballymun, both locally and in the Dublin newspapers. I was aware from eyewitness evidence by Gerard Dowler, a resident of McDonagh Tower in Ballymun Town Centre, that there were allegations of harassment of some of the kids of families resident in the Towers by some wild youths reputedly staying at Fr McVerry's hostel flat. Other claims of active use of condoms, etc., in the stairways were also made. Supervision of the flat was not what it should have been. One problem that was obvious to me was that Fr McVerry, in his zeal for reform of the system and for immediate action, was impatient to say the least with residents and others who might raise any questions which he regarded as obstacles to his particular solution whether in Ballymun or in Whitworth Road, Drumcondra. We publicly suggested that each child should be professionally assessed and psychiatric and psychological disturbances identified and appropriately addressed. Otherwise merely providing a short-term roof over children's heads would prove futile.

The Dunsink Dump is always a source of local controversy. In the Valley Park district near the tiphead, a number of residents were known to have cancer and some had died while very young. There was a suspicion with some which turned into a belief with others that the cancers were connected to their proximity to the dump. This was also a concern in the Abbotstown and Ratoath area. However, when it was clear that the cancers were widely different in their type and site, I told some of the residents quite frankly that it was most unlikely but not impossible that the dump was at fault in this instance. That opinion was not what some people wanted to hear because many people do not like their pet theories questioned or refuted. Lying for votes has never been my way and giving a grossly misleading opinion purely to ingratiate yourself with the voter is simply wrong. The following day John Grundy phoned me to tell me in no uncertain terms that I was an idiot for saying what I had about the dump as a cancer risk in the area and that I had lost a lot of votes as a consequence. He had got an earful from some locals who felt I was covering up for the Corporation and that I did not care because I lived east of the village. With some, you just cannot win!

Our campaign director was Liam Pike who works in RTE in production which frequently took him away on location with 'Glenroe' to exotic locations in Wicklow. Liam organised the canvass of Finglas East with the help of his wife Katie, Odran Reid, Louise McKeever, Frank Lynch, Geraldine Holihan and others. The Finglas East branch moved to the other ward primarily to help Roisin Shortall. Des O'Malley was told by me to concentrate his efforts on Ballymun where Joe Doyle, Frank Rock, Helen Fields Molloy, Paddy Dunbar, the Costellos and Gerry McCarthy were his main helpers.

The Finglas strategy was crucially wrong in deciding on a detailed canvass and follow-up of every house in Finglas South because we thought that this was an opportunity to establish a vote where Proinsias deRossa had cleaned up in the '89 General and European Elections. We knew that local schoolteacher, Pat Carey, was personally popular there but we totally underestimated the extent of his electoral strength which was largely independent of his party. The other factor which was a real bugbear was the persistence of a low voter turn-out at around 40-42% in the general Finglas South area. This contrasted with the higher turnout of around 47% in the wealthier areas in Finglas East.

Going door to door in the Wellmount district on warm, bright, sunny evenings was a real pleasure. Many people were basking outside in the late evening sunshine and were happy to talk and give their verdict on the world at large. With Helen and George Metcalfe, Gerry Doyle, Tommy Dunne and Jimmy Somers both SIPTU officials, Bill Hughes from Clonsilla, Andy Earley, and Paul Norton all regularly appearing for action, the campaign was very pleasant. Jimmy mentioned me over to his car boot one evening and handed me a gift wrapped red SIPTU tie which I was very pleased to accept. Wear the tie at any meeting with Paddy Donegan or Tom Dunne and they cannot resist making a smart comment. Billy Attlee asked me more than once at the RDS where did I get the tie? Somers, guilty again! I have noticed since the OBU became a reality that union officials pay (or should it now be a remuneration package) always gets a few snide sideswipes from permanent officials current or retired, when a few pints have been lowered particularly after funerals. The current lot are never a patch on Larkin or Connolly or Fintan Kennedy or Ruairi Roberts or whoever, all the way up to Mickey Mullen. I have always had a lot of time for John Carroll myself. The late Michael Mullen would have been very pleased to have completed the merger with the FWUI. He certainly told me in his own imposing flag-draped office on the top floor of Liberty Hall that such was his ambition. The view in the summer from that office is magnificent especially looking downriver when the weather is clear and the sun is sinking in the west — the Miranda Guinness, the Lady Patricia, the East Link Bridge and on out to the Poolbeg. We also received help when they were available from Reggie Moore, Dick Slevin, Gerry Juhel, Tom Lynch, Alan Talbot, Frank Lynch, Geraldine Houlihan, Bridie O'Reilly, Sylvia Byrne, John Elliot, Lorraine Curtis, Willie and Pat Kelly, Gerry and Betty Maher and a number of others. Compared to ten years earlier, the population in Finglas West has aged and many of their children have married or emigrated and moved away. The whole area is much quieter and there is far less vandalism. This was in contrast to the crowds of children and barking dogs in Finglas South and Ballygall. Dog bites were a real hazard on the hustings as was the risk of vandalism to cars.

Having Andy Earley, Bill Hughes and Paul Norton available in the afternoons was a godsend because it made canvassing so much easier. Lack of manpower can be demoralising to the psyche. I have been out canvassing and postering alone on many occasions in the past and it can be a bit tedious even to the dedicated and determined.

On Saturday the 20th, Barry Desmond brought his Eurobus to the Janelle Shopping Centre and around to Finglas village, all decked out in posters, blaring the appropriate message about our wonderful candidate to all and sundry. He provided a few thousand canvass cards with a Barry Desmond and candidate joint photo which we used in the area east of the Finglas Road immediately. I was still getting some flak over the Fairbrothers when canvassing people who happened to be members of the Gardai living in Cremore and in Finglas East.

We were lured into a false sense of security when a poll in the local *Finglas New Paper* with one week to polling day showed Carey heading the list on 25% with us second on 14%. Liam Pike, however, kept insisting that we would be lucky to get the bottom seat and he was so right. We ran a final handout urging people to 'Join the dramatic swing to your Labour candidate, Finglas is voting Labour!' That swing announcement was unfortunately for me just one election too early.

By the last week of June, the voters were becoming battle weary, listening to a constant barrage of vote for Zig or Zag in language varying from a polite request to a military order. Canvassers reported all sorts of amusing anecdotes. Comments like 'Jayzas missas, lets hoied, here's more a dem bloody politicians... chancers! Ye never see dem except in elections! etc ' were commonplace. The Drake Inn cynics were saying that the handiest way for Finglas to avoid five years of leaflet overload and letter box fatigue was to elect two Fianna Failers who live in County Meath and a Fine Gaeler living in Rathmines, all of whom presumably would go home sometimes!

Another night, while we were having a few drinks in the Willows Pub on Sycamore Road after canvassing, Paschal O'Reilly came over to tell us that Roisin Shortall was a certainty and that I might come unstuck or so he hoped. I had heard from David Costello that the Shortall campaign was like an efficient military operation and that she was going to do well, this information came as no surprise. Also Des O'Malley was forever phoning me complaining about Shortall ignoring him as a Labour candidate, another sure sign of her efforts.

Polling day on the 27th June was the last occasion for the voter gauntlet outside each polling station. Barry Road polling station was in St Joseph's National School . There were seven-feet-high railings along both sides of the road and these were solidly festooned with posters of every political persuasion. The lamp-posts were also chock-a-block and there was no mistaking the site of the action. To confuse the issue, the entrance to the school across the street was postered by candidates for the North county area for which this was a small polling station. I spent a large part of the day along this road with Proinsias de Rossa and his main men Brian Whelan, Tommy and Aiden Hughes, Jim Tunney and John Costello acting for Taaffe, Dermot Flynn from Mellowes Road an ever-present stalwart gentleman for Fine Gael, others for Harry Fleming of Sinn Fein and Barney Rock of the PD's, Kevin Kenny, Maura and Jimmy Monahan for Noel Cloake, Pat Carey and Pat Grant had two personal supporters each, and James Freeman was pushing the whole FF Ticket. I was also helped at various times by Tommy Dunne, Gerry and Betty Maher and by a few lads like Sean Fannin and his pals, well known for downing a few pints in the Drake Inn. This was a hell of a gauntlet for the average voter to face. Bits of paper with Vote No. 1 and a name with or without a photograph were pressed into the palms of as many as possible accompanied by a curt exhortation for Pat Carey or Mary Flaherty or Lucy O' Neill, etc. This was often responded to by determined nods of Yes! or a lowering of the eye line and a shrug of the shoulders or a comment 'You'll be all right there Frank, Bill, or whoever'. There was a long pathway up to the school door and some canvassers were chasing voters nearly into the building. The duty police had to ask them to cool it at times and when I complained to the Gardai about voter harassment, the comments from some WP people were not very friendly. All of this street theatre must have looked quite hilarious to any visitor from Mars. It probably resembled the parallelogram in Croke Park with the ball on the way – all elbows, shoving and shouting. We always had a manpower shortage to cover all of the polling booth gates for the whole day. Often because organised reliefs did not arrive in time or when the poll was low people simply became bored and drifted away for a while either home or to a local pub for a battery recharge. How important all of this effort really was, is impossible to guess but if one party does it, we all must follow suit. However, Barry Road was in a gauntlet class out on its own in North-West. There were about 5,400 voters registered there and the turnout was usually about 42% in Locals. The tallies showed that Fianna Fail, de Rossa, Labour, and Sinn Fein got a good vote there. I knew that we would be in trouble at the count on the following day because of the low number of people approaching the Barry school gateway from the Finglas village side where our tallied vote at previous elections was quite good. This was in contrast to the consistent arrival of voters from the Barry and Plunkett areas to the north and west where the Workers Party and Pat Carey of Fianna Fail had good pockets of support. Pat Carey had found particular favour through an association with Northway Rangers Schoolboy Football Club and through clever use of his council position to steer lottery money in the right direction. Mary McDermott was a popular local personality and a key person to target because she was chairperson of the Northway Estate Residents Association and was co-ordinator of the Arts in the Finglas library building. She was featured in the Carey paper at just the right time to maximise the impact. Proinsias de Rossa gave the impression of supreme confidence in the re-election of Lucia O'Neill and even he must have been surprised at the count when the 68% transfer of votes from Sam Jordan the second Workers Party candidate, a taxi driver from Berryfield, Finglas South was needed to secure her election.

The Count

The count in Bolton Street was interesting and tense. I polled about 300 votes less than expected given all the circumstances. We did not anticipate the enormous Pat Carey success even though we knew he was certain to poll very well. In casual conversation with Bertie Ahern during the morning, he indicated that he would not be surprised to find himself in coalition with the Labour Party nationally – very prescient of him. Later in the morning, I met Eamonn O'Brien who felt that he was in for a real battle with Labour's Des O'Malley in the Drumcondra five seater. Pat McCartan of the Workers Party looked pale and drawn. He was an excellent TD yet he was very worried when I met him; he succeeded in retaining his seat in the end.

Liam Pyke, Odran Reid and I sat out the transfer of votes knowing the inevitable but hoping against hope for an electoral reprieve which never came. Jim O'Higgins from Fine Gael wanted to talk but I was quite unable for polite conversation. Choked you could say. I was to say the least very disappointed. Before the final distribution began, I left Bolton Street College and walked over to the King's Inn pub with Gerry Doyle. I congratulated Roisin Shortall and her people were jubilant. That was the beginning of my end in the Labour Party even though I did not yet realise it. We were wrongly congratulated on winning by a number of Labour members from other constituencies because I was presumed to be a certainty to win. Well, that made the evening even harder so I went off home alone. Gerry Doyle stayed to hear some of Ruairi Quinn's comments to his entourage in the pub. Ho Chi was out of the traps head hunting. What a Jack Russell!

13
NEVER GIVE A SUCKER AN EVEN BREAK – A LESSON IN DESELECTION

The Locals in Dublin

In the June '91 local elections, Labour in Dublin City did very well and recovered the huge losses suffered in 1985 increasing from two to ten seats. The Labour proportion of the quota varied from 0.29 for Cecelia Larkin in Cabra to 0.93 for Michael Conaghan in Ballyfermot. From 0.4 to 0.6 of a quota included Derek McDowell, Des O'Malley, Tormey, Joe Costello, Mary Freehill, Dermot Lacey, Paddy Burke, and Tommy Broughan. Michael Conaghan, Sean Kenny, Joe Connolly and Ruairi Quinn did even better. However, no Labour candidate reached a quota on the first count. Thus, with local factors considered, it was a fairly even performance across the city and was very encouraging for the future.

CAP Tax and Smokes

EC tax harmonisation has been used as a reason not to increase the tax on the old reliables. These two habits are the countries main addictions and should be discouraged by the government. The relationship between price and consumption is well known and I had hoped that the minister would seek a derogation from EC tax harmonisation law, hit them in the budget and target the money into community care. The Community spends £7.3 million (11 million ECU's) on its anti-smoking campaign. This may seem impressive but smoking is said to kill 400,000 Europeans per year. Despite this, the Common Agricultural Policy supports tobacco farming in disadvantaged areas, particularly in France and in Italy with subsidies totalling about £950 million. In relation to the area being cultivated, tobacco is Europe's most heavily subsidised crop. Ironically, demand for dark European tobacco has fallen while the popularity of the light Virginia type has increased and the EC has become the world's largest importer of tobacco.

In the *Irish Times* on November 13th, I wrote that 'Commissioner McSharry's CAP reform should include the staged abolition of the tobacco subsidy. The money saved would be better spent on income support and retirement pensions for tobacco growers. The EC must stop subsidising this industry.'

Gay Rights

In November, Odran Reid wrote as PRO of the Finglas Branch of the Labour Party to the *Evening Herald* in support of legislative change in the treatment of homosexuality to comply with the ruling from the European Court regarding the Norris case. He was attacked by a correspondent who suggested that homosexuality was a curable disease and referenced Liz Noonan's vote as a reflection of the public view of lesbianism. In a reply in the *Evening Herald*, I pointed out that the electoral performance of Liz Noonan in Dublin South-East in 1982 could in no way be considered a referendum on support for homosexuality. I do not believe that it is the business of the state to interfere with adult relationships. Before someone shouts HIV/AIDS, heterosexual HIV transmission in the severely affected areas of Central Africa is the real problem. It is dangerous nonsense to equate HIV infection with homosexuality. Decriminalisation of homosexuality is different from encouragement. I wondered did the attitude of Mr Tunney represent the only Fianna Fail view on the issue? Some of the actions of left-wing councils in England in relation to gay rights were obviously an over-reaction which I do not condone and have no relevance to changes in Irish law. Homosexuality could be considered to be simply one end of the normal spectrum of human responses.

The General Medical Services Contract Row

The GMS capitation scheme was introduced in 1989 and was underfunded from the start. Despite the department's claims that the contract was attractive for the GP's because there were new conditions for holiday locums, study and maternity leave, pensions, practice nurses, etc., the truth was that the capitation rates agreed were inadequate. The GP's decided that they would possibly withdraw from the scheme in April '92 as a form of protest. Their Irish Medical Organisation representative said on television that they would continue to see their publicly-funded patients who could pay them and claim back the money from the health boards.

In a letter to the *Irish Times* 'I was agog at such ignorance. Doctors should have been aware that people are only eligible for Medical cards because of their very low incomes and as such could clearly ill-afford GP fees, however reasonable. The GMS payments were less than half the economic rate but effective patient bullying seemed to me, unethical.

The threat, if it was not idle, must be a source of real anxiety to many. While doctors have no obligation to work for nothing, each is ethically bound to offer the best treatment possible to each patient. It was the government and the tax-payer who must be convinced of the validity of the GP's claim, not the GMS patient who is the most vulnerable figure in the whole wrangle. Patients are also voters and should be mobilised to lobby politicians on the issue and should certainly not be abused. I opposed the withdrawal of services by doctors in any dispute with third party payers'. The following day after this appeared in the *Irish Times*, Catherine Monahan of LMFM radio from Drogheda interviewed me on the GP's threat and I ran through the arguments.

Within two days, Drs Tony Feeney of Lucan and Owen Fagan of Mullingar had replies published in the Letters column. Tony Feeney made the valid point that if the government was forcing him to discriminate between GMS and private patients because it was not possible to fund his practice from the low receipts in the public sector then he saw it as his duty to withdraw. This is, in my view, a wholly honourable position and he gave examples of the relative cost of procedures in primary care as against the same procedure, i.e. removal of moles carried out in hospital. There is one catch there, if the mole was malignant then the degree of recommended excision depends on the depth of the mole's invasion of the skin and underlying tissue. He claimed that we had a first-world hospital service but a third world community care system. That was a gross exaggeration.

Dr Fagan agreed with most of the points I had made and went on to state that 'realistically it seems very unlikely that, while the service continues to be provided in a satisfactory manner, any improvement will be made in the GPs' conditions of employment'. Therein lies the rub. It is clear that some doctors consider themselves in the employment of the state whereas I consider doctors are retained by patients for professional services. The patients either pay directly or through a third party. These two positions are fundamentally different and lead to a different attitude in dealing with third party payers such as the GMS Payments Board and the VHI.

Dr Kieran Gaine who was in my year in UCD Medical School, also weighed in from Mullingar. He claimed that following the GP withdrawal from the GMS that 'No patient will go untreated and uncared for, irrespective of means'. Dr Feeney again retorted in the same forum and pointed out that the debate had gone on for five or six years. Both he and Dr Gaine suggested that my attitude was coloured because I might be looking for votes.

I replied again through the *Irish Times* that in pursuing the GP's pay claim, 'the IMO GP group announced its intention to withdraw from the General Medical Services and to charge GMS patients for services that the GP's would no longer be contracted to provide. The GMS patients could then claim a refund from the health boards. At present, the health boards take between five and nine months to pay for contracted services.

The GPs' proposed resignation seems simple in theory but in practice the following may happen. The GMS patients are unlikely to be able to afford to pay but may choose to forego other commitments to pay the doctor directly or the doctor may hand them a bill which they may then present to the health board for payment. Would the health boards be obliged to pay any doctor not currently under contract and at the private consultation rate? This rate varies from place to place. Direct refunds to patients may be impossible due to retention tax law. Some patients may have to go to the Community Welfare Officer to seek assistance which is discretionary. Of course, GMS prescriptions could no longer be used, therefore local pharmacists would have to be paid for filling private prescriptions. Again with what? Under the 1970 Health Act, the Department must provide a service including pharmacy services. How would this be done? So how would the poor patient, in the middle of all this chaos, simply cope? Another problem might arise if the GP's were asked to leave publicly -owned dispensary premises.

The Health Act 1970 abolished the 120-year-old dispensary system and replaced it with the GMS choice of doctor scheme, with the declared intention of ensuring that no distinction would be made between public and private patients. However, I, like Dr Arnold Relman former editor of the New England Journal of Medicine, believe that doctors, whether salaried or not must first of all be advocates for all their patients. A comprehensive service for all is the only means by which doctors can demonstrate that the welfare of all their patients is of equal concern. I do not consider the withdrawal of services on financial grounds appropriate to professional medical behaviour and last summer in the *Irish Times* (July 30th, page 10) I pointed out the inevitability of conflict between doctors and patients on the one hand and administrators acting for Government on the other as long as resources are inadequate to meet patients' medical needs.

In her book '*Health, Medicine and Politics in Ireland 1900-1970*' (p.283), Ruth Barrington commented that 'this role of the state as the sole mediator in Ireland between doctor and patient may have contributed to the particular vehemence of the struggle between successive governments and the profession over extending entitlement to free medical treatment'. Doctors must never act against their patients' interests and should never allow the above assertion to become a reality. Honest and open public debate may convince the public of the validity of the GPs' case but an ill-conceived and messy withdrawal of services will certainly fail. Remember, patients have votes, as was shown to some effect in Roscommon in the last general election'.

Dr Feeney was quite indignant and in a further comment announced the closure of correspondence on the grounds that I was a full-time consultant earning a very large salary by any standard. This was another assumption on his part as I had a principled objection to the new 'Common Contract' and had not signed it. However, I finished by suggesting ways that the GP's could get politicians to negotiate. The British Medical Association has used poster campaigns in surgery waiting rooms when in conflict with central government and there are other ways also which involve snarling up the administrative system. A key reason for the formation of the Irish Hospital Consultants Association was the realisation that consultants could not ethically withdraw services from patients. Strikes or strike threats by doctors have occurred in 1912 over David Lloyd George's Insurance Act, in 1973 and in 1987 by non-consultant hospital doctors over pay and conditions. In 1974 consultants threatened 'action' over patient eligibility for 'free' hospital services. I also pointed out that GPs are the bedrocks of medical services and their actions reflect on all doctors.

I debated the possible consequences of doctors resigning from the GMS with Dr Cormac McNamara, the President of the Irish Medical Organisation on the Marian Finucane 'Liveline' programme on RTE Radio 1 on 2nd January 1992. He got about 65% of the time available and avoided directly confronting the points I had made. He has been a Fianna Fail activist in Waterford and could not be considered disinterested as Dr O'Hanlon was still the Minister for Health. The programme producer Julian Vignoles enjoys verbal 'blood sports' when medics are having a barney. The IMO's positions in the Consultant Contract negotiations were unhelpful to those of us who were opposed to a bureaucratic takeover of medicine. A year later (reported in the *Irish Press* of 4th February 1993), Mr Justice Lavan described Dr McNamara's evidence in an injury compensation case as 'bizarre and unreliable'. This doctor was still IMO President at the time. Further comment from my point of view would be superfluous.

I know from some GP friends of mine that some of the participants in the *Irish Times* newspaper correspondence were annoyed. The Department of Health's attitude places the GP negotiators in a very difficult position but principle should not be sold for expediency (money). This row was not resolved until about one week before the November General Election when a 17% pay rise plus some trimmings including drug targets and practice rebates was agreed.

Rock 104 and Joe Duffy with Gaybo on Booze at Christmas

As the Christmas season approached, the police crackdown on drunken driving was in full swing. You could not be sure of avoiding the boys in blue and their road blocks no matter what turns you took. If you were caught there was no wriggling out. Even great men in Leinster House were caught and convicted. Buses, taxis and sober drivers were the order of the day. The Mothers Against Drunken Driving (MADD) were winning.

Aine Ni Bhriain phoned me and asked if I would do a piece with Colm Hayes on his show on Rock 104 in the Ballast House early in the morning. I drove into town at about 7.20 am before the traffic. Stereo Steve was out on the Swords Road in their Space Wagon brandishing a live mike and the fun started. The idea was that the Hayes kid would drink normal cans of lager until he registered over the breathalyser limit. Superintendent Ray Campion of the Garda Traffic Department explained the law and Garda Noel Snow operated the breathalyser. We all had a good bit of fun and the callers into the show added greatly to the two-way crack.

Stereo Steve appeared back into the studio and he started on the cans of low alcohol lager and the breathalyser was not impressed. Nothing happened but the bold Colm Hayes got himself an early lager hangover that day. I hope he was really getting the Dart home after the show. He was in rare old form by ten o'clock.

About a week later, Joe Duffy called and we did a similar show live from the Chancery Inn on the Quays as part of Gay Byrne's morning radio programme on RTE1. Joe Duffy was in great form and was fascinated by the low alcohol lagers. Ray Campion turned out to be involved in rugby refereeing and knew my brother Peter in that capacity. The Holsten lager rep arrived into the pub during the show and gave us all a few packs of their products which were piled high in the corner. The number of serious drinkers in the pub at that hour of the morning never ceases to amaze me. Joe Duffy spoke to a number of them on their alcohol tolerance and Noel Snow again administered the blowing into this bag stunt again. I brought the cans of lager out to the lab in Beaumont and the lads relieved me of their weight. I never saw them full again. You could never trust lab technicians with free cans of beer!

More radio booze was available on Colm Hayes' Show on Rock 104 on Christmas Eve when he arranged a breakfast cocktails session. Every poison was available and there was a cocktails expert mixing them on the spot. Some visitors lowered a good few and many of the concoctions looked lethal. The one thing very noticeable was just how good the morale was in the studio. Rock on lads! Cocktail drinking – that was some way to start Christmas Eve!

Two Candidates in Dublin North-West at the General Election?

In late September, Paddy Donegan suggested that it was past time to try to come to some constructive arrangement with the Shortall camp in the constituency as there was an AGM due soon. This was held on the 14th October and Liam Pyke was elected chairman with Mrs Angie Daly as secretary. She worked in Head Office for about 10 years in a secretarial position in which she looked after the membership register. Therefore, she was in pole position to monitor any moves within the constituency which would affect the political position favoured by Head Office. Mrs Daly's election was inevitable at that time because she was nominated by Finglas and had the backing of the Militants in DCU and Finglas East.

On 22nd October, Gerry Doyle, Paddy Donegan and I met Fergus Finlay in Buswell's Hotel to discuss what should be done about the constituency. The Drumcondra Branch was due to be affiliated as it contained Roisin Shortall and her supporters. This would have given them a four against three advantage at constituency council. We decided to form new branches and to have these passed through the Organisation Committee where Pat Magner was in the Chair. The idea was that we would then be able to ensure a two-candidate strategy which I thought would be necessary to win a seat because the constituency had been lengthened to include a major portion of Drumcondra where Roisin Shortall had lived. The assumption was that Labour would be the 13-16% band nationally in the next election. The issue was discussed further on the night of Dick Spring's ten years in the Dail celebration dinner in the Burlington Hotel later that month where Neil Kinnock gave an entertaining and amusing speech. It is a great pity that a man of his soul never succeeded in making 10 Downing St.

What to do in North-West was again discussed over tea with Dick Spring and Fergus Finlay in the Dail restaurant on the evening following the Labour Party Christmas party in December. I told them that I had organised enough people to form two new branches and that we were making progress. I also told Fergus and Dick that it was fairly obvious that Ruairi Quinn and Ray Kavanagh were operating their ventriloquist tricks from afar. I could name the political dummies but the laws of libel, etc.!!!

Ruairi Quinn came to North-West in late November to deliver an address on his answer to unemployment. I was underwhelmed to say the least and so were many on my side of the house, but they were too polite to say so out loud. Paul Tansey's book *Making the Irish Labour Market Work* would have provided a lot more meat for discussion. Vague analysis and blancmange solutions will never cure any economic problem.

1992

1992 arrived and our electoral strategy was under severe stress. Sufficient local people had been contacted by the turn of the year to allow us to go ahead with meetings to formally set up the new branches. We planned to reconstitute the former branches called Wadelai and Poppintree. Gerry Maher and his family agreed to be core members of the Wadelai Branch to get things going. He was a former local election candidate who had been defeated for the final seat without being eliminated in the 1979 local elections in Finglas. The constituency secretary was informed in early January that the branch had elected interim officers and now wished to affiliate to the Constituency Council at the mid-month meeting. The list of new members was supplied with money for membership fees and signed membership details.

The new branch's request was ignored and a letter of protest was immediately sent to the General Secretary, Raymond Kavanagh, at Head Office asking him to have the Administrative Council affiliate the branch. Nothing was heard.

Ina Gould and Barney Hartnett agreed to organise a reconstituted Poppintree Branch. Ina had been the Branch Secretary of that particular group earlier and was a local election candidate in the politically grim year of 1985. We had no problems getting former members to support the new effort. Barney Hartnett had left the party about 8 years earlier and after meeting with Helen Metcalfe and I was keen to get going again. He was the long time editor of the *Ballymun Echo* and his doggedness and determination on national political issues was well known in 'The Mun'. Des O'Malley was very worried that the new branches would affect his power and influence particularly in Ballymun despite every reassurance. Des was told about which people we had approached when we were ready to go despite him being constituency organiser because his political reactions had become so unpredictable. Des was obsessed with opposing Ms Shortall and simply did not believe that I would be deselected.

Roisin Shortall, Des O'Malley and I met the Organisation Committee in 88 Merrion Square on the afternoon of Wednesday 15th January. The issue was what, electoral strategy should be used in Dublin North-West to ensure success in the next election. In the chair was Pat Magner and around the table were Anne Byrne from Wexford, Raymond Kavanagh, Ruairi Quinn TD, Paddy Murray SIPTU in Dublin and John O'Brien SIPTU from Wicklow. Shortall wanted one candidate, O'Malley and I wanted two or more. I had written an analysis piece on the constituency which included statistics and the details of the Militant disruption for their perusal – another exercise in futility. I was the last to be called in and on entering the large first floor room, Ruairi Quinn was on my right and immediately flashed a thumbs-up sign under the cover of the table top. What a hypocrite! I knew exactly where he stood but exactly why he stood there I had no idea.

Deputy Quinn

Tony Phillips, a friend of mine, is a Welshman and a journalist on the *Yorkshire Post* in Leeds. He is a Welsh Rugby Union supporter whom I first met at Headingley and Roundhay rugby clubs in Leeds around twelve years ago. He always phones me when he's in town. Wales again beat Ireland at Lansdowne Road on a typical January Saturday afternoon. Tony asked me around to meet him on Sunday night at Campbell Spray's house in Heytesbury Street. Campbell is the Deputy Editor of the *Sunday Independent.* Surprise surprise, Deputy Quinn and his wife Liz were there.

So I took the opportunity to discuss the North-West situation. Ruairi was affable and agreeable as is his wont and I thought that he agreed that there should be two candidates. So I immediately wrote to him the next day pointing out what I thought was said.

Dear Ruairi,

I was delighted to meet yourself and Liz .... etc. I was equally pleased to hear you agree that there should be more than one candidate in Dublin North-West to maximise our chances of victory in the next general election, given the local reality in the constituency.
Your support for the ideal of agreed candidates along the lines of the mechanism for selection for the Drumcondra Ward in the last local election as the most amicable way of resolving potential local conflict was very welcome.
I hope you continue to support a dual candidate strategy for North-West in your position on the Organisation Committee.

Yours, etc.,

One week later Quinn replied:

Thank you .... etc

I found our discussion about the situation in Dublin Northwest very interesting and useful.
However, I have a different recollection to any conclusions that might have been reached. As far as I am concerned the only conclusion that was agreed unanimously, between the two of us, was that we should do everything to ensure that the Labour Party wins a seat in Dublin North-West whenever the next election takes place. I did not express a clear preference for either a one or two-candidate strategy. Clearly, that is a matter that has to be decided, in the first instance, by the Organisation Committee and ultimately the Administrative Council.
I was rather surprised to get your letter as it appeared to be in the form of a formal note confirming the conclusions of a formal meeting when in fact what you referred to was an informal discussion. It is for that reason that I feel obliged to reply formally to your letter as in all three paragraphs you attempt to suggest that I had given a commitment to you to support a two candidate strategy for Dublin North-West.
This is not my position then or now. My concern is, and has always been to ensure that the Labour Party adopts the strategy most suitable to win a Labour seat in every one of the eleven Dublin Constituencies.

Yours, etc.

I replied immediately :

> Thank you for your interesting reply to my note of January 21st re: our conversation albeit informal about Dublin North-West.
>
> You most certainly did agree that more than one candidate would optimise the Party's chances of general election success in Dublin North-West. I looked for no commitment from you, only consistency.
>
> My note was in essence accurate. I was neither lying nor confabulating.
>
> Yours, etc.

All of this cross correspondence was copied to Pat Magner. I'm sure it had at least some amusement value. It's not only football that's a funny old game.

The Finglas branch was anything but united in its attitude to the candidate issue. I met Paul Brien and Paul Malone in the Royal Oak Pub on Finglas Road in late January to discuss the possibility of a deal if they would start to reattend Finglas Branch meetings. Paul Brien said he would agree and Malone agreed to consider the matter further.

The resignation of Charles Haughey as Fianna Fail leader on January 30th added urgency to the situation. That night I attended the Larkin Memorial Lecture delivered by Alexander Cockburn in DCU and the political discussion afterwards was very interesting. I have no doubt that Des Geraghty, then of the Workers Party, would have made an excellent TD. I did not think that SIPTU should place any obstacles in the way of its officials being elected to public office for whatever party. The General Officers should remember that the membership votes all the way across the political spectrum. It is utter humbug to suggest that they are all true Labour. The number of Labour votes in 1987 was 114,551 in 1987 and 156,989 in 1989 and these figures are less than the total membership of the old ITGWU alone.

I continued to support local developments and the Finglas environmental improvement with tree planting was launched at the Spanish Convent in February and the community's desire for change continues to grow. A large and growing core of Finglas people deeply care for their own environment. All the local political contenders attend these gatherings and the extent of personal friendships and antipathies are obvious for all to see.

A group from the constituency met some of the members of the Organisation Committee and only Helen Metcalfe and the Constituency Chairman, Liam Pike, argued cogently for two candidates. The others supported Roisin Shortall. The Organisation Committee later recommended that there be only one candidate.

From the end of January, Des O'Malley was supposed to prepare a report on branch reorganisation but Des never got around to the task and resigned suddenly within weeks giving his opposition to coalition as the precipitating factor. Most of us considered that there was another more substantive reason – Des wanted a nomination and saw too many obstacles in his way. At the February constituency meeting, the Wadelai Branch was added to the agenda for discussion. There was general disagreement about the issue and it was put on hold. Betty Maher appealed against the decision of the Constituency Council not to affiliate the branch to Pat Magner and Raymond Kavanagh at the Organisation Committee and at Head Office. She made the point that there could be only one substantive reason for this. It could crucially affect the decisions made by those who currently have delegate votes at the council. There had been no objection raised to the Drumcondra Branch recently and no action had been taken against branches which contained Militant members. The Wadelai branch contains people who campaigned in the last two elections in the constituency and in Gerry Maher, it had a previous local election candidate.

Frank Rock and I left the list of names, interim officers and subscriptions for the Poppintree Branch into Angie Daly's house in Fairways Estate. The Constituency met on 18th March and Odran Reid and Peter Daly for the Finglas Branch proposed that, 'No new branches should be formed, ratified or accepted for consideration in Dublin North-West until the constituency review can be completed and discussed'. This motion was talked out and withdrawn. They also had another 'that the Constituency Council calls on the Constituency Organiser to complete the Constituency Review and report to the July Constituency Council meeting'. They also wanted a selection convention in May.

Later in March, Paddy Donegan, Gerry Doyle, Frank Rock, and myself met Anne Byrne, Pat Magner and Fergus Finlay to again discuss the worsening situation from our point of view. We checked to see from what date Head Office considered the Drumcondra Branch ratified and 14th October was given. Therefore, from May the Shortall camp would have a majority provided the Militants were not expelled. Henry Haughton, an AC member from Labour Left, had been attending the meetings for some reason and frequently pontificated on the rules and the role of the AC. Such interference would not have been tolerated in a commercial organisation. Haughton had been anti-Spring for years and would have not shed any tears if the four votes in Tralee in 1987 had gone the other way. Politically, he often occupies areas that would be complete virgin territory to me. For Henry, Frank Buckley, Emmet Stagg and their mates, the sights on the east side of the Berlin Wall must have left little room for 'Doubting Thomas's'. Emmet's pal, Michael Taft dived into Democratic Left when de Rossa formed his breakaway from the Workers Party in March. Stagg then left the Parliamentary Labour Party for a while but the Labour membership in Kildare indicated its solid support for the

Party and discretion being the better part of valour, a chastened Stagg was later readmitted to the Parliamentary Labour Party. His former 'Man-Friday' finished as the unfortunate Eric Byrne's agent in the marathon recounts in Dublin South-Central while Emmet got a half-car as a Minister of State for Housing.

On March 24th I again met Dick Spring and we discussed the whole issue. He suggested that maybe I should rationalise my position, step back and try to secure a Senate nomination with his support. I really wasn't that bothered because the messing in the Labour Party seemed very trivial compared to events in the real world. Clearly, since many of those that I dealt with in the Party took no notice of the human condition, I wondered why I had bothered with them for so long.

The long-running Beaumont Hospital saga took a turn for the worst on the 30th March when Sean O'Laoire the neurosurgeon was suspended from duty, a decision from which I formally dissented at a meeting of the Medical Board. Brendan Howlin put down markers on the O'Laoire situation the following week in the Dail. The atmosphere in the hospital was tense to say the least. Within days Neil Kinnock had been defeated in the British General Election and that defeat would not be good for Ireland. The British Labour Party lost even in the throes of an economic depression and we were literally shocked at the outcome. Anne Byrne, Pat Magner and Fergus Finlay had been all ready to go across to London to celebrate the victory that never was.

My wife Helen was very ill at home during this period and needed a lot of medical and psychological support. Spasms of severe pain, nausea, vomiting and terror were very frightening for her and her welfare; politics was not the priority. Loss of appetite and weight loss were forcing her to try to take as much liquid food as possible and she struggled to count in as many calories as she could knowing that there was a daily shortfall. Pale, gaunt and weak but absolutely determined, she said that she did not want to die and wanted to believe her cancer could be arrested with chemotherapy. Our son Tommy's welfare was her big concern and she so much wanted to live. But in her heart of hearts she knew that she was in real trouble. The mirror would not lie. John Hyland, the surgeon who had operated upon Helen the previous May admitted her to St Vincents in early April and she never came home. A week later she phoned me in Beaumont and asked me straight if she was going to die. I was choked then and I still am. Helen called Tommy and me into her room a week before she died to tell him why she was going to die. He had no idea and was absolutely devastated. It was a very private family moment which I could never forget. She died peacefully on Monday 4th May in the early morning.

The funeral in Mount Merrion was an ordeal and I am grateful to family and friends for all the support at the time. The day Helen was buried was the day fixed for the North-West selection convention at the Willows Pub. The Labour Party postponed it for five days.

Selection Convention

The General Secretary presided at what we considered a charade. Firstly there was an open vote on the question of one or two candidates. Then the vote on which candidate was taken by written ballot and the result was the same for both questions. The selection convention was lost by four branches to three. Each branch had four votes so we lost 16 to 12. There were approximately six Militants voting for Roisin Shortall at the meeting. On the previous Saturday, Gerry Doyle, one of my supporters from the Ballygall branch had seen Michael Murphy, the secretary of the Finglas East Branch and a delegate to the selection meeting selling Militant in O'Connell St. This was reported to Head Office. Alan Bermingham a delegate from DCU subsequently signed himself 'Militant Socialist co-ordinator' in letters to the press. The other Militant activity is detailed in earlier chapters.

The following day I had lunch in Leinster House with Dick Spring and Brendan Howlin. I told them that other than three people, I had continued to receive the active support of all those who campaigned in the 1989 general election. This take-over of the constituency could not have happened without the active connivance of Head Office. Two Head Office employees were delegates to the selection meeting. When one is the membership secretary, the old axiom of 'you can't beat Tammany Hall' becomes true. Therefore, any counter-measures that we tried to take were easily frustrated.

The Ballygall, Ballymun, and Santry/Whitehall Branches were very annoyed and had a joint meeting following which they wrote to Dick Spring and to Niamh Bhreathnach, the Party Chairman:

> We the undersigned three branches are very concerned about the consequences of the outcome of the recent selection conference and in particular the process by which the decision was reached.
>
> We feel that the single candidate strategy will destroy whatever chance there is of winning a seat in the constituency at the next general election. Since the new constituency boundaries were published, our branches have consistently advocated the necessity for more than one candidate as a prerequisite for victory, given the diverse nature of the local population structure.
>
> We have referred to the process by which the decision was made. It is rather strange that DCU, a branch which has taken no hand act or part in constituency activities, can suddenly appear at a selection convention with four delegates. In past elections, they could not even produce four people to help in the campaign. Regarding the Finglas East Branch, it is well known and has been reported previously in writing to the General Secretary that the Militant influence there is very strong. A third voting branch (Finglas) had to depend on two paid Head Office officials to complete their delegation of four people.

The fourth branch, Drumcondra, the formation of which we welcome, had very recently become eligible to vote and it is rather strange that the selection convention was convened to coincide with this fact.

We are not writing with any sense of pique, antipathy or animosity towards the selected candidate, Roisin Shortall. Our three branches are on record in stating that Labour's best chance of winning a seat in Dublin North-West is a Shortall/Tormey ticket.

Our three branches are long established and consist of a majority of members who have consistently worked in Labour's cause from bad times to good, when we only missed a seat in the last parliamentary election by 54 votes. For these reasons our members strongly recommend that Dr Bill Tormey be added to the ticket. This letter is written only in the interest of the Party and not of any individual candidate of member.

This letter was co-signed by the three branch secretaries.

Two Ballymun Branch members Paddy Dunbar and Joe Doyle called to my house on a few occasions pledging their support for me usually after a discussion in the Comet pub on the Swords Road. They were urging me to immediately declare myself as an independent Labour candidate. Their lack of sincerity would quickly be exposed. Meanwhile, Mary Flaherty and Proinsias de Rossa were having leaflets delivered and Roisin Shortall announced herself as a candidate. After the late Jimmy Tully's funeral on the coast at Laytown, the Labour Party's long-term hardcore membership found it incredible that I had been deselected and said something would be done.

The three branches met jointly in the Autobahn Roadhouse on Glasnevin Avenue and a parallel constituency council evolved. The Finglas *Local News* phoned to enquire what I was doing in the next election and I told them I was running. The Maastricht Referendum was passed with the minimum of interest in North-West. As far as I could ascertain, nobody in the local Labour Party campaigned. I felt that we should vote Yes, and I asked all our local supporters to do so because the brotherhood of man is important and I believe in the European ideal. Nationalism is an international disease. Respecting difference is the key to co-existence and near neighbours have a historic tendency to war. A single currency is an absolute necessity otherwise economic and monetary union is meaningless. Dick Spring told me on the phone that he was not surprised that there was a minimalist campaign for Maastricht as that was the situation in many constituencies. It was a strange episode considering the seriousness of the issues involved. Michael Freeman and many in Fianna Fail were personally against the Treaty but decided to keep their views private. In a nationalist party like Fianna Fail, I would be surprised if their grassroots members felt any different. If Fianna Fail has any real core value, it is nationalism.

In early July, the shadow three-branch constituency met and there was general ire that neither Niamh Bhreathnach nor Dick Spring had replied to the joint letter. The particular annoyance was that the long-time Spring loyalists were being ignored. Anyway, from the motions and agreements at the February and March constituency council meetings, July was the month that the new branches could be passed by the constituency. Gerry Doyle was to introduce the issue under 'any other business' and we were to say nothing and have our full delegate numbers there. On the night, we all turned up and had a clear majority. Then, believe it or not, the secretary did not appear and there were no minutes. The Shortall camp was shocked but they persuaded the chairman, Liam Pike, to rule that in the absence of the secretary, Mrs Daly, any decision would be postponed until the September meeting. I told Roisin Shortall at the constituency council that I totally abhorred her brand of political ethics which would have been more appropriate in another larger party.

In September, the minutes produced were at variance with what our whole group had remembered and with what was written in our notes. Our strategy was to agree the affiliation of the new branches and to pass a motion to the effect that there should be two candidates. There was never any intention of attacking the candidacy of Ms Shortall even though she was not exactly flavour of the month with us. It was suggested that we take over existing branches for the same purpose but this would have been very difficult or impossible because Mrs Daly was in the sentry position as membership secretary in Head Office.

The other part of our strategy was to compete with the other parties on the ground with literature. We decided to try something different. The 'Loose Cannon' was the title and it was to be a mixture of local facts and information mixed with satirical comment on national events. Des O'Malley's description of Albert Reynolds as 'Reckless, foolish and unwise' was a propagandist's treat and Reynolds' retort months later in October when he described Des O'Malley as 'Reckless, irresponsible and dishonest' just shows what the last few months of the FF/PD coalition must have been like. Des O'Malley must have felt like pleading 'Come back Charlie all is forgiven'. Some of our ideas and characters were loosely based on Dermot Morgan and Gerry Stembridge's 'Scrap Saturday' and the style was easy to write. *Private Eye* and the *Phoenix* were good teachers. We produced about 16,000 of these double A4-size leaflets and distributed them, starting in the last week of August. George Metcalfe did a lot of the work as he was out of work. The leaflet was produced by Frank Rock, Chairman of the Bill Tormey Supporters Club and no political party was appended. We were easily able to drop the whole area in less than two weeks. I was very impressed. Three editions were produced before the election unexpectedly arrived. The reaction from the public was mixed. Many loved it and phoned to say so. Others said it was too disrespectful of politicians and should not have been written by a medical person. I confess, I enjoyed it myself.

Some of the Fianna Fail local lads complained if one was mentioned and another left out! Anyway, it kept us in the frame in the locality.

Liam Deegan, the Cappagh Avenue newspaper letter writing 'hurler on the ditch' was provoked by the 'Loose Cannon'. He frequently returns by post many of my leaflets delivered to his door with anti-Labour comments scrawled across them. These were often unsigned but his hand writing is recognisable so I found his number on the electoral register and wrote to him. In the course of his reply he said that he voted for Mary Flaherty of Fine Gael. That cleared up my curiosity regarding just which conservative party he supported.

The Shortall camp was not happy. Oh dear! At the next constituency meeting in late September, Roisin Shortall's Drumcondra Branch introduced a motion to effectively ban the leaflet. However, they were unable to win their argument because they were tied in knots over the right to freedom of speech. Precedents including our own fringe Labour Left and the Tribune Group in England were cited and the question was put: What article in the Labour Party's constitution was being breached? They tried to rule that 'leaflets produced by any individual branch or member shall have the approval of the director of elections prior to distribution'. We also told them that 'the loose cannon' was a 'publication' and not a leaflet. Is it a biscuit or is it a bar? Interestingly, John Horgan, the former TD and Senator turned up at the meeting in support of Shortall. Even after a year, Ms Shortall gave the impression of being interested only in local ward matters and rarely gave a view on issues of national controversy. She could have been in Fianna Fail without hardly changing a word.

It was also interesting to have Henry Haughton suggest to me that I should resign from the Party in the interests of peace in North-West. That was an interesting angle from a member of Labour Left on a mission of effective political sabotage. If I hadn't had so many other problems from family, to Beaumont to Shamrock Rovers at around the same time, all of these people would have been more vigorously fought.

We would have been quite happy to explain what had been happening in North-West to the Administrative Council but we were never asked.

Last Throw From The Parallel Constituency

On 7th July, branch representatives met in the Autobahn. The Donegan family, Maura Doolan, Michael Hopper, Tom Dunne, Gerry Doyle, Andy Earley, Eithne Costello, Maria Hedderman, Helen and George Metcalfe, Paddy Dunbar, Joe Doyle, Frank Rock and myself. After a lot of discussion over what should be done next, there was much annoyance at the discourtesy shown by the lack of a reply from Dick Spring to the joint letter. But there was a feeling that a small group of representatives should ask to meet him to try to resolve the candidates' issue. We also heard that a whispering campaign of rumour and smearing had been started in the central party against me. Fergus Finlay heard some of these and asked me directly if they were true. One involved the General Secretary, and I phoned him directly to kill it stone dead. This kind of tactic shows just how far some people are prepared to go to succeed. The *Phoenix* magazine published some of the story at the end of August but it was never followed up.

The following agreed note went to Niamh Breathnach and to Dick Spring in September:

> We are all long-serving and faithful members of the Labour Party in Dublin North-West. We are writing to you to express our grave disquiet and concern about what has been happening in this constituency.
>
> It has been brought to our attention, specifically, that Dr Bill Tormey is widely regarded in the Party as having alienated the membership in Dublin North-West. It appears to be believed that he has little or no support here, and that the overwhelming view of the constituency is that we should run only one candidate – and that that candidate should be anyone except Bill Tormey.
>
> These rumours are false. All of us who have signed this letter believe that Bill Tormey has been most unjustly treated. In fact, we believe that the treatment meted out to him is entirely unworthy of our Party. Bill Tormey has held this constituency together since the day he first came here. He 'inherited' a constituency that was bitterly divided and demoralised, and largely by his own efforts, he has put us back into a position where we were only 54 votes short of a seat at the last election.
>
> In all that time he has given unstintingly of himself. It was his generosity of spirit that encouraged us to mount the kind of election campaign that we ran in the last local elections, with Bill opting to run in the most difficult ward area, in the belief that the strategy would win us two seats. Few of us knew at the time that those elections were going on that Bill was also coping with a very traumatic personal situation, which consumed time and emotions.
>
> Nevertheless, the strategic decision almost worked brilliantly. If Bill had been elected then, we believe there would have been no question of his being deprived of another opportunity to win a Dail seat. In fact we know that he would have insisted on two candidates because he, like us, believed that that is in the best interests of the Party. Instead he has been rejected and vilified, portrayed as someone who constantly alienates support, and has noone but himself to blame for the fact that he is not on the Party's ticket.
>
> We have all had our fights and arguments with Bill. But we all respect him and support him, and we all believe that he has fought for the Party like few others. To such an extent, in fact, that we believe a decision not to run Bill Tormey will be the death-knell of the Party in this constituency.

> Please believe us when we say that a strong representative view of the Party membership (the long-serving membership who have been through good times and bad) wants to see Bill Tormey on the ticket. We believe that the two-candidate strategy is appropriate to this constituency, and we undertake to work might and main to make that strategy work.
>
> We know that the decision to add Bill is in your hands. We are asking you, as long-serving members who represent a broad strand of opinion in the Party locally, to adopt a two-candidate approach, and to add Bill to the ticket. We would very much welcome the opportunity to meet you before the decision is made, if you think that would be helpful, to emphasise our support for Bill and a two-candidate approach.

Niamh Bhreathnach replied:

> Dear Member,
>
> Thank you for your letter received in September regarding your request to consider adding Dr Bill Tormey to the Election ticket for the Labour Party in your constituency.
>
> As I indicated to the AC in September, following the recommendation of the Organisation Committee that one candidate be selected in your constituency, I intend to adhere to this decision.

The irony of all this is that Labour could possibly have won two seats in North-West with the right strategy in 1992.

The Ballygall Branch met and decided to propose Frank Rock and Helen Metcalfe respectively for Chair and Secretary of the Constituency at the AGM in October. We wanted to show the Ballymun people just how great was the lack of magnanimity in the Shortall camp. True to form these people gobbled the bait. The constituency was £50 in credit at the AGM. Given the size of the official Labour Party campaign mounted within weeks of that meeting, borrowings or donations must have been in many thousands. Mr Mangan was made Chairman and I was quite surprised to see him standing with SPUC people tallying William Binchy votes at the NUI Senate Count in Carysford, Blackrock in February. We really had minimal interest in who the new officers would be.

The Sean O'Laoire neurosurgery enquiry was continuing through July, August and into September at Blackhall Place and I gave evidence on his behalf towards the end. The verdict against O'Laoire came as a considerable shock to me. I am absolutely convinced that all such enquiries including those held by the Medical Council should be open and in public because justice, as well as being done, must be seen to be done. Transparency in procedures is important to allay suspicion and innuendo.

Emigrant Votes

The proposition that every Irish citizen should have the right to vote seems simple and fair but apparently not to the government. The Electoral (No. 2) Bill published in December 1991 ignored the issue of votes for emigrants.

In the *Sunday Independent* in January, I wrote that 'the issue itself is far from simple. If our overseas citizens were allowed to register at an Irish embassy for a postal vote at their previous Irish address and did so in large numbers then the constituencies would quickly require redrawing. In which constituency would Irish citizens without a previous Irish home address register? Given the very large number of Irish emigrants and Irish passport holders overseas, the number of TD's would have to be significantly increased or the population number per TD would have to be allowed to go out to the constitutional maximum of 30,000.

Again this would require constituency boundary changes. Would the children of emigrants under 18 years be counted because otherwise the quotas in emigrant areas would become relatively high? A special emigrant constituency with the number of seats determined by the number of our overseas citizens including minors registered at our embassies is one solution.

Another, perhaps more realistic response might be to reform the Senate and give emigrants a directly elected role there. The electorate would be elastic in the way the university panel electorate is at present and the number of seats fixed. Flexibility would also be available in the number of constituencies. One might represent those resident in Britain and Europe, another those in North America, etc. Either way a referendum would be required. I suggested that it be held when the Maastricht questions were being put.' This whole issue remains unresolved because people once gone are easily forgotten. They no longer have to be given Irish social welfare payments and they don't vote. As Donal McAmhlaigh, when living and working in Northampton, put it *Dialann Deorai.*

Turning a Blind Eye

Because many of our laws are an absurd intrusion into the personal lives of citizens, there is an unstated convention that law enforcement agencies should turn a blind eye to many social arrangements. By February 1992, Harry Whelehan, the Attorney General, threw the system into convulsions.

The Attorney General's action in the X Case was perfectly valid legally but in a real sense it was a breach of the unstated 'mind your own business' convention. It may force the public to reassess our general acceptance of 'Irish solutions to Irish problems'. Imagine the consequences for our society if there were prosecutions for bigamy following foreign divorces finalised while the parties were still resident in the state, or following Catholic Church nullity rulings.

Regarding abortions, should the state consider paying GCHQ in Cheltenham, which taps telephone traffic across the Irish Sea, to pass on the calls from this country to nominated telephone subscribers in certain British cities? Would the Gardai be asked to further investigate any such calls if there were grounds for suspicion? Where does this leave prescriptions for the 'Morning after' pill?

Will there be prosecutions of homosexuals before the Dail finally gets around to complying with the rulings from the European Court? Will assaults committed on football fields under the nominal jurisdiction of various sporting bodies now be subjected to court proceedings? There are clearly limitless possibilities for proving the old axiom that 'the law is an ass'.

Was this another fundamental shift in our rapidly changing culture? When the country is faced with future social choices in the personal behaviour area then Charlie Haughey's Irish solutions answer will no longer suffice.

Supporting the Bank Officials

The Irish Bank Officials Association found themselves in an awkward situation because the upper echelons in the banking business have learned how to divide and conquer and also that they can hire away with 'yellow pack' staff and still get by. It is easy to say that staff have to move with the times but the banking sector in the Republic is very profitable and not particularly industry friendly when compared with the Germans and Japanese. I felt a good deal of sympathy for the AIB staff walking up and down outside the branch on the Swords Road while other supposed colleagues worked on inside. Obviously, the Associated Banks had effectively broken the power of the IBOA. No more prolonged strikes like those in the '70s with the lads off working on the building sites of England while Job Stott did the business at home.

The *Irish Times* on 14th March editorialised on the subject and I felt that the picketers deserved more support. I responded – 'Dragging up old Ned Ludd as an aphorism to prod the IBOA in the *Irish Times* editorial is a little short-sighted when the 300,000 unemployed barrier is about to be breached. The switch in employment from heavy manufacturing industry and farming to services has been gathering pace, and unless we redefine employment, there will be no chance of giving every citizen the dignity of work.

The behaviour of people at both ends of the earnings spectrum arises in this dispute. For example, the banks employ lower-paid bank assistants to increase profits and pressure other officials, but top management appear unaffected by the ICI affair, US takeovers, Goodman, etc. It clearly seems fair game to exploit the least- powerful employee.

By contrast, the professional elite can command huge fees as witnessed by the question of value for money in the Greencore affair. Monopoly licensing bodies in the professions are crucial in restricting numbers and controlling real competition. These professional monopolies will have to be broken in the public interest if legal and financial services are to be provided to the wider public at affordable fees. Bank management policy in Ireland is very cautious and contrasts sharply with the proactive attitude of the financial institutions in Germany and Japan to their indigenous manufacturing industry. Does anyone believe that real banking competition exists in Ireland? Bank profit performance in Ireland contrasts sharply with their overseas results.

The bank strike appears to be concerned with the real industrial question of the next century: How can we give more power, responsibility and control to workers in industry without introducing chaos? Survival of labour unions is important to limit the gap between a dictatorial small upper-management, upper elite and the many anonymous badly-paid operatives on the shop floor. Industrial democracy is still important and worker morale is a key element in the success of any industry. The banks should, in their own interest, negotiate not bully.'

Banking and other personal services industries will be the major employers of the future and it is important that their workers' rights are not trampled upon. Young turks may gobble up old 40-year-olds but the gap from 24 to 40 years closes quickly. When the 40-year-old financial services wizards begin to be made redundant due to burn-out and are then replaced by the next batch of 24-year-olds then and only then will they appreciate the value of the IBOA and their like.

The *Guardian* newspaper Banned for a Day in May !!!!

True to form the unbelievable happened. Having been a *Guardian* reader for the past 15 years, I never imagined that the paper would be banned for a day in this glorious republic due to an abortion clinic advert. It is only when the thought police interfere directly in one's own existence that the brutal absurdities of life in this country are rammed home. Theory becomes reality. I felt personally insulted by that episode. I used to believe that there was a tacit understanding that clearly absurd laws would be ignored. Now that events have effectively demolished that cosy idea, it is urgent that the Dail legislate in the interests of all of the people. Having voted down Labour's Bill on the right to travel and information, it is a bit 'Irish' of Mr Reynolds to claim that the issues would be dealt with before the end of the year. 'Irish Solutions' and double think and talk are wearing a bit thin.

Private morality should be exactly that, private. It is now entirely possible that some women's magazines, medical journals, other newspapers and periodicals and telephone directories for virtually every country in Europe may be seized by our moral guardians.

Further European integration might just save us from ourselves. I confess to the feeling that my mind lives on a different planet to the certainty of the one true faith brigade in this country. Poor Ireland!

Albert did manage his referendum in November which left him in essentially the same position as if he had nodded through the earlier Labour Bill in the Dail.

Social Welfare Cuts – When 'Social Insurance' Is Really Not Insurance

The whole constituency was up in arms at the proposed abolition of unemployment benefit following redundancy which was paid for the first 15 months. With the money, there was time to seek another job or to start your own business. These payments are made from the social insurance fund and are not charitable handouts. This benefit was to be withdrawn in the new year of 1992 and lump sums would be means tested before any unemployment assistance is paid.

Voluntary redundancy would become a rarity, and lump sums a rapidly reducing asset. If PRSI is, in reality, only an income tax, it should be abolished in the interests of honesty and administrative simplicity.

From April, when Charlie McCreevy 'reformed' social welfare payments 'McCreevy's Dirty Dozen' cuts were born. This was an electoral godsend to Labour who exploited the situation ruthlessly. It will be interesting to see just how many cuts will be restored. Or will the dirty dozen be taken as read, only to return later in the same way as the 1987 poster, 'Health Cuts hurt the Old, the Poor and the Handicapped' returned to haunt Charlie Haughey in 1989.

Summer Heat and Political Comedy

Senator O'Foighil was alleged to be banned from the Senate for wearing a Bainin jacket but this was later stated to be incorrect by the Cathaoirleach. Mr Háughey's yacht *Celtic Mist* was boarded by the British Navy near Belfast Lough despite the fact that the British authorities had advance notice of who was on board. The sailors must have been crazy autograph-hunters looking for a signed CJH from the former President of Europe. I'm sure that running into the Navy was a lot softer than hitting the Mizen lighthouse rocks. Charlie is some character when it comes to offshore objects. I wrote to the *Herald* that 'like him or loathe him Charles Haughey is entitled to respect as a TD and former Taoiseach. That particular routine security check could only be defined as a nonsense.'

Then there was the 'Mug Town' episode from Councillor Taaffe who described a convicted drunken driver as 'a road traffic rapist' and then put a motion to Dublin City council that there should be a warning posted for tourists in high crime areas. You can just see it – a large sign – 'Beware, you are now entering Mug Town' or 'Only mugs go here'. This would be great stuff if it was written for *Private Eye.* Just the sort of thing needed to encourage the visitor. It might be more appropriate to police the area better so that natives, as well as map-bearing tourists, could feel safe.

It seems that Ballymagash is alive and well on Dublin City Council. There is a need for a supervised municipal camp-site in Dublin to bring us into line with the

European norm. I hope the councillors get Frank Feeley to act on that one.

Snobbery in Glasnevin hit the news again. I commented through the *Evening Herald* 'If a change of name from Ballymun Road to Glasnevin Road ensures a price bonus of £5,000 per house, then the Corpo should rename Ballymun Flats Glasnevin (or better still Glawznephin) Heights to get a similar bonus. Funny isn't it? Glasnevin which includes the definitive proof of 'Death the leveller' in Prospect Cemetery seems to be infected with a persistent strain of snobbery. At least Collins (Avenue) survived its University (Avenue) challenge!!! The street referendum failed to get the necessary majority.'

By mid-summer, the new Lord Mayor, Gay Mitchell, would love to give it a lash and have the Olympics hitting town if he had his way. He was serious. The cost of such a venture is such that it compared with the building of a cathedral in the jungle by Humphrey Boigny in Cote d'Ivoire in West Africa.

Martin Breheny in the *Irish Press* ridiculed much of the building mania that had recently swamped sports administrators. I commented, 'Rather than a proliferation of white elephants, it might be more appropriate to build small stadia in the larger urban areas linked to sports centres, conference halls, schools and colleges. When rugby and the GAA start to pay their players a major proportion of their income, then neither will be in a position for further major capital investment. Just look at the experience in soccer. The players get paid more than the gross gate receipts and the FAI itself could not afford a new stadium. If the GAA retain their sporting apartheid system, to which they are quite entitled, then Lansdowne Road or the RDS will have to be given priority, particularly as the Horse Show may be heading for Goffs.'

There were also some suggestions for 'pain-free health cuts' and with Dr John O'Connell as Minister, it was just what the doctor could order. Dr John had announced that he could very well 'go in and show them where cuts could be made. He could start by cutting hospital legal bills by ensuring democratic accountability for the actions of public hospital boards. Another pain-free move would be to prevent public hospitals hiring public relations agencies. Effective freedom of information should be available in the public interest. Each hospital should be called to account for its work each year, not by public statements from administrators but by each medical department accounting for its own annual activity. A new Dail committee on the health services would be the best forum and it could examine hospitals and call patients, medical, nursing and paramedical witnesses to get a clear picture of an institution's health care activity.

'The Adelaide Hospital should be left where it is in Peter Street. A happy hospital is sure to be more efficient, and cost effective than a divided monolith. Hospitals work better if their size is on a human scale and personal contact is retained', I noted in a letter to the *Irish Press* in August.

Healthy Cuts

The Minister for Health, Dr John O'Connell, again called for 'savings' in the health services that would not directly affect patient care. He should take note of a report in the British Medical Journal in September 1992 where auditors admitted that the Wessex Regional Health Authority in England wasted at least £20 million out of a total of £43 million spent on computer projects, and ask for an audit on the same subject across the country here.

The enthusiasm of departmental and other officials for collecting patient data for statistical monitoring purposes could mean that public funds are being spent on pet computer projects while other areas of direct patient care are being rationed.

Did the minister know the cost of the current and previously rejected computer projects in the Irish health services? He might very well be surprised. It is important that we get our priorities right when money is tight.

Local Fianna Fail TD, Michael Barrett Finally Cuts Loose After a Long Gestation!

The summer heat was still stirring in August when Senator Eamonn O Cuiv declared that, in the event of Irish re-unification, a 32-county State should consider re-entering the British Commonwealth. Enter Mr Michael Barrett TD to take off his political shirt and bear his republican chest. He said 'Britain is squatting in this country... they are occupying the six north-eastern counties of our country. We in Fianna Fail have always said that the British should leave in a peaceful way'. I wrote to the *Evening Herald* in reply:

> This stuff was irresponsible nonsense coming from a government back-bencher. It had been clear for some time that both the British and Irish governments will implement whatever solution can be agreed between the Northern parties.
>
> Primitive nationalist rhetoric should have no place in seeking a solution to a 23-year tragedy which had caused 3,000 deaths in the North up to that time.
>
> Whatever about the merit of the Senator's proposal, it did not deserve this kind of irredentist knee-jerk response. Mr Barrett is proud of his membership of SPUC. Well, I would like to live in a country where public representatives are equally careful about the effects of their statements on the born.

In fairness to Michael Barrett, it should be said that he has done a hell of a lot of social work particularly for widows and illiterate people in relation to pensions and other welfare payments over many years. He does, however, come to weekly public notice as a 'Minister of the Eucharist' at 'Our Lady of Victories Church'. That made him even more formidable electorally.

Sex, The Church and The Media

Sex was never far off the boil in the heat of the season. In the *Irish Independent* on July 15th, Fr Denis Faul described the public health policies of this State for the last 25 years regarding sexual matters as 'disastrous'. He wrote 'Politicians should not give people what they want, but what is best in the traditional life of the country and for the common good of the country'. He further inferred that condoms are pernicious items which destroy the health of our young people.

Fr Faul is a very brave man on issues affecting the rights and health and safety of his own Dungannon community but he had to be challenged on this stuff because of his influence.

The facts are that the republic has not had a happy time regarding legislation on sexual matters. The intrusion of the law into personal behaviour in a way that infringes human rights has resulted in people having to go to the European Courts to seek justice – the Magee and Norris cases are examples.

In a democracy, the whole point of elected politicians is that they should give people what they want while respecting the views of minorities. The other way is dictatorship. The Pope has reminded his followers many times that the Roman Catholic Church is not a democracy even though à-la-carte Catholicism is very common here now. It is important to separate church and state to avoid bigotry and intolerance. Fr Faul should realise that condoms are the final issue before sex not the initiator. People are not obliged to fornicate but may choose to do so. The state must allow those who do to minimise the possible consequences.'

Fr Tom Stack in his comments in the *Sunday Press* on August 16th on the deteriorating relationship between the Catholic Church and the media in Ireland ended by approvingly quoting Professor Joe Lee that 'the church is the main bulwark.......of the civil culture'. His objective was to try to end the growing rift between the official church and journalists. In an increasingly educated society where vigorous questioning and scepticism is replacing blind belief, his task is impossible.

Western culture is not hemmed in by state boundaries. Tolerance and the brotherhood of man are social democratic ideals that are fundamental principles of mainstream political parties who argue over the ever-changing uncertainty of policy details. Many western countries are relatively irreligious but full of ideological argument. They are not any less caring societies than here. Ideals are ultimately more powerful than institutions.

Religious belief is usually characterised by a certainty – we're right and by God, you must do as we say. Tolerance of non-believers is often very shallow. This philosophical imperialism often leads to an illiberal mirror reaction. Fr Stack must realise that the Official Church's constant patronising pronouncements on sexuality is a cul-de-sac up which even its own members do not wish to travel. That kind of authoritarianism is so easily ridiculed.

The failure of the Church to acknowledge error is very obvious in Ireland. Was the Co. Wexford schoolteacher Eileen Flynn treated fairly? Is denominational education a good idea in Belfast? Should politicians legislate for the whole community or for those Catholics who require legislation to prevent them transgressing Church laws?

Ecumenism, particularly with the Anglical Communion, would certainly benefit from reform of the authority freedom relationship in the Catholic Church but such reform is very unlikely under the primacy of Pope John Paul II. The Church must evolve to survive. Just as there was change when it became obvious that Galileo was right, current 'flat earth' principles will also have to be jettisoned in the interests of common sense. The Church may not be a democracy but all leaders have a habit of noticing where their own mob is heading and getting there before them.

The Jobs Crisis

Irish Gross National Product expanded by 3.6% in 1992 and a net 10,000 jobs were added to the economy. This is not a bad performance when the 2.2% and 0.7% contractions in the British and US economies are considered. The lack of jobs has resulted in Dail committees, the Culliton Report and ICTU statements all of which may give the illusion of movement on the problem.

It is self-evident that entrepreneurs are in it mostly for the money. Thus, the new 10% DIRT savings accounts which overly reward lazy owners of capital, effectively tells risk-takers that they are crazy. Reversal of this policy would be a very acceptable U-turn for job hunters.

After Maastricht, we must get our debt/GDP ratio below 60% to receive the full benefits of the cohesion funds. This is bound to cut government social spending on health, education and welfare.

I believe that a series of new public enterprises such as vehicle manufacturing, technology developments in medicine and sciences, in association with universities, new clean energy projects for export, etc. should be set up and workers paid on a performance-basis only.

These should be semiprivatised when operational and the capital rolled over to open further businesses.

If there is no state intervention the core unemployed have no real hope because even an extra 10,000 jobs per year would require 20 years for the numbers of unemployed to reach the 100,000 level that the former Taoiseach Jack Lynch defined as a resignation figure. 'Surely, the Lemass and Whitaker mould was not a once-off', I wrote in the *Sunday Independent* in August.

Albert's Jobs Tactics

Nero fiddled while Rome burned. Albert repeatedly told us that the 'economic fundamentals were in excellent shape'. Yet the Taoiseach appeared oblivious to the unemployment hurricane which raged all around him. The Dail was not recalled and the government appeared like a becalmed sailing ship. It had no policy other than do nothing and hope that the economy would be stimulated from abroad. It could be a long wait. The sixty substantive recommendations of the Culliton Report languishing on the shelves since January 1992 might not be fault-free but they were a reasoned response to a real crisis. What had been done about them since? Was the inaction inertia or merely incompetence? We just did not know. The 'Hail fellow well met', 'No problem' or 'Economic climate' stuff didn't wash any more. If the PD/FF coalition had no idea what to do then they should resign and let someone else try. This was ironic considering the Labour Party would resuscitate Albert Reynolds' career within five months in a new coalition.

The Currency Crisis

It was not necessary to be an economist to realise that a hard punt exchange rate policy was unsustainable in an economy with about 19% unemployed. It is easy with hindsight to say, 'I told you so' but in this one I did.

In September, I wrote in the *Sunday Tribune* that 'while the Central Bank should be congratulated for their technically-correct use of very high overnight interest rates to defend the punt against currency speculators, politicians should not try to pretend that Irish economic fundamentals were any more than incidental elements in preventing the local currency from falling through the ERM floor. Any gloating over the devaluation of sterling is seriously misplaced. Our exchange rate should ideally be a balance of convenience, weighing the cost of our foreign debt in dollars and Deutschmarks against the needs of our traders in sterling. We must keep the punt/sterling exchange rate some way below parity to preserve our competitiveness and avail of the inevitable economic recovery in the UK which remains our nearest neighbour and biggest market. Preserving jobs at home must be the first priority.

I still believe I was absolutely correct and I found it quite bizarre to hear the ICTU pushing hard through the turn of the year for a no-devaluation policy when jobs were going down the sluice and families were being crucified by high mortgage interest rates. Sometimes it is better not to ask the question, Why? The 10% devaluation in January told its own tale.

The GMS Mess Still Simmers in the Autumn

In the *Evening Herald*, I wrote that, 'I did not want to believe that doctors would strike for a GMS pay rise. In a country where social class is closely related to home address, does that mean that places of high unemployment with the knock-on high rates of illness and doctor visits are going to be effectively denied medical care? Frankly, I will believe that when I see it. GP's in poor areas are badly paid and are at the sharp end when it comes to getting hospital services for their patients who have to join the public queue, unlike those who can afford Plan D and E in the VHI.

But what about the average GP? If about 130 patients per week is an average workload and 66% are private at about £10 each, then working 46 weeks each year, the GP's earn £40,200 plus GMS, insurance forms, etc. Up to 50% of income may be paid on expenses – buildings, nurses/receptionists, malpractice insurance, registrations, equipment, locums, education, etc.

GMS payments are considerably lower than the comparable private consultation which means that doctors with large GMS lists are poorly paid. There are about 1.3 million patients with medical cards and the GP's were paid £39 million in 1991 for looking after them. This works out at about £30 per patient.' In the *Irish Press* I further commented, 'In a study accepted by both sides, Mr Foley of Dublin City University Business School reported that the net average doctor income from the GMS was, in fact, £16,000 per annum. But data published by the Report of the Commission on Health Funding shows that by 1987, GMS patients saw their GP an average of 6.5 times per year compared to a figure of 2.4 for fee-paying patients. Given that GMS patients comprise about one third of the population, then they would represent about 57% of the average practice workload and expenses.' New data is not available on the visitation rate following the belated introduction of repeat prescriptions into the GMS but it is hard to believe that the capitation scheme was agreed by the IMO negotiators in the first place without this facility. The distribution of medical general practice income is very uneven. Why did the IMO agree to this contract only a few years ago? The policy of successive governments has been to try to encourage GP care and to make hospitals referral and accident centres only. At present, self-referral to casualty in Dublin is a huge problem and is very costly. There is also a financial incentive towards direct hospital attendance because the £10 charge in casualty for non-medical card holders is nearly always higher than the fee for GP services locally. Referral without a GP note or without being an obvious accident or emergency should attract a penal charge in casualty. Otherwise, the hospitals are not serious about community care. As it is, you can read telling comments by some 'casualty' consultants that they are not in competition with GPs. Well wowee, imagine that!

GP morale must be sustained to encourage group practices and better community services. This will cost money initially but if the casualty charges are adjusted, it will be money well spent.

Euthanasia

After reading the evidence published in the *Guardian* in September of the trial of Dr Nigel Cox in relation to a woman with severe end stage rheumatoid disease, Dr Mary Chambers and I wrote the following comments in the *Irish Times*.

> The conviction of Dr Nigel Cox for using a KCl injection to end the life of a terminally-ill, long-suffering patient was correct in our view. Intravenous KCl can stop the heart and it has no role in pain relief.
>
> While a doctor's duty is to relieve pain and suffering, it is, however, not necessary to prolong existence when the quality of life is unremitting agony. Prolonging life by, for example, intravenous or nasogastric tube feeding in severely damaged patients is a separate issue.
>
> Pain can be very actively tackled using opiates by infusion pump if necessary. Local anaesthetics, spinal blocks, anticonvulsants, benzodiazepines, NSAI's and steroids can also be used at the appropriate time. Psychological support is also important.
>
> Some pain relief methods may shorten life by hours or days, but this is not their primary purpose. We do not believe that euthanasia, by whatever means, is an ethical medical activity. Doctors may often differ in their estimation of a patients prognosis.
>
> Where does the killing begin and end? Because some doctors in other countries participate in euthanasia does not make it acceptable to us.'
>
> Ms Sue Richardson from Dublin 1 replied describing Cox's conviction as a 'absolute disgrace' and said that he should be given a medal not a sentence. She claimed that in certain intolerable circumstances of pain and fear that euthanasia should be a right.

However, Dr Frank Hassett of Cahercalla Hospice, Ennis, Co. Clare (where coincidentally my grandmother died) wrote in support of our view and of his personal and professional experience. He described euthanasia as 'a negative solution to a difficult problem, better solved by positive action. What the terminally ill are crying out for is good palliative care. Thanks to the Hospice movement symptom control is now a fine art, with established protocols of care that are effective, appropriate and ethical'. Emphasising the dignity and respect for each person, he wrote, 'The end of life can be a meaningful and growth experience for the person, their family, the nurses and doctors. One is humbled by their bravery and the often unexpected strengths and reconciliations that emerge'.

We further commented. 'For patients to maintain trust in their carers, medical practice must retain the basic principle of 'primum non nocere' (the main thing is not to harm). The frightening effect of legal euthanasia on the aged and the terminally ill would cause much mental anguish, and undermine the trust that the sick place in their carers in trying to provide optimum treatment. Legal euthanasia would also facilitate the possibility that patients might be pressured by relatives and others to agree to euthanasia. The last report on the subject by the British Medical Association in 1988 agreed that not prolonging life is acceptable, whereas actively terminating it is not.

We recognise that euthanasia is common in Holland and that last month saw the publication of the Appleton international conference on developing guidelines for decisions to forego life-prolonging treatment. The conclusion was that, 'requests for active termination of life by a medical act which directly and intentionally causes death may be morally justifiable and should be given serious consideration'. However, there were a number of dissenting voices.

We believe that there are many areas where doctors can distort their clinical training – supervising the death penalty, involvement in torture, abuses of psychiatry as occurred in the Soviet Union, Dr Mengele's research, etc. Euthanasia is another.

The ethics of withholding care is not some distant and foreign issue. The queues for cardiac surgery in the public sector here in Ireland are the best publicised example. As medical science continually widens the therapeutic horizons, the rationing of care for whom by whom will become a huge ethical issue.'

Labour Candidates in Dublin

Eithne FitzGerald joined the Labour Party in UCD in 1967, one year before me. She was defeated four times in general elections in Dublin South before being elected with a landslide 17,256 in 1992. She was first elected to Dublin County Council in 1979. In 1989 Eithne got 4,134 in the Dublin South five seater and was surprisingly beaten by Roger Garland of the Green Party. Her previous totals were 1,258 in 1981; 2,388 in 1982; and 2,684 first preferences in 1987. That constituency has a history of building 'em big to knock them flat four years later. Joan Burton was a Party member since the 1970s and had received 1,256 votes in 1989 in Dublin Central before she won a County Council seat in 1991 in Mulhuddart. She was only shaded in Central by Joe Costello on 1,305 in that five seater. In 1987 Costello received 767 first preferences in Central. The Labour total for Costello and Mary Freehill in Central in '87 was 1,399 in comparison to 3,337 for Jimmy Somers in 1982. Derek McDowell joined the Labour Party about 1981 and won a council seat in Clontarf in 1991 when Michael O' Halloran retired. Derek McDowell had contested North Central in 1989 with Michael O'Halloran following the late exit of Flor O'Mahony back to Dun Laoghaire. He received the creditable total of 1,398 with O'Halloran going out on the 9th count on 5,136. Even Mervyn Taylor was defeated twice before being elected, once in 1973 in Dublin South County and again in 1977 in Dublin Mid County. Virtually anyone with a Labour Party sticker after their name would have been elected in Dublin in 1992.

The perplexing question remains: Why, when fully aware of the true situation in both Dublin North-West and at Head Office, did the Party leadership not use its powerful majority on the Administrative Council to rectify the position? Were the votes really available or were subfactions busy? Politics in political parties is a strange business. Sometimes a leader's support is made up of various cabals including his personal followers sticking together for convenience but there may be other players in the group with their own cliques and own agendas. Trade-offs may then take place in a fairly cynical manner. Awkward subjects may sometimes best be ignored and simply not confronted. Ironically the Organisation Committee recommended two candidates in Dublin West. In Dublin North-East, the Constituency Council's wish for two candidates, Sean Kenny and Tommy Broughan, was accepted. Sean Kenny incidentally ran unsuccessfully in 1989, 1987, twice in 1982 and also in 1981.

Appendix

G.1.

THE HIGH COURT

1990 No. 2592p

Friday the 20th day of November 1992

BEFORE MR JUSTICE JOHNSON

BETWEEN

DEREK FAIRBROTHER A PERSON OF UNSOUND MIND NOT SO FOUND SUING BY HIS FATHER AND NEXT FRIEND NOEL FAIRBROTHER SENIOR

PLAINTIFF

AND

IRELAND AND THE ATTORNEY GENERAL AND THE MINISTER FOR JUSTICE

DEFENDANTS

This Action being at hearing before a Judge and Jury of the County and City of Dublin on the 3rd 4th 5th 6th 10th 11th 12th 13th 17th 18th 19th days of November 1992 and this day in the presence of Counsel for the Plaintiff and Counsel for the Defendants

On the Application of Counsel for the Defendants on the 3rd day of November 1992 IT IS ORDERED that the proceedings herein be reported by a shorthand notetaker

On opening and reading the Plenary Summons herein the Pleadings thereon and the documents and exhibits adduced in evidence and on hearing the oral evidence of the Parties and before the close of the Defendants' case on hearing said Counsel respectively

And It Appearing that a settlement has been reached herein on this day

And Counsel for the Plaintiff intimating to

G.1.

THE HIGH COURT

the Court that an Application would be made in due course to have the Plaintiff herein made a Ward of Court and on said Plaintiff's Counsel's Application to amend the title of the proceedings IT IS ORDERED that the title of the proceedings herein be amended as follows:

"Derek Fairbrother a person of unsound mind not so found suing by his Father and next friend Noel Fairbrother Senior

Plaintiff

and

Ireland and the Attorney General and The Minister for Justice

Defendants"

~~and that a copy of this Order be entered up with the Proper Officer~~

And on further hearing said Counsel respectively the Court doth approve of the settlement herein in favour of the Plaintiff in the sum of £375,000.00 and costs on behalf of the Plaintiff

By Consent IT IS ORDERED AND ADJUDGED that the Plaintiff do recover from the Defendants the sum of £375,000.00 and costs of this Action when taxed and ascertained to include any reserved costs

AND IT IS ORDERED that the said sum of £375,000.00 be lodged in Court and placed on deposit pending further Order

P. Healy
REGISTRAR

A copy which I attest

Doc No. 78630 (CS)

Superintendent of Copyists